Stage Three
Riding & Stable Management

by

Hazel Reed BHSAI (Reg'd)

Nova Publications

Stage Three - Riding & Stable Management.
First published in Great Britain by Nova Publications, 1998.
Nova Publications,
Olive House, 22 Frys Lane, Yateley, Hampshire, GU46 7TJ, United Kingdom.
(+44) 01252 874981

ISBN 0952585-93-6
British Library Cataloguing in Publication Data.
A Catalogue record for this book is available from the British Library.

Typeset in Yateley by Dreke.
Printed and bound by Intype, Input Typesetting Ltd., Wimbledon, United Kingdom.

Illustrations by Hazel Reed and Tracey Humphreys.
Computer Graphics by Hazel Reed.

Contents

Foreword

To pass the Stage III Examination requires hard work and practical experience. These qualities need to be based on, and supported by, a sound knowledge of the various topics contained within the syllabus. This book satisfies that need.

As a sequel to the Stage I and II books, this volume has been eagerly awaited by many students working towards their Stage III Examination. It is written in a style that is easy to read and understand with all the information being presented in a logical way.

The need to have many books, each giving a little information is eliminated. Here we have all we require in one volume enabling more time to be spent on increasing the practical expertise.

Anyone reading this book, whether as a serious career student or as a horse lover seeking to learn more about the horse, will find it invaluable.

I recommend this book to anyone who gains enjoyment and pleasure from the horse.

Valerie Lee. B.H.S.I

Valerie Lee, BHSI

Chief Examiner

Acknowledgements

Thanks to:

Robert Pickles BHSI, Jody Redhead BHSAI, Margaret Heritage BSc, Derek Reed BSc, Jean Gill BHSII BHS SM, Robert Dibben BHSII BHS SM, Kimberley Brown, Stephen and Fiona Jones, Sarah Goodall BHSPI, Rachel Oldland BHSAI, Caroline Lycett BHSII BHS SM, Sarah Goodall and Simon Kirkpatrick-Smith.

Thanks for their help and support to John and Nereide Goodman and all the staff at Wellington Riding, and to Clive Duffin RSS, Farrier. Thanks also to Dr. Jamie Whitehorn, Ian Spalding, Diane Salt BHSAI (Reg'd), Rob Kennedy and everyone who helped us in the production of this book. Without the support of human and equine friends these books would never have been written. A special thank you to Sophie, Martyn and Helena who really do want their Mum back if she can ever stop writing books!

Grateful thanks go to Phillipa Muir, Michelle Johnston, Dr. Amy Jones, Jill Adams on Charlie Brown, Lucy Chalcroft on Bridget, Heather Mclaine on Sir Jellicoe, Vanessa Bertrand on Another Windjammer. Special titbits to Rufus, Wellington Oliver, Arken, Tosca and all those horses and ponies who, during the photographic sessions, had so much patience and good manners.

My special thanks and admiration go to Mark Massingham and his team at Intype Printers who are able to perform miracles and to whom I owe several bottles of champagne.

This book is dedicated to the memory of Keaghdance.

Note: Again we apologise to all fillies and mares for the use throughout this book of the male gender. Using 'it' cannot describe the horse, which is a living creature, so 'he', 'his' and 'him' with respect refers to all horses and ponies everywhere.

Cover photograph by David Hart, taken at Wellington Riding Establishment, Hampshire, England.

Introduction

The 'Stage III – Riding & Stable Management' is part of the series which includes the 'Stage I', the 'Stage II incorporating the Riding & Road Safety Test' and the 'Preliminary Teaching Test', (due for publication soon). These books direct and guide students through the British Horse Society Examinations to the Preliminary and Assistant Instructor qualification.

The series consolidates all the theoretical and practical data required from various sources. This includes a vast amount of personal experience from instructors, competitors, examiners, lecturers and horse owners.

Each book is designed specifically for the relevant Examination, detailing the information necessary for that level. Many students spend vast amounts purchasing a library of books that either give too much, or too little, information. It is then often difficult to decide how much depth of knowledge is needed. To provide the right amount of information not only saves time, but also helps students to learn the relevant subjects thoroughly instead of being confused with an overload of data. Students can then enter and take the Examinations with confidence.

Purpose of this Guide

The Stage III book is a continuation of the Stage II, expanding on the knowledge already learnt for that Exam and introducing the new subjects in the Stage III syllabus. It describes the equitation, flatwork and jumping, including the preparation the student will need for this standard. The stable management information is described, together with Exam tips, to help each student be mentally, emotionally and physically ready for the 'big day'.

Exams are not easy and students often become discouraged from taking another too soon (or even at all!). Though sometimes it is advisable to take a little time to recuperate, often the momentum is lost; the knowledge learnt at one level is forgotten and has to be learnt again.

The aim of the Stage III book is to encourage students to forge ahead, building on their previous knowledge and success. Written in a 'reader-friendly' style this book presents the information logically, practically, with interest and enjoyment. Students can continue towards a personal achievement and gain a British Horse Society qualification.

It also emphasises the need to *understand* the various aspects of horsemastership, fostering a desire to learn more about that wonderful creature, the horse. By increasing our comprehension, and that which we pass onto others, we may, in some small way, improve the lives of horses and ponies.

I hope this book will be enjoyed as much as the others in the series and, again, humour is used as a learning aid to emphasise relevant points.

The Stage I and Stage II Books

Inevitably for the Stage III, there is an overlap of information that is contained within the Stage I and II books. To avoid continuous repetition, which would be tedious and would create a vast volume, the relevant sections have been indicated by 'Revision' insertions. Students can read through and revise these areas from the earlier books.

The Stage I and II books are a useful addition to every student's equestrian library, for not only do they contain material necessary for the Stage III, they are also of tremendous value for the Preliminary Teaching Test. They cover the subject matter needed for the lecturette, explain about lungeing, safety and first aid. They also cover equitation, which helps the PTT candidate teach the group, private and lunge lessons.

Even when the student qualifies and becomes a Preliminary Instructor (PI) or an Assistant Instructor (AI), these books are both useful and informative. For all instructors and lecturers this series forms a solid basis from which they can teach their own students in all aspects of horsemastership.

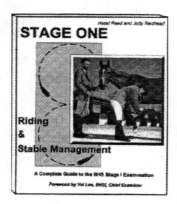
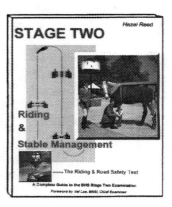

C H A P T E R   1
General Information

Achieving the Stage III, together with the Preliminary Teaching Test, enables the student to gain the Preliminary Instructor's Certificate and be officially recognised by the British Horse Society as a qualified instructor.

The Preliminary Instructor can then progress by teaching the number of required hours and become an Assistant Instructor. This qualification is well recognised throughout the world, offering career opportunities both at home and abroad.

For those candidates not seeking employment within the equestrian industry, but who may be returning to horses after a period of years, gaining the Preliminary Instructor's qualification is a personal achievement within their lives.

Eligibility

All applicants must:

* be a member of the British Horse Society at the time of application and on the day of the examination
* be 17 years or over
* have passed their Stage I and Stage II Riding and Horse Knowledge & Care

The Riding and Care sections of the Stage III can be taken separately if required, providing that the appropriate sections have been passed at Stages I and II.

The Syllabus

The riding section consists of flatwork, show jumping and cross-country. The Horse Knowledge & Care includes lungeing and the 'ride and lead' exercise.

Equitation

General   Check the horse's tack for fitting, including a double bridle. Alter if necessary. Assess and discuss the horses, their basic conformation, qualities, faults and possible methods of improvement.

Flatwork   The riders should ride the horses effectively and sympathetically through an independent, balanced and supple seat.

Each rider will work the horses in a snaffle and a double bridle. For a short period, some work will be required with the reins in one hand. The riders will also be asked to ride at some point without stirrups at walk, trot and canter. Spurs are not normally worn but riders should learn to ride with and use spurs correctly. The rider should assess each horse they ride and show that they understand the problems and can improve the horse's 'way of going'.

The rider should show accurate school figures, correct transitions and movements such as turn on the forehand, leg yield, rein back, lengthening and shortening strides.

Jumping   A course of show jumping fences up to 1 metre (3 feet 3 inches) and a cross-country course of jumps up to 0.91 metres (3 feet).

Safety   All riders should have an awareness of school etiquette and the rules when riding at competitions and events.

Horse Knowledge and Care

General Management

Candidates should show a level of responsibility, being capable of managing a number of horses and ponies in the stable and in the field; dealing with young, nervous or problem horses and those with stable vices.

Anatomy & Physiology

The horse's main muscles; how these provide movement, support and carry the rider. Structure of the leg below the knee and hock including the foot. An elementary knowledge of the horse's respiratory and circulatory systems. Conformation; the horse's action and footfalls.

Health   Taking and recording the horse's temperature, pulse and respiration rates. Administering medicines in water, in feed and by mouth. Parasites and worming procedures. Candidates should know the correct method of leading a horse in hand to check for action and possible lameness. Candidates are usually asked to do this in the Exam.

Candidates will be required to complete a written section on minor ailments and their treatments. They should also know when and how to call for professional help and the information to give.

Ride & Lead   Candidates will be required to ride one horse whilst leading another safely and efficiently.

Travelling   Practical knowledge of loading, travelling and unloading horses from a horsebox or trailer.

Feeding   Practical experience in organising and monitoring a feed room. Planning feed charts for various types of horses and ponies. Nutritional value of foods including grass in the horse's diet.

Fittening   Practical knowledge of a fittening regime from bringing the horse up from grass to competition standard. Looking after fit horses and their preparation for shows and competitions.

Saddlery   Tack up a horse for a dressage or cross-country event. Put on and fit a double bridle. Organisation of a tack room; storing saddlery. Types of bits for use on young, problem, and competition horses.

Clothing   Knowledge of use and fitting sweat and cooler sheets. Cleaning and storing rugs and blankets. Exercise bandages, putting on, fitting and uses, advantages and disadvantages.

Shoeing   Assessing a newly shod foot. Specialist shoes, studs and foot pads. Defective shoeing and effects.

Stable Design   Planning and organising a yard. Different types of stabling and materials.

Grassland Management

Managing and maintaining paddocks and fields.

Lungeing   Lungeing a horse for exercise with side reins, safety precautions for lungeing. Assessment of the horse on the lunge.

General Knowledge

Safety precautions and procedures when riding on the Public Highway. Accident procedures and the prevention of further incidents. Fire regulations and precautions. Knowledge of the aims and structure of the British Horse Society, the different departments, training, Examinations and approval of riding schools.

Note: though correct at going to press, and whilst every effort is made to keep these books up to date, the contents of the syllabus can change at any time. Candidates are always advised to contact the British Horse Society or the Examination Centre prior to their Exam to discover if any alterations or additions have been made.

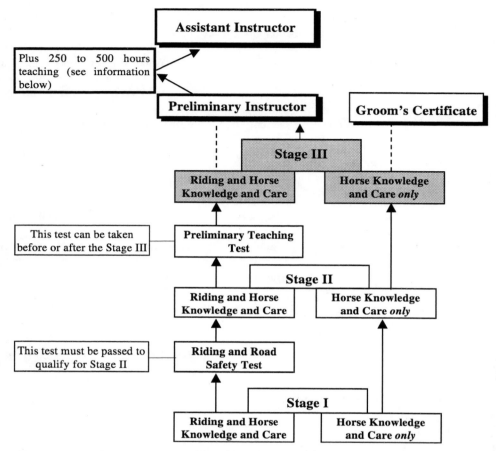

Figure 1: Table of BHS qualifications to Assistant Instructor level from January 1996.

BHS Examination Structure

To gain an Assistant Instructor qualification students must pass the Stages I, II, III Riding and Care, the Riding & Road Safety Test and the Preliminary Teaching Test. They must also complete a BHS Log Book to show that they have a specific number of hours of practical teaching experience. Those who teach at BHS 'Where to train' centres (listed in the 'Where to train' book) need 250 hours whilst those who teach at other establishments need 500 hours. Freelance instructors, teaching at various centres, will be able to count one hour as two when they teach at a 'Where to train' centre. Some of the hours required can be offset by attending teaching courses given by the British Horse Society.

A Groom's Certificate will be awarded to those candidates who pass the Care Sections in the BHS Stages I, II and III.

Requirements for the Stage III

One of the most important qualities each candidate needs for the Stage III, both in riding and stable management, is **confidence.** This should not be over-confidence or conceit but a quiet, positive confidence stemming from a belief in the student's own abilities and knowledge.

Stage III candidates are well on their way to becoming a Preliminary or Assistant Instructor. Most PI's and AI's will certainly be teaching whilst many may be employed to assist in taking charge of a yard. This could be a commercial business establishment with a number of horses and staff. The Examiners need to feel that each candidate is capable of this responsibility; that they have the knowledge and the ability in practical terms to take control of situations when they arise.

Another point is that candidates at Stage III will be expected to *think* for themselves. By this level most candidates will have had practical experience and will know that each horse is an individual; what works for one will not necessarily work for another. Whilst at the basic level there are rules, by Stage III candidates will have learnt to be adaptable and use alternative methods, keeping in mind the health of the horse and, most importantly, *safety*.

During the Stable Management section candidates should give their answers in a positive manner drawing, wherever possible, from practical experience. Candidates may also need to take control of a situation in the Exam with authority and tact. For instance when preparing to load the horse, if the group stand around looking lost and wondering what to do next, this will not make a good impression. It is better for one to take control and organise the others.

There is an underlying criterion in the Exam that, as well as being knowledgeable, the candidate should be capable of managing people. He or she should be able to organise people with tactful authority.

Where to Train

It is essential that the student trains at a centre that is *at least* a Stage III standard. The prospective candidate will frequently need to ride horses of this ability and, if possible, horses that are above this level. In this way the student learns to 'feel' the 'correct' movements, balance, rhythm, impulsion, working through into an outline. Until the rider has felt this he or she will have little chance of understanding, or working towards, a more correct 'way of going'.

The rider will also need to practise over Stage III show jumping and cross-country courses. A couple of jumps in a small menage will not give the rider the ability needed to negotiate larger courses.

There are establishments of high quality that do not offer the BHS Stage III but, while students will learn to a high standard at these, it is advisable that some lessons are taken at a Stage III Exam centre or college. Here the instructors will be conversant with the Exam and know the standard desired by the Examiners. Most centres will run courses, either full or part time. Many Agricultural Colleges combine other courses as well, such as secretarial, computer or business studies.

Preparation for the Stage III

Students working towards their Stage III will need to expand their practical ability and knowledge. Some of the theory covered at Stage II will be put into practice at Stage III. For instance, loading and unloading will actually be done in the Stage III Exam.

The practical sections will need to be learnt from personal experience gained from practical lectures, from working with and handling horses. It will also help to attend shows, either to compete or to groom for a friend.

The theory can be learnt from home study and from lectures. Some new subjects are introduced in the Stage III; other topics are an expansion of the knowledge learnt for Stage II.

For the equitation the rider will need to show an improvement in position and technique on the flat and in jumping. This does require lessons from a qualified instructor who is knowledgeable, experienced and technically able to improve the rider's position and expertise.

Assessment

Having decided to work towards the Stage III, the student should first have an assessment from a qualified BHS Instructor who is familiar with the Examination (preferably a BHS Intermediate Instructor or above). This will give an indication of the sections on which the student needs to concentrate and when he or she is ready to apply for the Exam.

The important point is to allow enough time to prepare fully. Each student can plan a timetable for riding and stable management lessons each week combined with home study sessions. Good preparation leads to knowledge and ability, which in turn leads to confidence. Confidence will give the candidate a positive attitude and consequently success in the Examination.

CHAPTER 2
Equitation - Flatwork

The equitation in Stage III includes flatwork lasting up to an hour, one show jumping round and one cross-country round. In all three disciplines the rider needs to show that their basic position is established, secure and in balance, and as a result of this, they are able to work the horse more effectively.

Revision

The following points were covered in the Stage I and II books and the student may revise these if necessary.

The rider's position, the natural aids, co-ordination of aids, the half-halt, straightness, circles and turns, transitions, school rules and commands, the horse's basic paces and their footfalls. Mounting, dismounting, checking girths and stirrups.

Preparation for Flatwork

All prospective candidates may start preparing for their Stage III several months in advance, planning a timetable of riding lessons each week. The training may include a variety of lessons: on the lunge to improve basic position and balance, private or semi-private lessons that allow more time to concentrate on the horse and group lessons to increase anticipation and adaptability when riding with others.

The group sessions should mainly be in open order, that is, working as individuals within the group. Students then become accustomed to working the horses on their own, learning to adapt their direction to accommodate other riders whilst keeping the work fluent and smooth within the space available.

Students need to ride horses of different standards, ages and types, to increase their experience of horses' paces and movements. It will also expand their recognition of problems, their repertoire of school figures and movements by which they can improve the horses.

Another aspect is 'rider' fitness. To develop fitness, students should ideally ride for at least three to five hours a week, more if at all possible. Going to the gym or doing aerobic exercises is commendable and will help with physical agility. The wrong type of exercise however can develop the wrong muscles making the rider literally too 'strong'. True rider fitness is different; it is not strength that a rider needs so much as suppleness, flexibility and technique.

A qualified fitness trainer will design a programme based on stretching the muscles and making the joints supple. The rider should also use exercises to build up stamina. Swimming is excellent, particularly as many riders suffer from back problems.

One excellent aid to progression is the video camera or camcorder. Being able to watch lessons on film, to slow down and replay certain parts, helps the rider to understand exactly what is happening. Taking a series of films over some months also shows the rider how much they are improving, which is not always apparent with gradual progress.

Stage III Requirements – Flatwork

The Stage III rider will need to develop:

a)   a balanced position with an established, independent seat.

b)   effective use of the natural aids and an understanding of their influence on the horse.

c)   an understanding and 'feel' of the horse's paces and movements.

d)   ability to ride with a double bridle. (Though not normally requested during the Exam, the rider should be able to demonstrate the correct use of spurs.)

The Rider's Position

The rider's position, at this standard, should be such that the rider is *physically able to sit in balance with the horse.* This means that the rider maintains a balance throughout the horse's movements, independent of the reins or gripping knees.

Often the term 'the rider's position' can convey the impression that there is one static pose that the rider should hold no matter what action the horse is performing. To try and keep one 'correct' position makes the rider rigid and stiff; the body is held against the horse's movement rather than flowing with it.

Whereas in the 'balanced position' the rider sits quietly and with slight, supple movements of the hips, soft relaxed thighs, and a light, carried upper body, allows the horse's action. Then the rider can begin to use the aids and work the horse with more effect.

To achieve this balanced position the rider has to develop the right suppleness and physical fitness, the ability to sit deep but lightly in the saddle. Lunge lessons with an experienced, qualified instructor, who is able to pinpoint problems and give the relevant corrections, are invaluable and will benefit the rider long after their Exam. The lunge horse does need to be supple, free moving and obedient on the lunge for the rider to gain the full benefit.

Alternatively, or as an additional exercise, riding in the school without stirrups for short periods of time helps to develop fitness and balance.

Once the basic flatwork position has been achieved and the rider has the basic physical ability to sit on a horse, finer and more subtle adjustments can be made.

The Hips

One of the most important areas for the rider is the hip or pelvic area. This forms the conjunction between the upper and lower body and any displacement in this area affects the whole position.

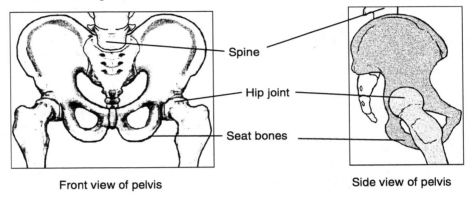

Front view of pelvis   Side view of pelvis

The lower part of the pelvis contains the seat bones, which lie in contact with the saddle. Through the development and increased suppleness of the pelvic area and hip joints, the seat becomes 'deeper', more in contact with the saddle.

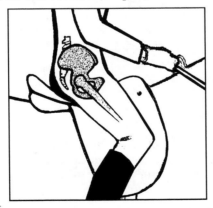

Here the pelvis is kept upright in a 'natural' position. The rider's body is straight and central in the saddle

Any tilting of the top of the pelvis forwards or backwards will affect the rest of the posture.

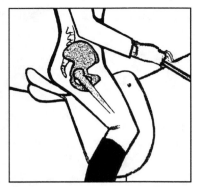

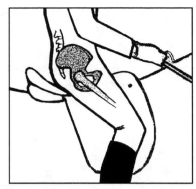

With a hollow back, the top of the pelvis is tipped to the front. The upper body is normally leaning forward.

Hunched or 'chair' seat: top of pelvis tipped backwards. Back is rounded, body collapsed and the rider's weight lies heavy on the saddle.

When the horse is at halt or moving in straight lines the rider's hipbones should be level.

One hip should not be higher or lower than the other hip. If more weight is placed on one side the rider will be sitting unlevel and will normally compensate for this by displacing another part of the body.

For instance if the weight is placed on the left seat bone, the rider's body will be heavier and lower to the left. The rider will normally lean over to the right to compensate and, in effect, will 'collapse' the right hip.

Also both hip bones need to be **in line**, that is, one hip should not be further forward or further back than the other.

If one hipbone is further back than the other, the rider will normally compensate by twisting the upper body and bringing one leg forward.

The 'pelvic twist' can be evident from the position of the rider's body; the spine may be twisted the shoulders unlevel and the head tilted to one side. The hands may either be held at different heights or one in front of the other.

To help recognise and correct these faults the horse should be brought to halt and held by someone for safety.

The rider, sitting naturally, can then feel the projecting hip bones just below the waist by placing a hand on each bone. The rider should be able to feel if the hipbones are level and in line with one another.

Sometimes the displacement can be so slight that it is difficult to detect. The seat may also feel level because the rider is accustomed to sitting that way.

In all cases a good instructor will be able to detect and correct faults with the hips and seat.

Once the rider has corrected any faults, the position may feel 'unnatural' for a while until the muscles are developed. This is especially so if the rider has been riding in this position for some time.

Another problem with the pelvic area is tension. The pelvis consists of many muscles, tendons and ligaments that link it with the spine, legs and other parts of the body. Any tightening of the muscles in this area can affect the whole position.

It also influences the horse. A tight, clenched seat will restrict the movement through the horse's back. The horse will normally try to take his back away (hollow) from this tense area.

Sometimes, riders suffer from tension in the seat and pelvis through trying 'too hard'. Think about 'fluffing' out the buttock muscles rather like a hen fluffs out her feathers.

The Seat

The seat should be 'soft' and inviting to encourage the horse to raise his back and to allow the energy to flow through from his hindquarters. The rider will need to maintain or improve the mobility of the hips, keeping them supple.

One exercise, which the rider can do whilst dismounted, is to walk by swinging each hip forward. Many people walk by pushing their shoulders forward, whereas if the hips are used this increases their flexibility and can improve posture. Walking in this manner seems to automatically bring the shoulders back and the head up.

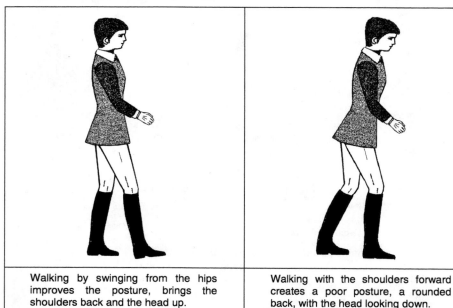

| Walking by swinging from the hips improves the posture, brings the shoulders back and the head up. | Walking with the shoulders forward creates a poor posture, a rounded back, with the head looking down. |

With the pelvic area supple, mobile and relaxed the rider's hips move in rhythm with the horse's movements. The rider can then begin to develop an awareness of the horse's paces.

Feel the horse move in the walk; his hind legs should gently push the hips very slightly forwards and backwards, one side then another.

In sitting trot this is emphasised even more by the two-time pace. In the canter the inside hip is pushed gently forwards and backwards in rhythm with the leading leg.

Once the rider has developed this feel (and this can be quite exciting at first!) he or she can then learn the art of **sitting quietly**. This means **allowing the horse to move the rider's hips** without restriction, keeping the seat soft and supple in the saddle.

The word 'soft' is often used in equitation; it is meant to convey a feeling of 'controlled relaxation'. The word 'relax' often means droop or letting go completely, whereas soften means to release the tension without collapsing or drooping.

The Legs

Basically the leg position is influenced by the hip area. With a soft, deep seat the legs can gently wrap around the horse's sides. The thighs will lie 'softly' against the saddle with the thigh muscles relaxed. The knees, slightly bent, will be pointing towards the front. The lower legs can 'cuddle' the horse's sides, in readiness to give the leg aids. The toes should be pointing towards the front, with the heels slightly lower.

Any tension in the thighs, normally associated with tension in the seat, affects the position and effectiveness of the lower leg. Tight thighs and gripping knees will result in bringing the lower leg away from the horse. This tension also restricts the horse's energy.

It will help to occasionally do the 'legs away' exercise to stretch and release the hips and thighs. **Gently** take one leg at a time slightly away from the saddle, keep the knee pointing forwards and slowly stretch the leg outwards and down. Keep the seat relaxed and soft throughout this exercise.

Another problem, also originating from the hip area, is when the rider's feet (or one foot) points outwards. The rider will grip or clamp the legs onto the horse, again restricting forward movement.

To improve the leg position, each hip joint can be gently rotated by taking hold of the thick muscle at the back of the thigh and *slowly* bringing it back and out. The flat of the thigh should now lie against the saddle, the knee and foot be pointing forwards.

Stiff, tense ankles also cause problems, preventing sufficient depth of seat. Rotating the ankles slowly to release the tension and to supple the ligaments and tendons in those areas can help the rider to flow with the horse's movement more rhythmically and fluently.

The Upper Body

The upper portion of the body should be carried upright with the rider sitting up straight. The ribcage should be open and 'free' with the shoulders back and relaxed. The upper arms will lie naturally against the rider's sides, the elbows bent and the lower arms following the line through the hands and reins to the bit.

The rider's head is an important point of balance; being quite heavy it influences the posture. It should be carried upwards, straight from the shoulders. If the head is tilted forwards the rest of the body has a tendency to 'crouch' forwards and hunch. The shoulders will sag and the back slouch.

It may help to look at a point where the horse will be in about three strides time. Some riders prefer to watch the horse's ears but this may tend to focus on the horse's head and bring the rider's own head down. It is better to look over and beyond the horse's ears, to think forwards.

For turns and circles the rider's should softly follow the intended line around the curve. The head should not be turned stiffly and rigidly round in an effort to bring the rest of the body and the horse around with it.

The Hands

Once the rider has achieved a correct, balanced body the hands can be positioned in the right place, just in front of and slightly higher than the pommel. (It is becoming apparent how important the basic seat is for the rider.)

The hands should be about five inches apart; (approximately the width of the horse's mouth) positioned either side of the horse's withers. They should be level, that is, at the same height. The reins can now be sufficiently short without the rider compromising the position by being pulled forward.

The wrists should be kept straight but flexible with the lower arms, wrists, hands and reins making a straight 'line' to the bit.

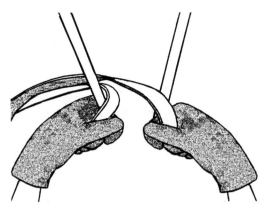

If the rider has to curl the wrists, holding the hands near and into the body, then the reins are too long. The action of the arms will be compromised.

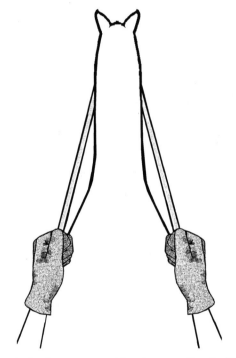

The hands should remain in the same position but not fixed. They will need to have slight mobility but always return to the same area. Release any tension in the lower arms by consciously relaxing the muscles in this area.

Another problem stems from tension in the rider's shoulders. Gently rotating the shoulders slightly, or moving one shoulder then the other up, back and then down smoothly, helps to release this tightness.

Weight and Lightness

The rider then learns to 'carry' his body; this in turn encourages the horse to carry himself. Only when the rider has self-carriage, can the horse have self-carriage.

The horse's back is not the strongest part of his anatomy and if the rider is slumped, his full weight and that of the saddle will be taken by the horse's back muscles. Imagine this being coupled with a rigid, tight hip area and no wonder the horse hollows in an attempt to keep his back away from pain. The horse's movements will also be impeded if this weight is not in balance but is constantly shifting backwards and forwards and from one side to another.

At Stage II the rider was creating a lightness from the waist upwards, by imagining the weight dropping down from the shoulders, into the seat, legs and heels without losing the height of the upper body. The Stage III rider can now progress with this in mind, by beginning to carry the upper body. Keeping the body 'light' the rider invites the horse to round his back into a 'soft' seat.

Sounds simple, but even for natural riders, and definitely for those of us who have to struggle, the correct body and seat positions are only developed through good instruction, physical exercise, riding fitness and with thought.

Once the rider's position comes into balance and harmony with the horse, the aids become more effective. In some cases the aids can also become lighter and more subtle because the rider's position is more efficient.

The Aids

The aids are the language by which we communicate our wishes to the horse. By Stage III the rider is learning to use the aids in different ways, in co-ordination with each other and with more refinement.

The Seat

The rider at this level is beginning to learn about the influence of the seat by developing an awareness of the horse's movements through the hip area. Though eventually the developed seat becomes the rider's most important aid, at this standard it is used sparingly through the weight aids and as part of the co-ordination of aids that compose the half-halt. The rider should concentrate on keeping the seat soft and supple to allow the horse's movements through his back.

The Weight Aid

An extension of the seat aid is the body or weight aid. It may be difficult to envisage the horse feeling anything through the thickness of a saddle and numnah, but with all the weight of the rider and saddle on the horse's back any movement, even slight, is definitely going to be felt. It is therefore important that the rider first learns *to sit quietly* with his weight carefully distributed and kept in balance.

The rider can begin to learn the effect of the weight aid and how this is used *with discretion.* For instance, to ask the horse to circle or turn, the rider's weight needs to be rearranged in such a way that the horse can move around the curve easily. The rider achieves this when giving the aids for a corner or turn.

The rider's inside leg aid is applied in the region of the girth, thus keeping the inside hip in the forward position. The *rider's outside leg is moved slightly back, just behind the girth.* This places the rider's weight fractionally to the inside, allowing the horse to redistribute his own weight and keep in balance around the circle or turn.

At the same time the rider's inside shoulder is brought slightly back and the outside shoulder slightly forward, in other words the rider's upper body follows the turn. This allows the hands to guide the horse around the turn. The shoulders should be kept level as any tilt or lean one way or another will detrimentally affect the horse's balance.

All weight aids should be smooth, slight and comfortable for both rider and horse.

The Legs

With the pelvis, thighs and knees relaxed, the lower legs are able to come into closer contact with the horse's sides. The leg aid can be applied with the inside of the leg or calf by 'nudging' inwards. This is much more relaxed and kinder on the horse than a kicking aid. The degree of the nudge can be varied from a light touch for the sensitive horse to a firmer, more assertive nudge for the horse who refuses to listen and respond.

For riders who tense when using the leg, try consciously relaxing the leg then nudging inwards, now release, nudge inwards again, and release.

The Hands

As the rider improves, the hands develop 'feel'. Sometimes the hands are talked about as a separate entity but actually they are part of a whole system. They are a segment of the rider's position and can reflect any faults in the posture.

The hands should be thought of as an extension of the shoulders, the upper arms, the elbows and the lower arms. Any stiffness or tension within the shoulders or elbows will be reflected in the hands.

The shoulders need to be relaxed (imagine a 'sponge type' feeling in the shoulder blades). The upper and lower arms should feel relaxed and 'elastic'. Think of the arms as a pair of side reins with an elastic stretch. The side reins are not rigid; they have a certain amount of 'give' but neither do they flop and become too loose. The elbows should be bent so that they do not 'lock' and go rigid.

Many times pupils are told they have 'hard' hands and this can create an everlasting fear within the rider. So much so that riders are often afraid to use the hands at all.

It is more true to say that riders either have 'cultivated' or 'uncultivated' hands and that this often stems from good or poor instruction. Every rider can achieve cultivated hands and will learn through progression, instruction and through their own consideration exactly how 'feel' can be learnt and achieved.

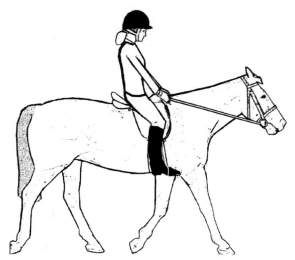

The horse's shoulders and forward movement are blocked by the tense, rigid hands. The rider's body stiffens in the attempt to 'bring the horse's head down' and the rider's attention is downward rather than up and forward.

The problems begin when the rider actively uses the hands with force or roughness. This may not be intentional but any rider who tries to force the horse's head down with stiff, straight, locked arms is restricting the horse. The rider's body locks into a strained posture and rigidity sets in.

The hands are an integral part of the rider's aids and *should always be used in conjunction with the other aids.* The thought aid comes first, the seat with discretion, the legs and then the shoulders; arms and hands control the energy and ask the horse to respond.

The 'mind' Aid

This is the most important aid; the rider should be able to think, be observant, perceptive and decisive. He or she will need to plan ahead, be adaptable and assertive in a quiet but positive way.

Before every aid is given the rider should think about the action first. Horses at times do seem telepathic, for on occasions it only takes a thought for the horse to respond; perhaps the rider thinks and subconsciously moves the body. For whatever reason, the horse can be extremely sensitive to the 'thought or mind aid'.

As the rider progresses, one of the most important qualities will be positive self-criticism. The rider needs to constantly assess his or her own position, the horse's 'way of going' and to be aiming for improvement positively.

Another necessary quality is self-discipline. The rider will need to be strict about correctness and accuracy in both his own position, his plan of work and in the horse's 'way of going'.

The Voice

The voice is mainly used when training or lungeing horses. In flatwork the use of the voice is discouraged, mainly because it is penalised in dressage competitions where the horse has to show his education through response to the other natural aids. It can however be used sparingly to praise or reprimand.

Co-ordination of the Aids

The aids are always used in co-ordination with each other to convey the rider's message just as words are used together to form a sentence. Developing this co-ordination of the aids is rather like learning a new language.

At the start we learnt the basic aids and their uses rather like the alphabet and how to make up small words. Later on we learnt to use some of the aids in combination rather like joining words together to make sentences. At Stage III we are learning to co-ordinate and combine the aids more effectively to build sentences into paragraphs.

The aids are used in combination with each other. If one aid is used without another, this aid becomes strong. There are times when an aid needs to be applied more firmly than the others to make the horse obedient; the other aids, however, should also be used in support.

Though used in co-ordination, the aids are not applied simultaneously. The time lapse may be very short; the more subtle the aids the more quickly they can be applied one after the other. For example the rider applies the thought aid, the seat with discretion, then leg, then hand. To use all together would confuse the horse; rather like trying to speak all the words in a sentence at once. Another analogy often used is that to apply the leg and hand aid together is rather like pressing the accelerator whilst putting on the brakes.

The Half-Halt

The most important co-ordination of aids is the half-halt. This is used before any change of direction, pace or movement or even within a pace to improve rhythm and balance. The rider momentarily sits a little taller, straightens the back, applies the leg aids and gives a squeeze and release on the reins. The effect is that the horse brings his hindquarters up underneath him, engaging his hindlegs and lightening the forehand.

This makes it so much easier for him and his rider to perform any transition, movement or change within a pace. The rider should practise this half-halt frequently, feeling the change in the horse.

Eventually the rider applies this 'aid' automatically whenever and wherever it is needed. The half-halt can be applied hundreds of times in one hour's schooling, which goes to show just how important this aid can be.

It should become an instantaneous, subtle message invisible to all except the horse and rider just as if the rider were whispering the horse's name to attract his attention before asking him to do anything.

Using the Aids

There is one more important point about using the aids – once applied the aid should be released. The application of aids then becomes more refined and subtle; apply – release, apply – release. The release of the aid is as vital as applying the aid in the first place.

Even when a stronger aid is required this is given more firmly then released. Any aid applied and constantly maintained becomes tense and restrictive making the horse resistant. This 'apply and release' also allows the rider to be more relaxed.

One important lesson the horse should learn is obedience to the aids. If the rider applies an aid, which the horse ignores and gives a firmer aid without response, the whip should then be used to insist on obedience in support of the rider's demand.

The Quiet Rider

The next important stage is to ride quietly. The rider needs to be in balance with the horse and maintain the soft supple position without any unnecessary movement. On trained or more sensitive horses even a tiny shift in the weight will ask them for a movement or reaction. Sitting quietly may be one of the more difficult aspects of riding that we have to learn, because quietness is not rigidity or static stiffness. It is compliance with the body to the horse's movement, acting with a small area of the body when, and only when, the rider needs to ask the horse for an action.

Any great degree of movement or fast, jerky action in the rider will unbalance the horse. For instance many riders are seen to 'rock' their body when the horse is in canter in an attempt to keep in balance or make the horse more active. Riders often use their legs or hands too much, their body constantly shifting to maintain position.

Imagine someone chattering on and on for hours, eventually the person listening will 'switch off'. If a rider is constantly bouncing, rocking or moving around on the horse, the horse will ignore a slight weight aid. Now if someone quiet suddenly speaks and says something of interest, this will be heard. The quiet, balanced rider will receive a response even from a slight change in weight.

Stage III Riding - Flatwork

The flatwork section of the equitation lasts for up to an hour. The riders are required to ride three different horses, at least one in a double bridle, with approximately 15 to 20 minutes on each horse. This is usually in an indoor school, but may be in an outdoor menage or arena. The instructor in charge either allocates a horse or invites the riders to make their own choice as to which horse they wish to ride.

The Examination

By this level riders are expected to show more competence by the way in which they structure and plan their work, by the way they adapt their skills to improve the horse.

Each rider should begin by checking the tack, fit and condition (fitting a double bridle is explained in the chapter on Saddlery). The rider can also make a quick assessment of the horse at the same time, his colour, gender, estimated height, basic conformation, possible age and type. The age will not need to be known with any accuracy but a quick peep at the teeth, if possible, when the rider checks the bit, should give an idea of youth or age.

The rider should also organise and make alterations to the tack quickly and efficiently, and be prepared to mount on the instructor's command.

When the horse is wearing a double bridle, the rider mounts holding the bridoon rein only. The curb rein should remain on the horse's neck near the withers, so that it does not slip down towards the horse's head and become unsafe. Some riders prefer to hold both reins but this can place pressure on the horse's mouth and, should he move, may cause pain if the curb becomes too tight.

The Double Bridle

The main methods of holding the reins are:

1. The bridoon rein passes between the ring finger (third finger) and the little finger. The curb rein goes inside the bridoon rein and is held between the middle finger (second finger) and the ring finger.

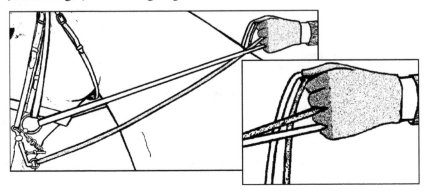

2.   The bridoon rein passes outside the little finger. The curb rein passes inside the bridoon rein and is held between the ring finger and the little finger.

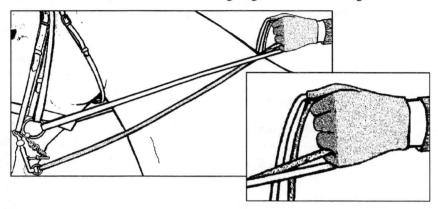

In both cases the reins then pass inside the palm exiting the hand between the thumb and index finger with the bridoon rein on top.

3.   The reins enter the hand as in example 2 and exit with the bridoon held between the thumb and index finger and the curb rein held between the index and middle finger.

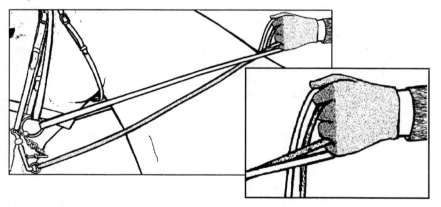

Any of these methods is correct; some riders prefer one way to another. In the first method the bridoon is held in the same position as the snaffle. In the second some riders find it easier to act on the bridoon by movements of the little finger only.

The third example keeps the reins separate making it easier to adjust the length of one rein without affecting the other rein. It also means there is a light pressure on the curb and any feel exerted on the curb rein can be given with sensitivity by the two middle fingers.

Riders should experiment to discover the method that suits them and which they can use with the best effect.

Using the Double

The double bridle is designed to have a more precise and refined effect on the horse through the added pressure points of the two bits. It allows the rider to work with a 'finer', more subtle and lighter feel.

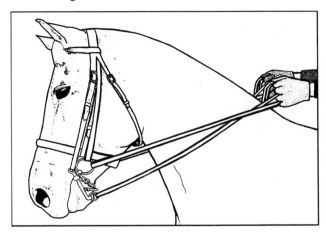

The hands should hold the reins firmly but gently. Imagine holding a small child's hand whilst crossing a busy road, firmly so that the child does not escape but gently to avoid crushing the small fingers.

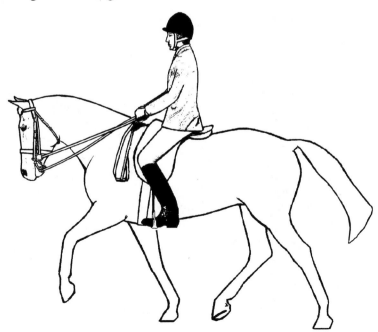

The contact needs to be constant, that is, allowing the horse's head movements but maintaining the same amount of 'feel' through the reins.

It is now more important than ever that the rider creates the energy with the legs and works the horse into an inviting hand. The horse's head should never be forced down.

Riders are often afraid of using the double because they are aware of its stronger action. However, not using it at all can also be detrimental to the horse. The idea is to provide the energy and activity from behind, encourage the horse forward and allow him to round his back. Then, with a 'contained feel' of the bridle, the rider keeps the horse between 'leg and hand'.

The rider maintains a contact with the bridoon rein and has a longer, lighter curb rein. Some horses object to the influence of the curb bit and chain, 'backing off' the bridle, coming behind the bit to evade, or lean down on the hand. *In these cases the curb rein can be loosened slightly.*

The rider may need to be firm but never strong. Ask and release and always use the legs before the rein aids. A horse controlled by the bridle alone will refuse to go forward actively. The word for riding with a double bridle is 'tact'. The use of the double bridle and the feel of two reins in the hand can be unusual at first. The rider does need to practise constantly using the double bridle before Exam day.

Spurs

The spur is used for the same reason as the double, to give a lighter, more refined leg aid. Technically riders can be asked to wear and use spurs during the Stage III. In practice this is rare as many horses at Stage III level are not accustomed to riders with spurs. It is important though that riders learn and practise using spurs, especially when using a double bridle.

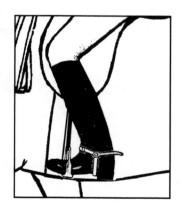

The leg aid is given with **the inside of the calf of the leg,** *not the heel.* In this way **the inside of the spur will lightly touch the horse's side. The toe should be pointing forward so that the heel is not turned in and does not dig into the horse's side.**

The Flatwork Session

At the beginning of the session, the instructor in charge may specify one rein for all the riders to work on, in open order. Alternatively, riders will be asked to work on both reins. Riders will be expected to work safely around the other riders in the school.

The rider should begin to assess the horse first at walk. Feel how the horse uses himself, whether or not he feels stiff through the back or shoulders. He may feel a little tense, but then the rider may be tense too, which is not surprising. The horse may need a *slightly* longer rein to loosen his body and shoulders.

Alternatively the horse may be striding on too fast, or taking short rapid steps in which case he will need a contact and a half-halt to slow the walk down. Remember to look up; as well as watching for the other riders in the school, this will correct the riding position. It is easy to become focused on the horse's head or neck and look down.

Using the school

Efficient and effective use of the school will help both horse and rider. The rider needs to work immediately on obedience from the horse, improving his suppleness, his balance, rhythm and tempo.

1. Ask the horse to go into the corners, as far as he is able at first, testing his response to the inside leg and rein.

2. Walk a 20 or 15 metre circle, ask the horse to bend his body around the inside leg, controlling him with the outside leg, whilst he accepts the inside rein and the outside rein contact. The rider can now assess if he keeps his rhythm and tempo whilst on curves, or whether he becomes slower and stiffer.

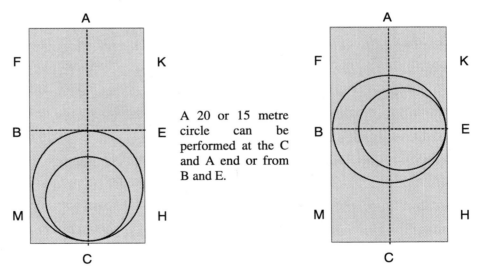

A 20 or 15 metre circle can be performed at the C and A end or from B and E.

3. Come across the school and on the centre line ask for halt. It is important to check the horse's response to the aids in downward transitions. If the horse stops suddenly with a jerk, he needs more leg. If he ignores the aids and resists, he needs more and possibly stronger half-halts. He must listen.

4. Check the horse's response for the upward transition to walk. If he is sluggish or reluctant, use the whip to insist he responds quickly.

5. Throughout all these exercises the rider should be 'feeling' the walk, assessing the speed, tempo and rhythm.

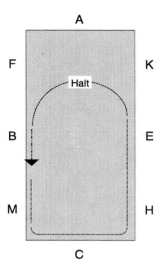

Trot work

The riders will be requested to work on into trot fairly quickly. Ride a variety of school figures similar to those described for walk.

Avoid like the plague trotting large around the school continuously, this does the horse little good and the rider even less in the eyes of the Examiners.

Other exercises at trot include:

1. Shallow loops (3 metres to begin with then 5 metres) down one long sides of the school; gives the opportunity of bending the horse's body first one way and then another.

2. These loops should also give an idea as to the horse's stiff and looser side.

3. On a large circle, shorten the stride for four or six strides, then lengthen for four or six strides and repeat.

4. Decreasing and increasing circles. Starting on a 20 or 18 metre circle, decrease the circle and leg yield out to the larger circle.

Keep the trot active, rhythmical and balanced throughout all the work.

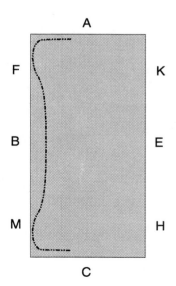

Change of Rein

When changing the rein use a short diagonal, the line between E and B or a demi-volte and incline back to the track. When riders change the rein by a long diagonal or the centre line they almost always find someone in their path.

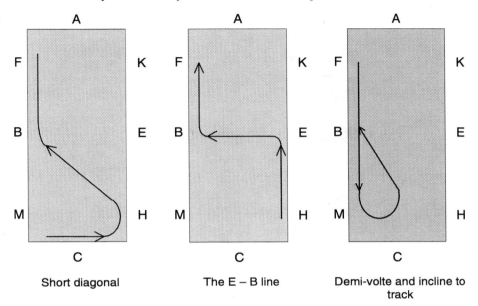

Short diagonal	The E – B line	Demi-volte and incline to track

Canter work

The instructor in charge will normally ask for some canter work on the first horse. Again use the school to its best advantage. *Avoid, at all costs, cantering round and round the track.*

1. Check the horse's straightness by cantering on an inner track down the long side.

2. Use 18 to 20 metre circles, and half circles across the school.

3. Canter 3 metre, shallow loops down the long sides, (an introduction to counter canter).

4. Slow the canter down slightly for two or three strides then on again. Do this slowly and gently or the horse may fall into trot.

5. Use transitions to and from trot. Check the horse's response to the aids in the upward transitions. If he is unresponsive correct with taps from the whip behind the inside leg.

    (Make the downward transitions in the centre of the school across the centre line to avoid impeding other riders on the inner or outer tracks.)

6. Continue to assess the horse.

Riding with the reins in one hand

The riders may be requested to ride with the reins in one hand during walk, trot or canter work around the school. This is to assess the rider's control and balance.

The reins and whip should be held in the outside hand. If the reins are held in the inside hand the rider will tend to twist his body.

Riding without stirrups

Riders are normally requested to ride in walk, trot and canter without stirrups, on the first or second horse.

Assessment of Horses

By the end of the session the rider should have made an assessment of all three horses.

1. The three paces. Assess which were the best paces and which the worst. For example: this horse had two good paces, the trot and canter, but his walk was poor.

2. Balance, rhythm and tempo; which horse had the more balanced paces. For example: the first horse had good rhythm and balance in his trot work, the second horse had an unbalanced canter.

3. Assess which is the horse's stiff side, which the soft.

4. Were the horses forward going or sluggish?

5. How good was the lateral work, transitions, their general 'way of going'?

6. How did each horse respond to the natural aids?

7. How could each horse be improved and what exercises would be beneficial, for instance, work over poles?

8. What type of plan the rider would consider using to improve each horse in the future. *Lateral work* improves the horse's suppleness and flexibility. It increases his obedience to the aids. *Pole work* improves the horse's paces, rhythm and balance and makes him use his legs, hocks and back more efficiently. *Work on the lunge* can improve the horse's balance and rhythm in paces and transitions. Transitions, shortening and lengthening stride can improve the horse's responses to the aids and encourage him to be more forward going. Hacking or featuring some different routine in his work can help a horse revitalise if he is stale and can make him more forward going.

The type of horses that will be available for the candidates of the Stage III will vary. The majority will be the Welsh Cob, Irish Draught cross Thoroughbred type, but there could be a full Thoroughbred or Anglo Arab. There may occasionally be a Warm-blood but this is not usual.

Normally the horses are school horses aged from 7 years old to aged schoolmasters. They should be capable of performing leg yield, turn on the forehand, rein back and of attempting shortening and lengthening of stride. Some will be accustomed to a double bridle.

Most will be capable of working in an outline, though some will be more difficult, stiffer and less educated than others. Most will also be steady, some forward going, others sluggish or lazy.

Candidates should practise riding and assessing the range of horses that are likely to be included in the Examination. They will then have the preparation necessary to warm up and work different types and breeds of horses, those of different ages and with varying degrees of suppleness.

Exam Tips

The most important aspect of the Stage III flatwork (and the jumping) is to be positive.

Have a definite plan in mind for the flatwork session. You can design your own plan of work to include a warm-up phase, an assessment and working towards improvement phase. This plan can be created some weeks before the Exam so that you can practise it in lessons, learning it rather like a dressage test. In the Examination you may be asked to warm the horse up in walk and trot only, or in walk, trot and canter.

The work plan may include:

1. Walk – assess pace. Check own position whilst loosening horse on a long rein down one long side of school. Take up reins.

2. Check the horse's straightness by walking on an inner track down the long side of school.

3. 15 metre circle on short end of school. Check bend, balance, rhythm and tempo.

4. On into trot work – 3 metre shallow loop on long side of school, circles at both short ends. Ask the horse to bend into the corners.

5. Come across the school to ask for downward transitions to walk and upward transitions again. Try transitions to walk and halt in the same place.

6. Canter, check transition. Canter on an inner track to check for straightness. Include circles and 3 metre shallow loops. Transitions to trot and walk.

7. Repeat the exercises in the other direction when requested to change the rein.

Design a plan that works the horse in all three paces, on both reins and which includes some school movements such as leg yield or turn on the forehand within 15 minutes. The time does go quickly, but this is the period you will have on each horse in the Examination.

Having a plan of work will help to focus your mind on the job. It will give you a structure to work within and make you more efficient at working the horse. Remember also safety. **The school rules are important at Stage III**. You need to be aware of the other riders in the school when working in open order, at different paces, often on different reins and performing school movements, such as leg yield.

Some riders concentrate so much that they forget there are others around them, but any rider who makes a downward transition directly in front of another, who impedes or rides too close to another horse will be deemed unsafe.

You will need to be positive and use the space available. There are those riders, though, who think that 'assertive' means 'aggressive' and charge around the school without consideration for the other riders.

No rider should ride in such a way as to be a danger to others. All riders at Stage III should ride with care, attention and safety. Keep your head up, watch for the other riders and be adaptable, use the school intelligently.

CHAPTER 3
Equitation - Paces

The horse's quality of work is important because he needs to exercise in such a way that he uses, and therefore strengthens, the correct muscles. To achieve this the rider needs to know how the horse should work and how to ask for this quality of work throughout all the horse's paces, transitions and school movements.

The Horse

This section will describe the horse's 'way of going', the paces that the rider should work towards achieving and the basic school movements required at Stage III.

Calmness and Relaxation

This is the first important aim for both horse and rider. The horse should be relaxed and calm, free from tension. For this, it is necessary for the rider to be calm and relaxed. Any tension within the rider can be transmitted to the horse, and a tense horse will be stiff and tight. Similarly a tense horse may result in a tense rider.

As part of this calmness and relaxation, at the beginning of each work session, the rider should ask the horse to move forward freely. The horse needs to move within his own rhythm on a long rein, into a light hand contact. This may be a little slow or fast and on the forehand at first but the rider should allow the horse to release any stiffness and tension for the first minute or so. The rider can also use this time for his own relaxation and release of tension.

The rider needs to take the contact up slowly and gently so that the horse is encouraged to bring his weight off the forehand and redistribute his balance. The horse can then carry his own weight and that of the rider more equally on all four legs. Once the horse has become more supple through this relaxation period, the rider applies the aids to ask the horse to work.

Forward Movement

For the horse to achieve balance in his paces, for him to work correctly and perform school movements and figures satisfactorily, he must first be moving forwards freely. This again stems from obedience to the aids, from calmness and relaxation in his mind and physical frame.

It is essential that the horse is obedient to the rider's aids. If the rider has to apply the aids frequently and firmly this will create tension.

The horse should be pushing forwards from his hindquarters, freely through his back and into the rider's inviting hands. The rider needs to maintain his own balanced position so that the horse can move with activity. If the rider is constantly trying to maintain his balance, perhaps by holding onto the reins and gripping with the legs, this will cause tension and consequently restrict movement.

A relaxed, obedient horse will be a pleasure to ride, responding to the rider's aids with a free, forward movement, creating harmony in both rider and horse.

Straightness

Another important aspect is the horse's straightness. It is essential that the horse is 'straight' if he is to work correctly.

Straightness basically refers to the horse's 'line' from poll to tail. To be straight this line should be uniform throughout the body, retaining its integrity when working on straight lines, circles and turns. The horse's hind feet should follow in the same track as his fore feet.

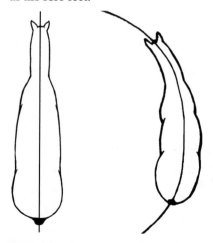

The horse, as in humans, has a naturally better side, similar to being right or left-handed. Even young horses favour one side, and as the horse grows older this one-sidedness can become more pronounced.

The horse will find it easier to work on one rein rather than the other. In one direction the horse may feel stiff and unyielding. The rider will be able to recognise which is the stiffer rein and can work to assist the horse on that side to prevent crookedness.

Where the horse may show his crookedness, in particular, is on straight lines: the inner track or centre line of the school.

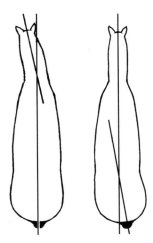

In the first picture the horse is bent at the withers.

In the second picture the horse's hindquarters are swinging inwards; this is a common fault at canter.

On circles and turns, because of his shape, the horse may deviate from the straightness. The horse finds it easier to bend through his neck rather than his body. He can 'fall out' through his outside shoulder, or swing his hindquarters away from the curve.

To compensate for the horse's crookedness the rider should first ask the horse to move forward with activity.

Then the rider can with the inside aids ask for correct bend whilst maintaining the integrity of the horse's 'straightness' with the outside aids. The rider is, in effect, helping the horse to use his body more correctly so that the horse can work the right muscles and develop fitness. This, in time, will make the horse work with more ease and to a higher level.

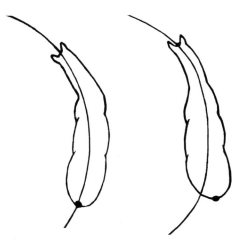

Balance, Rhythm and Tempo

A horse is in balance when he is able to carry himself and his rider with ease, when he is able to use his body efficiently through all paces and transitions. Young or untrained horses are often unbalanced, taking most of the weight on the forehand. They will often lose their balance in transitions. Through training and developing the correct muscles the young horse learns to use his hindquarters so that the weight is distributed more evenly.

Rhythm is the pattern of the footfalls in any pace; for instance at walk the rhythm is four time, 1-2-3-4. Tempo is the frequency or speed of the rhythm. Balance, rhythm and tempo go together, they cannot be separated. A horse who is unbalanced cannot work in a rhythm or with an even, constant tempo. A horse who changes the rhythm or the tempo of a pace, faster, slower, faster, slower – cannot keep in balance.

The rider needs to assess the horse's balance, rhythm and tempo at each pace. The rider then expands on this by keeping the rhythm and tempo when performing school figures and movements, for example on a circle or turn.

To create quality of work, the three principles of calmness, forwardness and straightness are important if the horse is to achieve the correct balance, rhythm and tempo in his paces.

The Paces

The walk

At free walk the steps should be ground covering, relaxed with a regular, rhythmical four-time beat, each foot should touch the ground at separate times. The rider should practise feeling the rhythm.

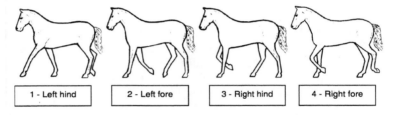

| 1 - Left hind | 2 - Left fore | 3 - Right hind | 4 - Right fore |

The walk is the most important pace as a naturally poor walk cannot be improved to any great degree and a good walk can be spoiled by bad training or schooling. Many horses do have a poor walk especially at the beginning of a schooling session.

Some horses start rigid with a fast, short-stepping gait. The rider should slow the tempo of the walk, encouraging slower but longer steps to create balance and rhythm. A horse who is stiff or tense along the back or shoulders can be improved with slight bending exercises **for the whole body**. The rider can ask the horse for bend with the inside leg and rein aids controlled with the outside aids. The shallow loop or serpentine exercise down the long side of the school has this effect.

A sluggish walk can be improved if the rider thinks of that 'coming home from a hack' walk that most horses give. The steps are longer with the horse using his shoulders and hindquarters with more effect. The rider can imagine this type of walk for a moment, take a deep breath and relax. Amazing how this works!

When the rider asks for a free walk on a long rein, the rider's hands should follow the movement of the horse's head. If the hands are kept still, even with a long rein, this restricts the horse's free movement, prevents him lengthening his frame, stretching downwards and forwards.

The Trot

The trot should be a rhythmical 1-2 beat with a moment of suspension between each beat. The pace should feel active with the horse pushing forwards with his hindquarters. This pace should have swing and spring. Again the rider should feel the rhythm.

If the horse is stiff and tense, often the tempo of the pace is too quick, the rider needs to correct the rhythm and balance by slowing the trot with a half-halt but asking for more impulsion with firmer leg aids. Flexing exercises, shallow loops and serpentines, lateral movements such as leg yield, can help to make the horse more supple.

The sluggish horse will need activating with firmer leg aids and possibly a series of transitions to increase obedience. Often a sluggish trot is helped by a period of canter.

The Canter

The canter should be a steady three-time rhythm. The pace should feel forward, active, free, fluent and light.

A horse who is stiff through the canter may be improved by shortening and lengthening the stride. Circles and 3 metre shallow loops on the long sides of the school will help with suppleness.

For the horse who speeds on too quickly, the rider should sit tall and straighter in the saddle. Riding large circles to help the horse's balance. Sluggish horses may be improved by successions of transitions and by shortening and lengthening the stride.

Some of the problems with canter originate from the transition. Sometimes the horse is not given sufficient preparation; then the aids are applied too strongly because the rider is afraid that the horse will not listen and perform the transition well. The previous pace needs to be active first; then the rider balances the horse with a few paces at sitting trot.

It is the inside leg applied on the girth that asks for impulsion; the outside leg is **stroked** back behind the girth. If the outside leg is used too actively to kick the horse, he may swing his hindquarters in and become crooked. Literally stroking the outside leg back softly along the horse's side is sufficient.

The inside hand, as well as asking for slight bend in the direction of canter, gives slightly at the moment of strike off allowing the horse his forward movement. The outside hand should maintain the contact to keep the horse 'straight' and in balance.

Once the horse is in canter, the rider maintains the impulsion with *an allowing seat and the rhythmical nudging of the inside leg aid.* The inner seat bone should feel as if it is being pushed forwards. The rider's *outside leg should remain passive*, softly in contact against the horse's side.

Downward Transitions

Downward transitions are achieved through preparation and maintaining the horse's rhythm and balance. The originating pace is slowed slightly and the horse encouraged to bring his weight into balance, lightening his forehand and bringing his hocks underneath him. The rider needs to think of bringing the horse into the transition starting with his hindquarters. The rider sits up tall and straight, maintaining the leg contact so that the horse can step under himself, raise and round his back and keep his body weight in balance.

Some horses have a tendency to fall onto the forehand in downward transitions, pulling the rider out of balance. This may be caused by incorrect aids, particularly pulling back on the reins. If the horse is stopped from the front backwards he is bound to fall onto the forehand; he then rushes on to regain his balance.

For the transition to halt the rider should again think of 'hindquarters to forehand'. The rider uses a half-halt, sits up tall, so that the horse can bring his hindquarters underneath him. The leg aids are given equally to ask the horse to go forward into the halt. The rein aid should be a momentary resistance with equal pressure, then release.

School Movements

During the Stage III flatwork the riders will be requested to perform some school movements, the turn on the forehand, the leg yield and the rein back. In this section these movements are explained with descriptions of the aims and benefits.

Turn on the forehand

This is an introduction to lateral movements. It teaches both horse and rider the co-ordination of the aids and improves the horse's obedience to the inside leg. In practical situations this movement is used when opening and shutting gates.

The Aim

The aim is to ask the horse to move his hindquarters sideways, with his inside hind leg stepping across and in front of his outside hind leg. The hindquarters make an arc around the forehand. The inside fore leg continues to step on the spot whilst the outside fore leg makes a small arc around the inside fore.

The turn is named after the direction in which the horse's head moves. If the head is moving to the left, this is a left turn on the forehand; the hindquarters will be moving to the right.

The inside is the side to which the horse is bent. For a left turn on the forehand, the left or nearside of the horse would be the inside.

Method

First plan and choose a safe spot away from the school wall or fence and at a safe distance from other riders.

This movement is performed from halt, which needs to be a good, balanced halt. The halt should be sustained only for a moment or two.

∗   *Keep the seat level in the saddle*, the body upright and the shoulders level as well.

∗   With the inside hand ask for a slight flexion at the poll to the inside.

∗   Apply the inside leg slightly behind the girth to ask the horse to step over. Give this leg aid in a series of nudges, one nudge for each step across.

∗   Maintain a passive contact with the outside leg in readiness to control the speed of turn and to ask for forward movement once the turn has been completed.

∗   The outside hand will control the amount of bend and keep the horse relatively straight, apart from the poll flexion.

∗   Both reins are used with slight restraint (resist and release) to prevent the horse from moving forward.

∗   After the turn has been completed, the horse should immediately be asked to walk forwards actively.

Ask the horse to step across slowly, one step at a time. It is better that the horse performs one or two good steps than a number of poor ones.

To begin with ask for a quarter turn to feel if the horse is definitely moving his hindquarters laterally.

A quarter turn to the left, with the horse stepping his hindquarters to the right.

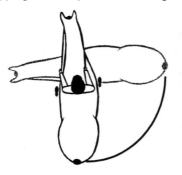

The horse is stepping across well with his hind legs. The inside fore is being raised and the outside fore will make an arc around it. The rider is leaning slightly too much to the left.

The horse can then be asked for a half turn (180°). This can be performed on the centre line or the line between E and B. The half turn can also be performed on the inner track to change the rein. In this case the horse should be positioned away from the wall or side of the school for safety.

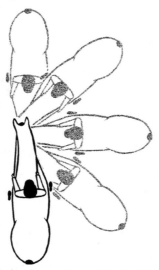

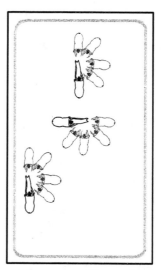

- If the horse is resistant, tries to step back or does not quite understand the movement at first, ask the horse to walk forwards and prepare again with a good halt before asking for another turn.

- If the horse spins around quickly the outside leg should be used to control this speed.

- If the horse shuffles round without using his hind legs properly increase the inside leg aid. If he still does not respond to the inside leg, tap him with the whip to increase his understanding and obedience.

Leg Yield

This lateral movement develops the horse's physique; helps to keep his body supple and is useful as a warming up or loosening exercise at the beginning of the work routine.

The Aim

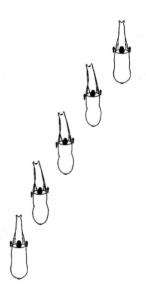

The horse moves sideways and forwards, crossing his inside fore and hind legs in front of the outside fore and hind legs. The horse's body is straight, apart from a slight bend in the region of the poll, away from the direction of travel. The rhythm and balance of the pace is maintained as the horse moves laterally with fluent steps.

Method

* First balance and maintain the rhythm of the pace.

* Make sure the horse is actively stepping forwards. This is most important for leg yield.

* Keep the body central in the saddle, the shoulders and hands level.

* Apply the inside leg in a series of nudges in the region of the girth or *slightly* behind. If the inside leg is brought too far back the horse may swing his hindquarters out.

* Keep the outside leg in contact with the horse's side to ask for forward movement.

* Maintain the contact with the inside hand as the horse moves away from the inside leg. The flexion to the inside should be slight, only the arch above the horse's eye should be visible.

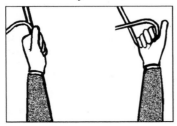

The outside hand indicates the direction of movement.

The palm can be turned upwards slightly so that the thumb is pointing in the direction of travel. The wrist should be kept straight and the arm relaxed.

Leg yield should be thought of as a forward movement as well as sideways.

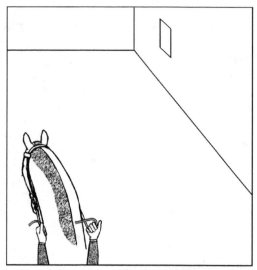

The rider can aim at a spot or marker on the wall.

It may also help to consciously think one step sideways, now one step forward, now one step sideways and so on.

The horse should move across the school with fluency, ease and with good pronounced steps.

When doing leg yield in trot the rider should ideally be in sitting trot. Use rising trot around the arena if necessary, then, as the horse is prepared for leg yield, the rider should go into sitting.

The rider is sat straight, her inside leg is slightly behind the girth and the horse is crossing well. The horse's head is slightly tilted.

Again the rider is showing a good position. The horse is crossing well. The horse could be asked for more flexion to the inside.

There are several places to perform leg yield within the school.

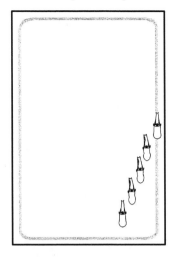

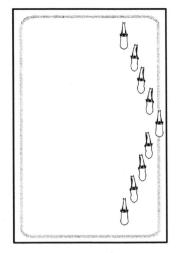

❖ The normal area to start is from the three-quarter line to the wall of the school. The wall acts like a magnet and the horse is encouraged to move across towards it.

❖ Leg yield to the track and then back from the track to the three-quarter line.

❖ Leg yield from the centre line to the three-quarter line.

❖ Leg yield one way for a few steps and back the other way for a few steps.

❖ Leg yield from a small circle to a larger circle. Start with a 10 metre circle and gradually leg yield out to 20 metres. Maintain the bend with the inside aids whilst containing the correct bend with the outside aids.

In the photograph the rider is applying the inside leg on the girth. The horse is bent around this leg and flexed to the inside (right).

Quality is better than quantity; a few good steps are more beneficial to the horse than several poor ones. If the horse can show improvement after performing leg yield a few times, this is progress. The rider needs to assess the horse's movement and correct any problems, if they should arise.

- If the horse does not move with fluent steps or loses the activity in the pace, the rider should tap the horse with the whip behind the inside leg. It may help to ride straight onwards actively and try again on the next inner track.

- If the horse races the leg yield, this is also an evasion. The rider should think of slowing the leg yield down, consciously ask for one step at a time.

When the horse performs well a rewarding pat afterwards with the inside hand will encourage him.

Rein Back

The rein back improves the horse's physique, develops his musculature, particularly around the haunches, stretches his top line and makes him more responsive to the rider's aids. The term 'rein back' is a misnomer as it implies that the back ward steps are requested by reining back. This movement is based on the seat and leg aids.

This exercise also develops the rider's feel for the horse and the influence of the aids.

It has practical uses, if the rider has to back when opening a gate or out hacking when the horse needs to be backed away from a dangerous situation or hazard.

The Aim

The horse moves backwards freely in a *straight line* responding without constraint or resistance to the rider's aids. The steps are *almost* in diagonal pairs.

Method

* Plan ahead and choose a safe spot normally on the inner track or across the school on the centre line. This movement is not normally performed on the track, unless so instructed to help with the horse's straightness.

* The horse is brought into a good halt, straight and level.

* Keeping the seat bones in the saddle, incline the upper body slightly forward. This lightens the seat, taking the weight fractionally off the horse's back to allow the backward action.

* Apply both leg aids slightly behind the girth in the same manner as when asking the horse to walk forward.

* Then, just as the horse is about to step forwards, resist with the hands in a squeeze and release action on the reins. This feel on the reins should be a gentle restraint and release, not a constant pull. With practise this becomes a subtle but positive aid.

Both leg and rein aids can be given for each step backwards, then released. Ask for three or four steps and then sit up straight again, ask for forward movement with the legs and allow with the hands.

Some horses do find this difficult through stiffness or tension along the back. The rider may ask for one step at a time and praise the horse if he responds, walk on and once more ask again.

Shortening and lengthening strides

Shortening or lengthening the horse's stride is a useful exercise for a variety of reasons. It improves the horse's balance and response to transitions. It improves the horse's physique and athletic ability building up the muscles when he shortens or lengthens his frame. It adds variety to the work. It can also make a sluggish horse think and move with more activity. It increases the rider's awareness of pace, rhythm and balance. In practice, varying the pace is used in jumping and in dressage.

The Aim

The horse is asked to decrease or increase the length of his stride. The steps in the pace should maintain the same tempo and rhythm.

During shortened strides the horse is taking shorter but higher steps. It is better to think of 'working towards collection' rather than the horse taking shorter steps. In collection the horse takes smaller strides but increases the elevation of the steps. The horse needs the same amount of energy, if not more, to perform collection, the steps going upwards and forwards with the horse 'rounder' through his back and frame.

The horse lengthens his stride by extending his legs, stretching his body frame to cover more ground with each step. During shortening and lengthening the strides, the rider is aiming to maintain the same rhythm and tempo of the pace.

Method

To shorten the stride, the rider needs to lighten the weight of his body. This allows the horse to round his back; the horse needs to lift his body to produce shorter steps.

* The rider achieves this by stretching his upper body, growing taller, whilst keeping the seat bones close to the saddle.

* Shorter, quicker leg aids are given, normally with a little more insistence, as the horse needs energy to spring himself off the ground. Many horses do find it difficult to maintain the energy required.

* The hands restrain and release lightly to ask the horse to come upwards and forwards.

To lengthen the stride the rider needs to sit a little deeper into the saddle asking the horse to lengthen his frame. The rider will often find it useful to do rising trot when lengthening the stride at this pace.

* Longer leg aids are given, that is, keeping the legs in contact with the horse's sides for a fraction longer in time.

* It is important that the rein contact is maintained; this prevents the horse running onto his forehand, losing his balance, becoming too long and flat. Think of giving sufficient rein to allow the forward movement without throwing all the contact away. It may help to think of giving the horse 75% of the contact whilst keeping 25% for the rider.

* The horse should still have the spring in his step whilst extending his whole frame.

Shortened strides are performed first to build up the horse's energy. Use the short sides of the school to shorten the stride and ask for lengthening down the long sides. Alternatively the shortening and lengthening can be performed on a circle. Shorten for half a circle, then ask for lengthening on the other half.

Both shortening and lengthening can be performed at walk, trot and canter, but for the Stage III Examination the riders are normally requested to show shortened and lengthened trot, occasionally canter.

Equitation Terms

There are some equitation terms that are often used and which, just as often, are misinterpreted. Many of these terms describe a 'feeling' between rider and horse that is difficult to clarify in words and which only becomes clear through experience.

Inside Leg to Outside Hand

This is a combination of aids to help the horse become straight and to ask him to use himself in a more effective way so that he can round his back. It also prevents him from 'falling in or out' around circles and turns.

The rider uses the inside leg whilst maintaining an elastic contact on the outside rein. This can work like magic; the horse shifts the weight from his inside and works both sides of his body equally. The rider still needs to think of using the other aids, the seat, the outside leg and inside hand when necessary.

Between Leg and Hand

This literally means the horse is stepping up from the leg aids into an inviting hand. He is submissive and responsive with all his energy waiting to do whatever the rider asks. This is a wonderful feeling. The rider sits light, supple, relaxed, thinking that he can now do anything!

To achieve this feeling needs work, both from horse and rider, and many horses cannot give a true 'leg to hand' feel because their muscular development is not sufficiently strong. It is possible, though, that every horse listens and responds to the leg and will work into the rider's hand contact.

First, the horse should be working correctly in the basics, that is he should be active from behind, coming forwards, be straight, working with rhythm and balance. The basics are so important for the end result.

The rider will need to be consistent in his demands, asking and tactfully insisting that the horse responds to the aids. The rider should not need to nag at the horse. If the horse does not step away from or respond to the leg aids, he should be reprimanded with the whip. It is more efficient (and less tiring) for the rider to insist on obedience from the start, than to be constantly niggling with leg and hand throughout the session. Once the horse has respect and is responsive, the rider will feel the energy at his disposal and the horse will be working between leg and hand.

Working in an outline

As the rider advances more emphasis is given to 'working the horse in an outline'. Unfortunately this term is often referred to as 'getting the horse on the bit'. For most riders (and horses!) this is disastrous because immediately the rider's focus is put onto the horse's head and neck.

We all have been terribly ashamed when, after ten minutes, the instructor yells that by now we should have the horse working 'on the bit'. So in a desperate attempt to comply we start fiddling with the reins, pulling, bending the horse by the neck one way and another, anything just to bring this horse's head down. Of course this has the opposite effect; the horse resists, hollows his back and up goes the nose.

So we need more impulsion, fine, let's kick the horse on and make him go faster; now try fiddling the head down, still no joy. The rider's arms tense, the shoulders lock, the body goes rigid and both rider and horse look miserable. At which point we tend to give up.

Let us start from the beginning.

The term 'on the bit' is a bad description; 'working in an outline' or 'coming through from behind' are more appropriate. The horse should be creating energy first with his hindquarters, pushing his body along by the hindlegs.

The rider needs to focus more on the horse's hindquarters than his front end. It may help to think about activating the hind legs and slowing down the front legs. This is achieved by the half-halt with the rider thinking of back and seat to steady the horse, legs to ask the hindquarters for more energy, hands squeeze and release (or even a resist and release). The horse needs to be in balance from his hindquarters through, maintaining a forward thrust with rhythm.

The horse needs to be 'straight' in his body. This may take firm inside leg aids, controlled by the outside leg and tactful use of the outside rein.

The rider also needs to think of lightening his body (not lifting it but feel a floating effect within the upper body), sitting up to invite the horse to round his back.

Without all this first the rider stands little chance of working the horse correctly except by forcing the head down which in turn prevents the energy coming through anyway.

It is like a jigsaw puzzle. If the rider tries to force the horse 'onto the bit' he is trying to do the puzzle from the inside out. Trying to fit the centre pieces in without first having found and put together the outside frame and corners.

Once the rider does receive obedience from the horse, working him to the best of his ability between leg and hand, in an outline, with calmness and relaxation then rider and horse arrive at their goal where two living creatures unite in total harmony. And no matter how short the period of time this happens, it is paradise!

Exam Tips

Why is equitation so easy to read about but so difficult to perform? Sometimes riders try so hard that every limb, muscle and nerve seizes up, the body refuses to accept commands from the brain and the ultimate goal seems as far away as it ever did.

Though all of us are striving to improve and, at times, have to push ourselves over the plateau, occasionally we need to find the balance between being positive without nagging or tension, asking for correct movements without pushing the horse too much beyond his capabilities. Ultimately equitation is sitting quietly *in balance* with the horse, applying the aids only when necessary but making the aids effective.

During the flatwork session, *do not become anxious if the horses cannot 'work into an outline'*. The Examiners are not looking specifically for a 'correct outline'; they do not expect perfection. The objective is that the candidate *knows the basic methods of working the horses towards improvement*.

You will need to assess the horses and show that you can use the school, school movements, transitions from one pace to another, and within paces to make the horses more supple, improve their balance, rhythm, tempo and paces. (Some of us become confused between rhythm and tempo. Rhythm is the regularity of the footfalls, tempo the speed of those footfalls. Think of a tune maintaining its beat for rhythm; the tempo is that same tune which can be played faster or slower.)

Do not worry if the horse finds it difficult to perform the school movements; the leg yield, turn on the forehand, shortening and lengthening or even a transition to canter. Use alternative figures and movements to help you and the horse.

For instance if the problem is achieving leg yield on a diagonal, take the horse onto a circle, decrease the circle then ask for leg yield onto a larger circle. Turn on the forehand can be improved by asking the horse to walk a square and, at each corner, ask him to step sideways for a couple of steps whilst keeping the forward movement. Shortening and lengthening can be improved by progressive transitions such as trot to walk to trot, then by direct transitions, trot to halt and halt to trot. This will prepare the horse for the transition within the pace. If the horse has a problem on the transition to canter, for instance he may continually strike off with the incorrect leading leg, try to leg yield from the inside leg for a couple of steps, then ask for the transition to canter.

Use your mind, think about the problem, its possible causes and try various ways to improve the horse.

CHAPTER 4
Jumping

This chapter covers the show jumping and cross-country information, Stage III requirements, planning and riding courses. Also included are some examples of the types of show jumping and cross-country courses that will be featured in the Examination.

Revision Stage II

Show jumping, the basic position, the rider's balance. The phases of the jump, how horse and rider change position during these phases. Course work, how to plan the approach to jumps.

Preparation for Jumping

As in the flatwork it is the basic position that is important. Students need to expand on the knowledge and physical fitness achieved for the Stage II, by consolidating their position, refining their style and building up their experience around courses.

As well as physical fitness the rider needs to build up stamina and suppleness. Gridwork, that is jumping a number of fences with related distances, is excellent. It also quickens the rider's responses to the horse's changing balance. Practising the cross-country position in a field, even without fences, develops the rider's balance and physique.

The rider will certainly need to expand their knowledge of different courses in various environments, in the school, outside menage, in a field and (groan) in all types of weather.

Some of the training for the cross-country may need to be planned for the warmer months as many centres conserve the ground by closing their courses during the winter and early spring.

The rider should train on as many different horses as possible, varying ages and types. This will increase the rider's ability at assessing the type of horse and his attitude to jumping.

The rider also needs to gain experience of horses in various environments and atmospheres. This can prove vital during the Stage III.

Though the horses certainly seem to know that Examination day is different, being plaited up, wearing smart boots and numnahs, some have no sense of decency and will still shy or be temperamental, even in front of the Examiners!

Competing at events, hunter trials, cross-country competitions or even jumping a clear round at a show jumping competition, will certainly be an advantage. This gives an idea of the type of atmosphere in the Stage III as well as expanding the rider's experience and building up confidence.

Competing gives riders an 'edge'; they learn how to acquire the best out of the horse. They become accustomed to being judged, jumping courses on their own and being watched by spectators.

During the spring and autumn there are many sponsored cross-country rides, which are less nerve wracking than competitions but which still offer valuable experience. Many riding establishments will take their horses and clients out on cross-country days, or hire a course for schooling sessions.

Stage III Requirements - Jumping

At Stage III the rider will need to show:

a)   a secure, yet supple and balanced position.

b)   effective use of the aids to ask the horse for a suitable pace around the show jumping and cross-country courses.

c)   an ability to inspect the courses and plan the routes, using the space available to present the horse at each fence with maximum advantage.

The three disciplines of flatwork, show jumping and cross-country should not be thought of as separate skills but in conjunction with each other. The knowledge, experience and ability learnt from one can, and does, complement the others. The balance developed on the flat and over fences helps the rider to become more in tune with the horse, creating an awareness of the different paces and the variations within paces. The aim in all three disciplines is the same; to ride the horse to the best of his ability with suppleness, discipline and sympathy so that both rider and horse can enjoy each other's company.

The Rider's Position

Theoretically there are three main positions referred to when explaining jumping – the light position used for riding the track, the more upright position taken on the approach to the fence and the jumping position over the fence.

The Light Seat

This position is used to keep the balance of both horse and rider around the track. The rider's light seat gives the horse freedom of movement whilst keeping the rider in the optimum position to alter to an upright or jumping position when required.

The rider's seat comes slightly away from the saddle by folding from the hips and bringing the shoulders over the knees. The line is now shoulder, knee and ball of the foot. The rider maintains a balance with the horse by keeping the weight down the leg into the heel through supple hip, knee and ankle joints.

The Upright Seat

On the approach to each fence the rider takes a more upright position, to keep in balance and to have more control from the seat. The rider may need to ask the horse for more impulsion or to alter the length of the stride. This position allows the horse to bring his balance further back, to lighten the forehand, in preparation for taking off with the forelegs.

These two photographs demonstrate how subtle the change in balance can be between the light seat and upright seat. On the left the lighter seat with the shoulders slightly forward, on the right the shoulders come back and the rider's weight is deeper into the saddle. The rider keeps perfect balance with the horse.

The Jumping Seat

The jumping seat allows the rider and horse to maintain their balance over the jump.

✳   The hips are moved slightly backwards, as the upper body inclines forwards from the hips bringing the shoulders just in front of the knees.

✳   The rider looks up and ahead, keeping the back straight.

✳   The arms and hands move to allow the horse freedom of his head and neck.

✳ The hands should be independent of the horse's neck; this can only be achieved by the rider's balance and security of seat.

✳ The hands give in the direction of the rein, that is, towards the mouth, halfway down the neck.

The rider, through experience, expertise and instinct, chooses the time to use the jumping position, to give with the hands and to maintain the balance through the flight.

The Rider's Balance

In practice what the rider is trying to achieve is a balance between these three positions over the various stages of the course. For instance the light position adopted on the track may need to be changed to a more upright position on a turn, to balance the horse. This may not necessarily be a complete upright position. It may only be a modification as much as the rider considers necessary to gain the correct pace and balance.

The three positions can be varied provided the balance is maintained between the rider and horse. The rider should avoid coming in front of or being left behind the horse's movement. (Naturally this does occur at times, to be in balance 100% of the time would be perfection.) What is important is that the rider is able to feel when they are out of balance and have the ability to quickly correct this.

Eventually the rider does not even think of changing position; he feels the balance of the horse, knows how and when to use his own body for control. The whole picture is then one of a flowing, fluid partnership where thought, telepathy and body language play the most important part.

To develop this balance the rider needs:

❖ A secure lower leg with the weight going down the leg into the heel

This is the rider's **anchor.** The lower legs need to support the body throughout the changes in position. The lower legs may be brought slightly more forward than in flatwork, more parallel to the girth.

The weight is pressed into the knees, the lower legs and the heels. The thighs are relaxed, lightly in contact with the saddle allowing the lower legs to come underneath the body and around the horse's sides.

❖ Supple hips

This is the **pivot point**. The angle of the hip closes, allowing the rider to fold. This changes the point of balance, lightens the seat to let the horse round his back when jumping.

❖   Supple knee and ankle joints

The **shock absorbers**. The knee and ankle joints need to be bent but not stiff and rigid. They need an amount of 'give' to absorb the concussion. Without supple knee and ankle joints the concussion makes the rider unbalanced and insecure.

Stirrup Length

It is important for several reasons that the stirrup length is sufficiently short. Closing the angles of the hip, knee and ankle joints centres the rider's balance over the knee and foot. The knee is pushed closer to the saddle and the thigh kept in front of the body providing more stability for the rider. It also gives the rider more mobility, a greater range of movement so that the jumping balance can be adopted with relative ease.

The rider, by being able to fold from the hips and give with the hands, can remain in balance with the horse around the track and over the fence.

Stirrup leathers are shortened by two to four holes from flatwork length, sometimes even more.

The rider may develop the correct muscles by riding with shortened stirrups either in jumping lessons, when hacking or for part of the time in flatwork lessons. Often at first the stirrup length for jumping feels too short, especially if the rider has been concentrating on their flatwork. Think about riding in shorter and longer stirrups for the same amount of time. For instance, if flatwork is practised for three hours a week, then shorter stirrups should also be used for three hours a week.

When the stirrups are too long the rider's legs are straight giving a tendency to stand up in the stirrups rather than bending from the hips. The rider can be forced behind the movement compromising the mobility of body, which then cannot maintain the balance or allow with the reins.

With stirrups that are too short the rider loses the stability of the seat and comes above the saddle. The lower legs are not secure and the aids cannot be given correctly or with effect.

These diagrams exaggerate the problems so that the incorrect positions are clearly visible.

Over a period of time the rider needs to find a stirrup length that maintains the stability of the position and is comfortable. This does depend on the rider, length of leg and style.

The Rider's Cross-country Position

When the rider adopts the cross-country position, the stirrups are at least one or two holes shorter than the show jumping length so that the angles at the hip, knee and ankle are slightly more closed. This is to maintain the balance with the faster, cross-country pace, to absorb the concussion and to give greater flexibility over undulating country.

The need to vary the position, as in show jumping, is even more relevant in cross-country. The rider needs to maintain balance on the track, and over fences, especially those with different take off and landing heights, for instance, drop jumps or steps. The lower leg may be brought forward slightly to give a more stable base for the body weight.

The hands follow the horse's head and neck. (In cross-country the hands may go forward more along the horse's crest, rather than down the neck. This helps the rider maintain his balance in the faster pace.)

The rider does need to be physically fit and supple to modify the body position when necessary with the minimum of effort and independently of the reins. The aim is to create impulsion and energy, allowing this to come through and be contained by the rider's balance. The reins should be in a light contact and the horse should feel as though he is springing forward in an easy active stride. The rider should feel in total control yet with enough forward activity that if the leg aids were applied, the horse would respond.

The Course

Once the rider has practised the positions and gained experience over various fences, work over courses should begin. The rider does need to think of the course as a whole, both for show jumping and cross-country.

There are six stages or phases of course jumping - the track, the approach, the take off, in flight, the landing and the recovery.

The Track

The track is the planned route at the start of the course, between the jumps and from the last jump to the finish.

The track is important, as this is where the rider uses his judgement to plan the approach into each fence. The rider should always use the space available to the best advantage.

It is therefore essential that the rider plans the route carefully, decides where to turn into a fence and thinks about the line to the next fence.

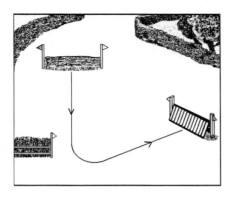 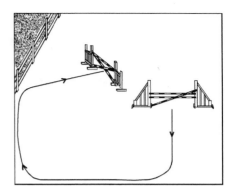

Here in the show jumping and cross-country courses, the planned tracks have wide angles and the approaches to each second fence is straight. The rider is making good use of the space.

If the rider misjudges the track, the approach to a fence may not be straight. If the fences are placed at an angle to each other there is often the temptation for the rider to swing around quickly. This results in an awkward jump or the horse running out because he has not been presented to the fence correctly.

A fence approached from an awkward angle, leaving insufficient space and time for manoeuvre, can make the fence much more difficult for the horse (and the rider).

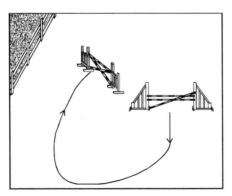 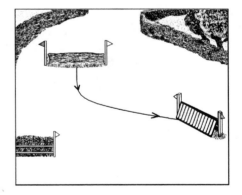

Here the track is badly planned with the approach to each second fence being too acute and sharp.

The Approach

This needs to be straight towards each fence and is dependent on the track ridden beforehand. For the last three strides of the approach the horse should be sufficiently set up by the rider so that there is no need to interfere.

If the rider correctly plans and controls the track and the turn before the approach then the line to the fence should be accurate. The rider should sit quietly, let the fence come to him and the horse.

The Take Off

Here the rider allows the horse to stretch his frame, lift the forelegs and push with the hindlegs over the jump. Many riders become anxious about the 'take-off point' and try to see 'a stride' before the fence. This can cause more problems than it solves. Some horses are more agile than others and have the ability to take off from a longer or a shorter stride. Some horses judge the stride and put in a half stride before the fence.

Being able to see a take off point and the stride beforehand comes from practice and experience. The essential point is that the rider assesses the type of horse and his style of jumping. Some horses are able to jump more effectively if the stride is shorter and bouncy, other horses need to lengthen their frame with a slightly longer stride. It is the rider's job to assess the horse very quickly and then ride the horse to the best of his ability in the style that suits him. This is much more likely to have success than the rider who constantly attempts to 'see a stride and take off-point' in front of the fence. This often makes the rider think of the bottom of the fence rather than over and beyond.

In Flight

The horse raises his shoulders and stretches his neck; his forelegs should be tucked up in front to clear the fence. The rider maintains a fold position in harmony with the horse allowing with the hands and keeping the lower legs secure.

The Landing

The horse lands usually on one foreleg so that all the concussion from the weight of horse, rider and tack is taken on one leg. This travels up the leg through the fetlock joint (which can sometimes almost touch the ground), the knee and the shoulder. The rider absorbs the shock through the ankle, knee and hip joints.

The rider should now be thinking of the next fence, the track and the approach, and should be looking in that direction.

The Recovery

The rider and horse regain control and balance. The rider returns to the light seat or the more upright seat depending on the amount of control necessary. Now the rider is planning the track towards the approach for the next fence.

Pace

The horse needs to be active, rhythmical and balanced. The pace should be forward going but steady. The rider will need to use the flatwork expertise in controlling and asking for the correct pace. The half-halt will be needed to ask the horse to use his hindquarters more effectively, to steady the pace and to improve the balance.

In show jumping the pace will need to be more 'collected' around the track; the fences are closer together and therefore there is less time to allow for control should the pace become too fast. The stride is shorter, with the hindquarters and hocks more 'underneath the horse'.

For cross-country the horse will be able to lengthen between the fences, his pace will be slightly faster, a rhythmical forward going cross-country canter. The rider still needs to control the pace; the horse should feel active and balanced.

Jumping at Stage III

Both the show jumping and the cross-country will normally take place in the morning before lunch. The candidates are divided into groups and, depending on the timetable, may be requested to jump immediately after their flat session. Sometimes the group who are scheduled for flatwork first, at 9.00 a.m., will jump as the last group, which necessitates waiting until 12.30 – 1.00 p.m. On other occasions the flatwork is completed for all groups before the jumping begins.

The show jumping course will be taken first, followed by the cross-country. Each candidate will be asked to ride one horse around the show jumping course and another over the cross-country course. Though the cross-country will continue in most types of weather, if conditions do make riding outside hazardous, there will be two show jumping rounds in an indoor school.

Inspecting the Courses

Every candidate will be given the opportunity to walk the courses either before the Exam starts in the morning or before the jumping begins. Candidates are strongly advised to arrive at the Exam Centre early, in time to inspect each course thoroughly. It is vital that all candidates walk and inspect the courses.

The Show Jumping Course

The show jumping for Stage III will consist of eight or nine fences up to 1 metre (3 feet 3 inches) in height situated in an outside menage, paddock or field. There will be a variety of fences, including a one stride double.

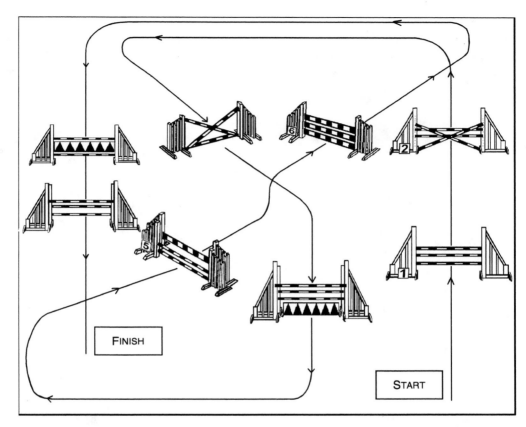

The fences are normally numbered but occasionally riders are asked to choose their own course around a set of fences that can be jumped from either direction. There may also be flags; the rider jumps the fences keeping the red flag to the right and the white flag to the left.

The Cross-country Course

The cross-country section of the Stage III consists of six to eight cross-country fences over varying terrain. Depending on the Examination Centre this could be part of an actual cross-country course or some cross-country fences built within a field. The fences will be no higher than 0.91 metres (3 feet). The course is normally numbered so riders will be able to take the jumps in sequence.

The cross-country fences will be fairly simple to negotiate and may include logs, brush jumps, tyres, straw bales, a small ditch or palisade. A jumping course can be thought of rather like a dressage test with the rider using markers either on the fence or in the field like the letters in a school. The rider should try and memorise certain points for turns and approaches.

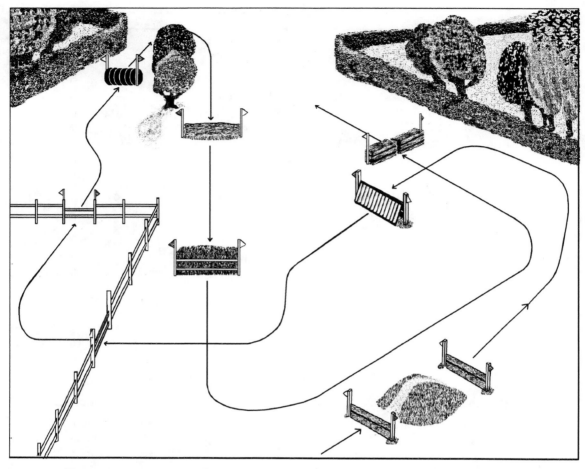

The Warm Up

After the riders have been allocated their horses and safely mounted, the instructor will explain about the warming up phase. The whole group may do this together or each rider will warm up individually before his or her round. **The warm up phase is crucial.** The rider has to evaluate the horse within the first few minutes: his paces, his balance and ability to turn into a jump. The horse will jump better if warmed up correctly and the Examiners can often tell how capable the rider is by the efficient manner in which they use their warm up period. The rider who prepares the horse competently and makes full use of the limited time to jump the practice fence gives a better impression than the rider who wastes time.

If the rider has warmed the horse up effectively, the practice fence should give a good indication of the horse's jumping style and should give both horse and rider confidence.

In the cross-country phase, the warm up period may be even shorter than for the show jumping, two to three minutes. The riders normally have a quick canter on both reins and then are asked to jump a practice cross-country fence twice. The rider needs to work the horse quickly and efficiently making use of the practice fence to obtain a 'feel' for the horse and his capabilities. One of the more usual problems for riders in the Stage III cross-country section is that the horse is not going forward actively in a good 'cross-country' canter.

Once the warm up is complete for both the show jumping and the cross-country and the course has started, relax, smile and enjoy it. After all jumping is fun!

Exam Tips

Preparation for jumping, once the rider has developed the balanced position, means good instruction together with practice, practice and more practice. This will increase the security of the jumping position as well as giving the rider experience over various types of fences and courses. The aim is to build up the rider's confidence and determination.

For the warm up phase for both the show jumping and cross-country have a quick plan in your mind. Include in this school movements and figures, such as circles or half circles in different paces. For example, depending on the space available, walk half a 20 metre circle then transition to trot. Trot around school then transition to canter. Canter around school and one twenty metre circle, transition to trot and change rein. Repeat on other rein and include some shortening and lengthening of stride in canter.

Transitions to trot, walk, trot and canter, assess horse's responses. Change rein and assess horse's shortening and lengthening of stride in this direction. If there is space, try the figure of eight exercise checking the transitions to trot and walk when changing the rein. Having a plan in mind will help to focus your thoughts and mind when assessing the horse.

Over the practice fence, check if the horse jumps better from a longer, more forward-going stride or a bouncier, shorter stride. This is your opportunity to discover how the horse jumps to the best of his ability. Have a canter around the perimeter of the jumps if possible so that the horse has a look at the fences.

Safety is obvious when working with others during the warm up phase of the jumping. Safety also includes being secure in your jumping position, guiding and controlling the horse around the show jumps and the cross-country course.

Keep the pace steady and fairly collected around the show jumping course. If the horse does become a little fast, ride a circle or transition to trot to steady the pace. In the cross-country phase the horse should be travelling at a good cross-country canter but again, not out of control.

Do not become anxious if anything goes wrong, such as knocking a fence down. If your position is balanced and secure, if you control the horse and plan a correct route around the jumps and fences you will be successful. Above all, remember to smile, relax and enjoy the jumping!

CHAPTER 5
Anatomy and Physiology

The horse's body consists of a series of systems such as the respiratory or digestive system. As well as being essential to life in their own particular way, each of these works in conjunction with and is interdependent on each other. When each system works to the best of its ability and in harmony, life is sustained and the horse is in good health.

If one system breaks down this affects others causing an imbalance and ill health. If the respiratory system does not function to its fullest capacity this affects the circulation, which in turn affects the brain, the muscles, the digestion and so on as in a chain reaction. To understand the anatomy and physiology of the horse, we need to learn the separate systems, their parts, their functions and how they influence each other.

The Muscular System

The muscular system is a mechanical device whereby the body creates motion within its parts.

Muscles are present throughout the body. They are categorised into three main types:

❖ The **involuntary** muscles operate by reflex action in automatic systems such as the digestive system and the blood vessels.

❖ The **cardiac** muscles are a special type of involuntary muscle only found in the heart.

❖ The **voluntary** or **skeletal** muscles are attached to the bones via tendons and move in obedience to the will, under 'voluntary' control of the horse.

The **skeletal system** consists of some **700 muscles** together with **tendons** and **ligaments**. The voluntary muscles are called 'striped' or 'striated' because they have a striped appearance. The involuntary muscles are not striped and are called 'non-striated' or 'plain'.

Functions of the Skeletal Muscles

The skeleton, made up of bones of different shapes and sizes, is the framework of the horse and, being a collection of separate bones, most are not connected to each other directly and cannot move of their own accord. Also, as bones are relatively rigid and breakable, any unnatural movement or undue force can cause damage and injury.

The skeletal muscular system **connects** the bones together, produces **movement** and provides **stability** by controlling and limiting that movement.

Formation of Muscle

The muscles are arranged in layers within the body. The outermost muscles are generally called **superficial** and those underneath are called **deep**. Where there are three layers of muscles, the central layer is termed **medial**. For instance, in the hindquarters the gluteal muscles are arranged as the superficial gluteal on top, the medial gluteal and the deep gluteal underneath.

Each muscle is made up of **long, thin fibres** bound together by **connective tissue** and arranged in **bundles**. These bundles form the '**muscle belly**'.

Muscles vary in size and shape. Some have long, flat fibres arranged longitudinally giving this type of muscle a wide range of movement. Some fibres are arranged at an angle to each other rather like a feather. These **pennate** muscles have a smaller range of movement but a stronger pull.

The brachiocephalic in the neck is long and flat. The common digital extensor in the foreleg is a pennate muscle.

How the Muscles Work

Each fibre has a **nerve supply** through which it is controlled. With exercise, the muscle fibres increase in size and strength, and the muscle itself becomes stronger. If the muscle loses its strength, through lack of use or a disrupted nerve supply, the fibres will weaken, wither and may disappear altogether.

Muscles are **attached at both ends** to the bones by **tendons**.

❖ In most muscles, one attachment is to a relatively immovable part of the skeleton; this is called the **origin**.

❖ The other end is attached to a moveable part of the skeleton; this is called the **insertion**.

❖ Some muscles are attached to moveable parts at both ends, for instance the brachiocephalic attached to the forearm and head, in which case either end can be the origin or insertion depending on which part is to be moved.

Extensor muscles at the front of the leg flatten and lengthen as the leg bends

Flexor muscles at the back of the leg contract and shorten to bend the leg

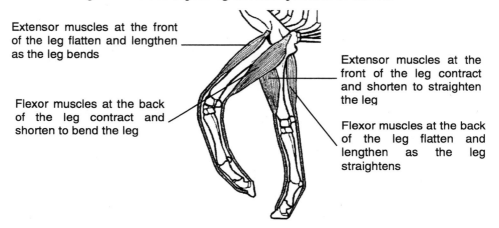

Extensor muscles at the front of the leg contract and shorten to straighten the leg

Flexor muscles at the back of the leg flatten and lengthen as the leg straightens

When stimulated by nerves, the fibres shorten and the muscle contracts, reducing in length. This pull brings the insertion point closer to the origin and the bone moves.

As muscles can only work by contraction, they are arranged in pairs with other muscles working in opposition to achieve the opposite action. For instance when muscles contract to bend a limb, the opposing or **antagonistic** muscles relax until the limb is moved as required. These antagonistic muscles will then contract to straighten that limb again.

The antagonistic muscles also act as a limiting force so that the limb cannot be moved to a degree where the joint becomes damaged. This arrangement of opposing, antagonistic muscles is essential to the efficient action of bones and joints. If this arrangement fails and both antagonistic muscles contract at the same time, the force exerted will be greater than the bone can take and it will break.

Tendons

Connecting muscle to bone are the tendons dense, white, fibrous tissue that can either be **cord shaped**, **ribbon shaped** or **flattened into sheets**. The tendons convey the force of the muscle to the bone. As muscles are bulky the tendons act by concentrating their pull to a small area of bone. Tendons vary in length; some are short whereas others are long conveying the muscle force to a bone at some distance.

Tendons are not very elastic and have a poor blood supply, which means that any damage can take a long time to heal. When a tendon passes over a joint the tendon is encapsulated in a sheath to protect it.

Ligaments

Ligaments are strong bands of fibrous tissue that have a variety of functions.

∗   In conjunction with certain muscles, they hold the bones together by binding the bones at joints, forming a connection that allows movement.

∗   They can also limit and control the extent of joint action and, in combination with muscles, attempt to prevent excessive and injurious movement. If a joint is forced beyond its capacity the ligament can become damaged or torn.

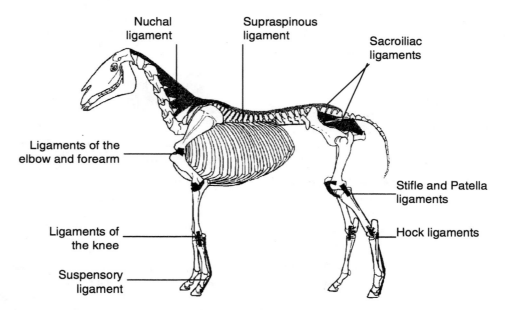

Skeleton of the horse showing some of the ligaments. The **nuchal** ligament in the neck and withers is modified to help the muscles support the neck and head. The **supraspinous** ligament holds the vertebrae in place. Ligaments at the joints, such as the elbow, stifle, knee and hock, hold the bones in place but allow a certain amount of movement.

∗   Other ligaments, such as the suspensory ligament, support bones and keep them in place.

∗   Ligaments act as joint capsules containing the synovial fluid that protects and lubricates the bones and cartilage.

The Muscles

There are hundreds of muscles within the horse's body. These diagrams show some of the more important.

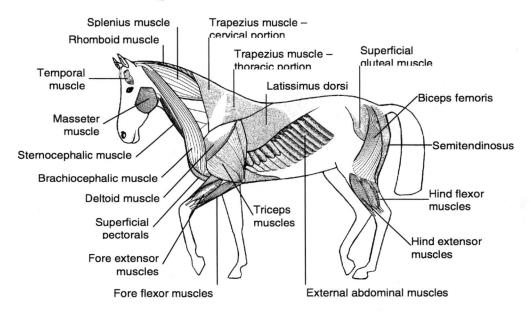

Splenius muscle
Rhomboid muscle
Trapezius muscle – cervical portion
Trapezius muscle – thoracic portion
Superficial gluteal muscle
Temporal muscle
Latissimus dorsi
Biceps femoris
Masseter muscle
Semitendinosus
Sternocephalic muscle
Brachiocephalic muscle
Deltoid muscle
Hind flexor muscles
Triceps muscles
Superficial pectorals
Hind extensor muscles
Fore extensor muscles
Fore flexor muscles
External abdominal muscles

Medial and deep muscles

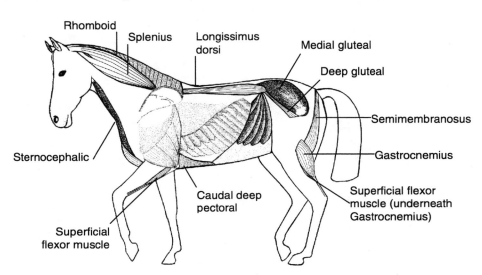

Rhomboid
Splenius
Longissimus dorsi
Medial gluteal
Deep gluteal
Semimembranosus
Gastrocnemius
Sternocephalic
Caudal deep pectoral
Superficial flexor muscle (underneath Gastrocnemius)
Superficial flexor muscle

Head Muscles

Masseter   large, dense muscles of the cheek. When the masseters on both sides work together the jaw closes straight upwards. When one masseter on one side contracts the jaw is pulled across to that side. So, when these muscles work alternately the jaw has a sideways, grinding action, which is important for the horse's digestive process.

Temporal   acting together with the masseters, these muscles help to raise the lower jaw, closing the mouth.

The weight of the long jaws and the molar teeth need several muscles to assist with jaw closure but the masseters and temporals are the most important.

As the jaw, in most cases, will open by gravity when the closing muscles relax, there is little need for large muscles to open the mouth and, therefore, only a few small muscles are involved.

Neck Muscles

Brachiocephalic   (pronounced brackyo-sefalik) so named from the bones to which it is connected, the forearm (brachium) and the back of the head (cephalus). This muscle can move either the head or the forearm, so the origin and insertion points are interchangeable. This broad muscle extends down the side of the neck over the shoulder to the forearm.

Rhomboid   (pronounced romboyd) also known as the rhomboideus muscle. This is connected to the occipital bone at the back of the head and the scapula or shoulder blade.

Splenius   situated on the side of the neck.

Sternocephalic   extending from the jaw to the sternum (breastbone).

Trapezius   this triangular shaped muscle originates in the neck and is divided into two parts by a tendon. Each part is named after the corresponding portion of the spine – cervical trapezius and thoracic trapezius. The cervical section extends from the lower half of the neck and covers the withers, overlying portions of the rhomboideus and splenius muscles. The thoracic portion lies over the withers and partly down the back.

Poorly developed trapezius muscles are often evident when the horse has a prominent wither and a ewe-neck.

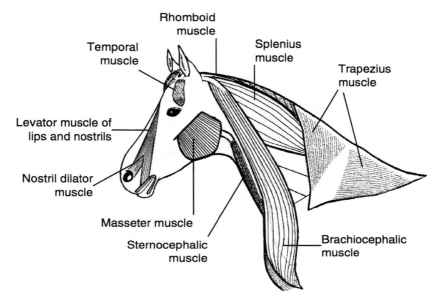

Diagram of head and neck showing main muscles including those activating the nostrils and lips

The neck is elongated in the horse because of his evolution. In a grazing animal the neck has to be the same length, at least, as the forelegs and the horse's legs evolved by lengthening to provide speed to escape predators. The neck also connects the head and body and, because the head is heavy, the neck has developed an extensive musculature to give mobility when grazing or watching for predators. The raising or lowering of this heavy head and neck can change the centre of gravity of the horse.

Trunk Muscles

Deltoid	originates at the scapula or shoulder blade and extends to the humerus.
Triceps	situated in the shoulder partly under the deltoid, attached to the scapula and the humerus and extending to the elbow.
Pectorals	these triangular muscles, attached to the sternum, pass to the humerus bones. These muscles are prominent in the chest area.
Latissimus dorsi	large, flat muscle connected by a wide, flat tendon to thoracic vertebrae and extending behind the shoulder over the ribs to the humerus. This muscle helps in supporting the rider.

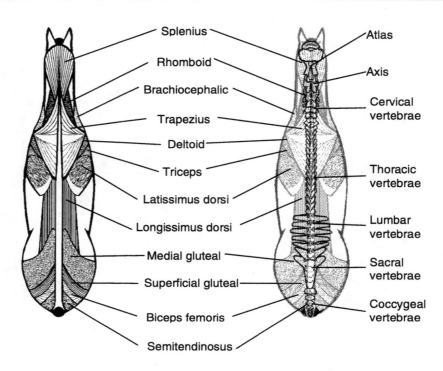

Top views of horse showing muscles and their position in relation to the spine

Longissimus dorsi the longest and largest muscles in the body, stretching along either side of the spine, they give the back its shape and support the spine. They are visible in the loin region. These are the main muscles that carry the rider.

Gluteal The superficial gluteal lies on top of the medial and deep gluteal muscles. These muscles are attached to the sacral area of the spine and extend to the point of hip and the femur.

Semitendinosus this long muscle extends from behind the hip at the top of the dock and connects to the stifle joint. The **semitendinosus** is one of the three muscles in the **hamstring group**.

The hamstring is the large tendon at the back of the hind leg.

Biceps femoris extending over the same area as the semitendinosus, this curves down the thigh and attaches in three parts to the femur and patella, to the tibia, and to the point of hock. The **biceps femoris** is the **major component** of the **hamstring group**.

Semimembranosus extending from the top of the dock (coccygeal vertebrae) to the femur. This is the **third muscle** in the **hamstring group**.

Gastrocnemius this muscle extends from the femur down the hind leg to the point of the hock.

The tendon associated with this muscle, fuses with the tendons of the hamstring group to form the Achilles tendon, one of the largest tendons in the body.

Intercostal these muscles are present in the spaces between the ribs and are used in respiration.

Abdominal there are several layers of muscles around and supporting the weight of the abdomen.

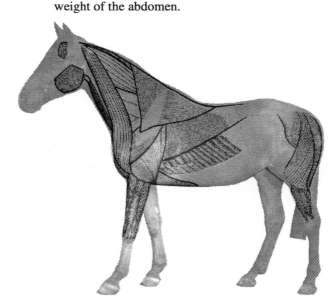

Leg Muscles

The leg muscles in the horse are all positioned on the upper leg; **there are no muscles below the knee and hock.** These muscles are arranged in layers, some under the surface of the skin, others situated deep, nearer the bones. There are several muscles in the foreleg but the main muscles are:

Foreleg

Common digital extensor front of forearm.

Lateral digital extensor partially underneath common digital.

Superficial digital flexor back of the leg.

Deep digital flexor back of the leg.

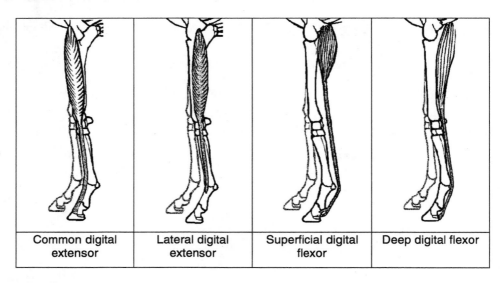

| Common digital extensor | Lateral digital extensor | Superficial digital flexor | Deep digital flexor |

Hind leg

Long digital extensor   front of hind leg.
Lateral digital extensor   underneath long digital.
Superficial digital flexor back of hind leg.
Deep digital flexor   back of hind leg.

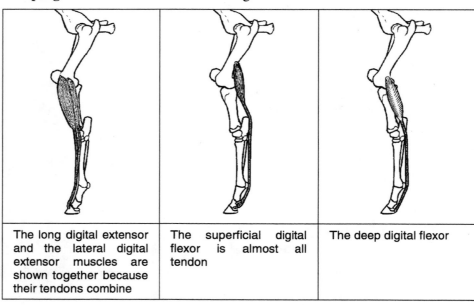

| The long digital extensor and the lateral digital extensor muscles are shown together because their tendons combine | The superficial digital flexor is almost all tendon | The deep digital flexor |

The muscles positioned in front of the legs are those which straighten the leg (**extensors**). The muscles behind the legs bend the joints (**flexors**). So the extensors contract, the flexors allow and the leg is straightened. Then the flexors contract exerting a pull, the extensors allow and the bones move at the joints to bend the leg.

As this chapter covers the names and positions of the muscles, so the following chapter describes how they act to create movement in the horse. Also included is information on the structure of the lower leg and foot, explaining which tendons are connected to which muscles and how these function in the complicated procedure of locomotion.

Exam Tips

There are hundreds of skeletal muscles in the horse's body; thankfully the Stage III candidate only needs to know some, in particular those that are involved in locomotion and carrying the rider. Trying to remember the names of muscles can be a headache, particularly if muscles have similar names or, as in some books, alternative names. Where possible, the alternative names have been mentioned but not too many as to make it complicated. Remembering one name for each muscle is quite sufficient.

Some muscles are named after the bones to which they are attached – brachiocephalic after the arm (brachium) and the head (cephalus); sternocephalic after the breastbone (sternum) and the head. Others are named after the action they perform – extensors extend a limb (straighten) and flexors flex a limb (bend). Remember front of leg E and back of leg F, or E comes in front of F. To distinguish between tendons and ligaments remember tendons '**tend on**' a muscle.

The Achilles tendon, the large tendon easily visible at the back of the thigh above the hock, is often termed the hamstring tendon, and vice versa. Basically, the tendons from the hamstring group of muscles join to form the hamstring tendon. Then the tendon from the gastrocnemius combines together with the hamstring tendon to form the Achilles tendon. This large tendon therefore can correctly be named either the Achilles or the hamstring tendon.

For muscles, devise rhymes or phrases which will help you to remember them. For instance for the muscles in the hindquarters, Gluteal, Biceps femoris and Semitendinosus, **GBS**, a mnemonic such as **Good Back Sides** may help you to remember their names and where these muscles are on the hindquarters. Similarly for the muscles in the forelegs 'CLouDS' Common and Lateral extensors, Deep and Superficial flexors; hind legs 'LloyDS' Long and Lateral extensors, Deep and Superficial flexors. Semitendinosus lends itself to five dinosaurs. Semi – ten, (half of ten is five) dinosus sounds like dinosaurs; semimembranosus to half a membrane. Anything that aids the memory is a useful tool in studying.

C H A P T E R   6
Movement

Movement is a complicated procedure; it is amazing how many muscles are involved in a simple action such as stepping forwards. Whilst some muscles are antagonistic and act in opposition, other muscle groups act together to create movement.

Locomotion

When a horse is **correctly** halted, with the hind legs and hocks underneath, the body is central with the weight distributed evenly over all four legs. With the horse so balanced, the power of motion comes from the hindquarters.

❖ The **hamstring group** of muscles, the **biceps femoris**, the **semimembranosus** and the **semitendinosus**, are the main important group to effect this propulsion.

❖ These muscles flex the **hip**, the **stifle** and the **hock joint** bringing the leg upwards and forwards.

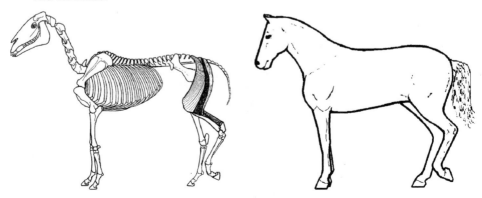

❖ The **flexor muscles** and **tendons** flex the **fetlock** and **pastern**.

❖ The **gastrocnemius** helps to bring the leg forward. It then assists in extending the stifle and hock joints.

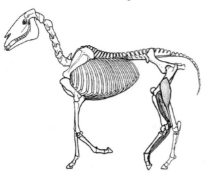 

❖ The hind leg is brought underneath the body and extended.

❖ The **gluteal** muscles act on the hip, the **gastrocnemius** and the **extensor muscles** on the leg to extend and straighten the joints.

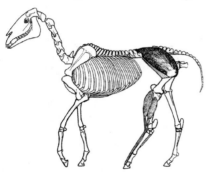 

❖ Once the leg is straightened it acts as a rigid lever pushing against the ground to move the body forwards. The **longissimus dorsi** supporting the spine makes the backbone relatively rigid so that the energy is transmitted to the forehand.

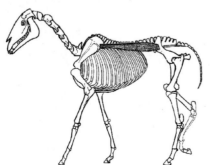 

Acting in accord with the hindleg, the foreleg is moved upwards and forwards.

❖ To lift the foreleg the shoulder joint must first be flexed and the humerus moved. The main muscle that does this is the **deltoid**. ❖ The **cervical trapezius**, supported by the nuchal ligament, draws the shoulder upwards and forwards then supports the shoulder and forelimb.	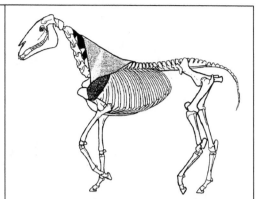
❖ The **triceps relax** to allow flexion of the elbow. ❖ The **flexor** muscles at the back of the leg **bend the knee** and the tendons below the knee bend the fetlock.	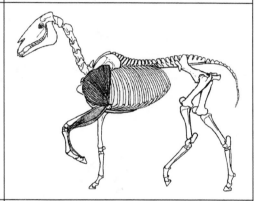
❖ The **rhomboid** muscles carries the leg upwards and forwards. ❖ The **brachiocephalic** carries the leg forward.	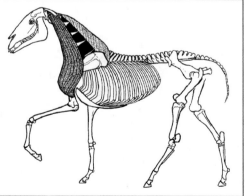

❖ Once in position the leg needs to be straightened. This is achieved by the triceps extending the elbow joint and the extensors straightening the limb.

❖ As the hoof touches the ground, the limb is supported by the tendons.

❖ The foot needs grip; if the foot slips the leg will not support the weight of the body and the horse will become unbalanced.

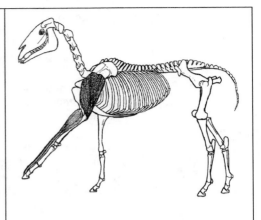

❖ Once extended the leg is rigid, relatively speaking 'fixed to the ground'. The whole body is now propelled forward, swinging over the limb.

❖ The **latissimus dorsi**, the **pectorals**, the **rhomboid** and the **thoracic trapezius**, together with a push exerted from the hindquarters, **act to pass the body over the leg**.

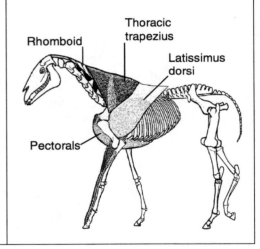

The forelimbs have no bony connection with the body; the horse has no collarbone. The body is supported and suspended by muscles between the two shoulder blades (scapulae) literally cradled within a muscular (the thoracic) sling. This allows a considerable amount of movement of the body in relation to the forelimbs. The body is literally swung over the leg.

The limbs, therefore, act mostly as levers, stretching forwards to cover the ground then straightening and fixing. In the hind legs the limb creates the impulsion, pushing the body forward. In the forelimbs the body itself is pushed or thrust forward over the leg.

This is a simplified account of the locomotion process. Many more of the muscles are involved, but this gives an idea of how the muscles work together to move the whole of the horse's body.

Variation of Movement

Muscles, as well as producing forward (and backward) movement, also create lateral (sideways) movements.

Some muscles (abductors) move the limbs away from the body

Some muscles (adductors) move the limbs in towards the body

Structure of Lower Leg

As there are no muscles below the knee and hock, movements of the lower limbs and feet are controlled by tendons attached to the muscles of the upper legs.

Bones

Below the knee and hock joints are the **cannon bones**, forecannon in the forelegs and hindcannon in the hind legs. These bones, though relatively slender, are designed to be weight carrying.

The two splint bones, situated on the outer and inner aspect of the cannon bone on each leg, are degenerated bones that have no function apart from helping to support the carpus and tarsus bones of the knee and hock joints.

Two sesamoid bones lie at the back of each fetlock joint.

Below this joint is the long pastern, the short pastern and the pedal bone. At the back of the pedal bone is the navicular, also called the distal sesamoid. Part of the short pastern, the pedal and navicular bones are classified as bones of the foot.

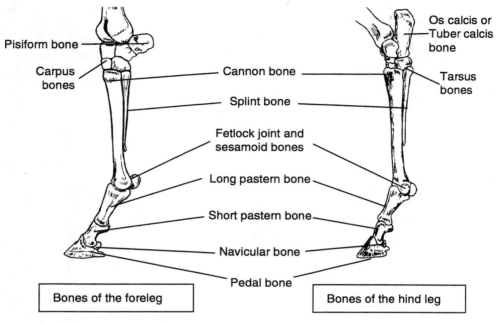

Pisiform bone	Os calcis or Tuber calcis bone	
Carpus bones	Cannon bone	Tarsus bones
	Splint bone	
	Fetlock joint and sesamoid bones	
	Long pastern bone	
	Short pastern bone	
	Navicular bone	
	Pedal bone	

Bones of the foreleg	Bones of the hind leg

Joints

The knee and hock joints are made up of a number of small bones to make movement easier. There are normally seven carpus bones in the knee and six tarsus bones in the hock.

The fetlock joint lies between the cannon bone and the long pastern. This joint can only move backwards and forwards.

The pastern joint lies between the long and short pastern bones.

The coffin joint lies between the short pastern and the pedal bone.

Tendons

The main tendons in the lower leg consist of extensors at the front and flexors at the back. These are a continuation of their corresponding muscles.

Common digital extensor tendon – in the foreleg this extends from the *common digital extensor muscle.*

In the hind leg the **long digital extensor tendon** *joins with the lateral digital extensor tendon* to form the *common digital extensor tendon.*

In both hind and forelegs, the tendon passes all the way down the front of the cannon bone and is finally attached to the top of the pedal bone. It acts to extend the foot, fetlock and knee joints.

Lateral digital extensor tendon – continuation of *lateral digital extensor muscle.* This tendon runs down the front of the leg next to the bone. It attaches to the long pastern and helps to extend the foot.

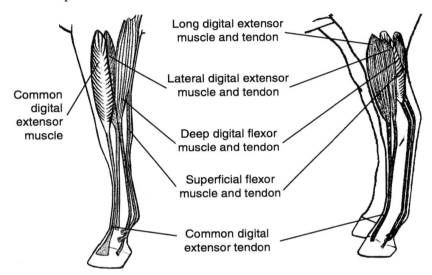

Long digital extensor muscle and tendon

Lateral digital extensor muscle and tendon

Common digital extensor muscle

Deep digital flexor muscle and tendon

Superficial flexor muscle and tendon

Common digital extensor tendon

Superficial digital flexor tendon – continuation of *superficial digital flexor muscle.* This tendon passes down the back of the leg. Just below the fetlock it divides into two, passing either side of the pastern bones. These branches divide again into two and attach on both sides to the long and short pastern bones.

Deep digital flexor tendon – continuation of *deep digital flexor muscle* passes down the back of the leg between the superficial digital flexor tendon and the suspensory ligament. It passes over the sesamoid bones, which act as a pulley to give the tendon a greater leverage on the fetlock joint and foot. The tendon then broadens out attaching to the pedal bone.

Ligaments

There are several ligaments within the lower leg and foot. Their functions are to connect bone to bone at joints, to keep the bones in place, and to maintain the alignment of the joints.

The ligaments around the fetlock, pastern and the coffin joints make connections between the respective bones, acting to support and protect them from abnormal action.

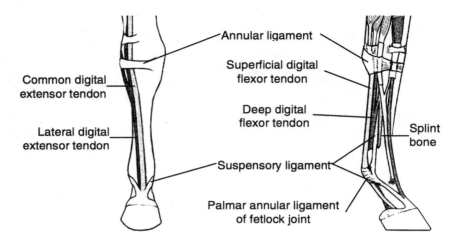

The sesamoid bones and the navicular are held in place by ligaments.

Ligaments also help to support and maintain the position of the tendons within the leg.

Suspensory ligament

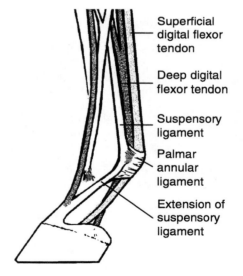

The most important ligament is the suspensory. This is a modified muscle possessing considerable elasticity. Originating at the back of the knee and hock, this ligament passes down behind the cannon bone. Just above the fetlock joint it divides:

❖ part attaches to each of the sesamoid bones.

❖ part binds with the palmar annular ligament around the fetlock.

❖ part passes round the front of the long pastern, either side, to merge into the common digital extensor tendon.

Part of the suspensory ligament at the fetlock binds with the palmar annular ligament and forms a ring through which the two digital flexor tendons pass.

The function of the suspensory ligament is to support the fetlock and prevent it from flexing too far down towards the ground. Even when the horse is standing there is tremendous downward pressure on the fetlock exerted by the horse's weight. There is even more pressure when the horse puts all his weight on one fetlock, for instance on landing after jumping.

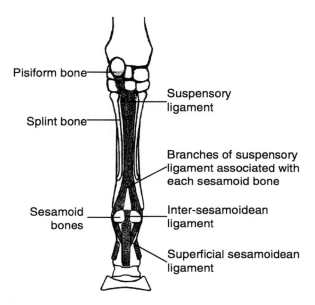

Pisiform bone

Suspensory ligament

Splint bone

Branches of suspensory ligament associated with each sesamoid bone

Sesamoid bones

Inter-sesamoidean ligament

Superficial sesamoidean ligament

Cartilages

This is a tough elastic tissue often termed 'gristle'.

It unites some joints together, acts as a buffer between joints, reduces friction within joints and, as it withstands certain compression, absorbs concussion.

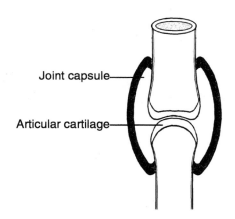

Joint capsule

Articular cartilage

Stay Apparatus

The stay apparatus is a system of ligaments, tendons and muscles that support the horse when standing, effectively locking the joints firmly into position.

The main component of this mechanism is the suspensory ligament. Acting in support are the check ligaments together with the superficial digital flexor tendon and the deep digital flexor tendon.

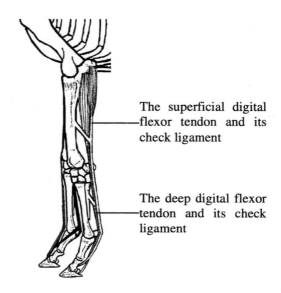

The superficial digital flexor tendon and its check ligament

The deep digital flexor tendon and its check ligament

Unlike other ligaments, which connect bone to bone, the check ligaments connect bone to tendon. They modify the action of the tendons causing them to 'check' or 'cut off' the muscular attachment above.

There is a check ligament attached to the superficial digital flexor tendon above the knee and hock. The deep digital flexor tendon has a check ligament below the knee and hock.

Basically when the body weight is placed in a standing position the check mechanism acts to lock the joints. The ligaments tighten and prevent the muscles from functioning.

So the muscle, tendons and ligaments of the skeletal muscular system act to give stability as well as movement. Another part of the horse's anatomy vital for movement is the foot. The feet bear the horse's weight, absorbing and transmitting the massive concussion of this weight when it meets and comes into contact with the ground.

Structure of the Horse's Foot

The horse's foot is an amazing piece of apparatus. It has evolved to bear all the weight of the horse on a relatively tiny surface.

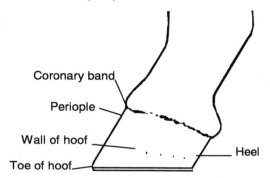

Coronary band

Periople

Wall of hoof

Toe of hoof

Heel

Coronary band – a band of tissue at the coronet that creates horn.

The hoof wall is made up of small tubes (tubules) of horn growing down from the coronary band. These tubules are held together by intertubular horn, a gluey, sticky substance secreted from the coronary band. This acts like cement binding the tubules together into a solid mass.

Periople - outer protective layer on the surface of the hoof, which acts like varnish.

This is secreted from an area just above the coronet, the perioplic ring. The periople regulates the moisture in the horn. It restricts excess evaporation from the hoof yet allows moisture to seep into the horn through osmotic action.

Hoof wall - the hard horn layer surrounding the hoof.

Horn takes from nine to twelve months to grow down from the coronary band to the toe. It takes a little less at the heel, around six months, because the depth is less. Diet is important for the healthy growth of new horn and a horse in poor condition will suffer from weak, brittle horn and ultimately poor foot formation. Damage to the coronet causes defects in the horn growth.

The wall is thickest at the toe and diminishes towards the heels. The wall extends around and forwards at the heels to form the bars of the foot. In between the bar and the wall is the seat of corn.

Sole of the foot - concave area between hoof wall, the white line and the frog.

The insensitive sole acts as protection for the inner, sensitive sole. It consists of a similar horn as the wall but is less strong, as it does not bear the same weight as the wall itself. The insensitive sole is constantly flaking away and being replaced from the sensitive sole.

The outer or insensitive frog - visible under the foot as a triangular shape extending from the heel to the toe with the apex about half way down the foot.

The frog has several important functions; it absorbs concussion, bears weight, provides grip, protects the inner, sensitive frog and it is vital to the healthy blood supply of the foot.

It consists of horn, similar to the hoof wall, but with a higher proportion of intertubular horn, which gives it a tough, rubbery, elastic consistency. It has three grooves, one either side (the lateral grooves) and one central groove. These grooves allow expansion of the frog on impact with the ground and also provide grip.

The white line – this is the division between the insensitive (outer) and the sensitive (inner) parts of the foot. It is visible underneath the foot, inside the hoof wall, as a layer of lighter coloured, waxy horn joining the sole and the wall.

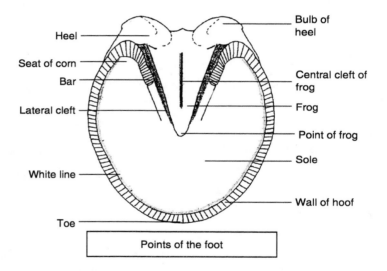

Heel
Seat of corn
Bar
Lateral cleft
White line
Toe

Bulb of heel
Central cleft of frog
Frog
Point of frog
Sole
Wall of hoof

Points of the foot

Internal Structure

Insensitive laminae - situated inside the wall is a layer of insensitive laminae. These tiny, spaghetti-shaped projections grow from the inner sides of the hoof wall and interlock with a corresponding number (around 600) of sensitive laminae.

Sensitive laminae - these are attached to the periosteum (the membrane lining) of the pedal bone. They are interwoven with the insensitive laminae keeping the wall of the hoof firmly attached to, and supporting, the pedal bone.

Sensitive sole - situated below the pedal bone, inside the insensitive sole, is the sensitive sole. Young cells are constantly being formed in the sensitive sole and these replace the layers of the insensitive sole.

Digital cushion – lies between the pedal bone and the deep flexor tendon. Also called the **plantar cushion**. This elastic, fibrous pad stretches from between the heels and extends around the pedal bone. It acts as a buffer to absorb concussion when the foot meets the ground. It also acts as part of the compression mechanism to push the blood back up the leg.

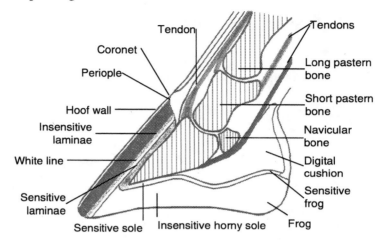

Sensitive frog – situated below the digital cushion, on top of and merging into the insensitive frog. New cells formed here replace the flaking layers of the insensitive frog.

Lateral cartilages - the two lateral cartilages of the foot are attached to the upper part of the pedal bone and extend upwards above the coronet. They protect the coffin joint and support the digital cushion. Their elasticity allows the foot to expand on impact with the ground thus absorbing some of the concussion.

Blood Supply of the Foot

The leg and foot are nourished by blood coming from the body via **the terminal or common digital artery**. This passes down the leg dividing into two branches at the fetlock joint. Eventually the blood vessels enter the pedal bone through small holes. This artery supplies all the tissues of the foot, the sensitive laminae, cartilages, digital cushion, joints, bones, tendons and skin.

The **coronary plexus** is a network of **veins** that takes the blood away from the foot and returns it to the body. Blood reaches the leg and foot by the pumping action of the heart and by gravity.

Blood is returned back up the leg by compression. As the foot meets the ground the impact is taken first by the hoof wall. The horse's weight presses down through the short pastern and onto the digital cushion. This causes the lateral cartilages to spread widening the heels and pushing the frog onto the ground.

This pressure effect of the foot is vital to the circulation of the leg. As the weight presses the foot down the blood is squeezed through the capillaries and into the veins, which do not have valves in this area. The blood is then forced back up the leg and oxygenated blood is encouraged to refill the arteries and capillaries. It may be possible that the action of these blood vessels also absorbs some of the concussion.

Nervous system

The leg and foot of the horse has two main nerves. These pass down the leg either side of the bones and split into branches serving all areas of the leg and foot.

Mechanics of the Foot

Weight bearing	The weight bearing areas are primarily the hoof wall, the bars, the frog and part of the sole nearest to the wall. In soft ground the sole will bear some weight.
Concussion	The parts of the foot that absorb concussion are the frog, the plantar cushion, the cartilages and the heel. The concussion then travels up the leg. The fetlock joint flexes to take the effect and eventually the muscles around the shoulder or hip absorb the remainder of the impact.
Anti-slipping device	The horse, in most cases, is prevented from slipping by the shape of the hoof, the shape of the frog, its lateral and central clefts and the concave shape of the sole.

Exam Tips

To learn every muscle and its effect on the horse's movement would take a lot of time and effort and is not necessary for Stage III. You will, though, need to learn the names of the main muscles, superficial and deep, their position on the horse's body and how they are involved in creating motion and in carrying the rider. You should also be able to show the position of these muscles on a horse and to explain briefly how these muscles work to perform their task.

It may help, after learning the information on muscles, to watch horses at work, during flatwork and jumping sessions. Videos can be useful, particularly if you are able to slow the action down and watch in detail how the horse uses the muscles for movement.

The structure of the leg below the knee and hock, and of the foot, external and internal, needs to be learnt together with the functions of the different parts and how they relate to the action of movement.

C H A P T E R 7

Respiratory & Circulatory Systems

In this chapter the respiratory and circulatory systems are explained separately, their parts and functions. Following this is a description of how the muscular, respiratory and circulatory systems, co-operate together and how each is dependent on the other for efficient functioning.

The Respiratory System

Oxygen, present with other gases in the air, is a fuel essential to mammals. Deprived of oxygen the body begins to deteriorate quickly; the horse will only survive for a matter of minutes. Brain cells begin to die rapidly and muscles stop working, which is serious for the vital organs such as the heart. To maintain life, air is inhaled, the oxygen extracted and distributed around the body. This is the prime function of the respiratory system.

Functions

The respiratory system is one method by which the body takes in a fuel and extracts waste products.

The functions of the respiratory system are to

    a)   take in oxygen

    b)   remove waste products such as carbon dioxide and water

    c)   regulate body temperature by taking in cool air and exhaling warm air

    d)   create sound

    e)   act as a sensory organ

The Upper Respiratory Tract

Air is taken in first through the **nostrils,** *not the mouth*. The nostrils can change shape when the horse inhales. During hard exercise, for example, the nostrils expand to inhale more air.

Lining the nostrils are small hairs (**cilia**) which, acting as a filter, trap dust and other foreign particles entering the system.

Continuing on from the nostrils are the **two nasal passages**, one for each nostril. These are separated by a partition made of bone and cartilage, the **septum**.

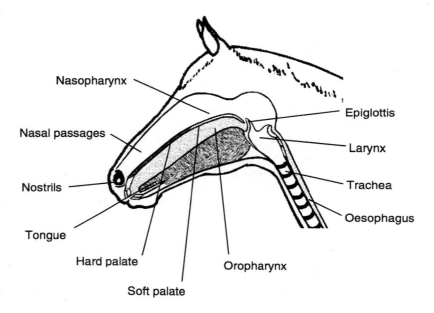

Dividing the nasal passages from the mouth is the **palate**. Towards the mouth the palate is hard but nearer the throat the palate becomes a soft, muscular membrane.

Behind the nasal passages is the **pharynx**, a single cavity divided horizontally by the soft palate. The top portion is the **nasopharynx** and the lower the **oropharynx,** at the back of the mouth. There are other **air-filled cavities** in this area, the **sinuses** and the **guttural pouches**.

Both the gullet (oesophagus) and the windpipe (trachea) start at the pharynx. The **trachea** is a tube kept **permanently open** by **rings of cartilage**.

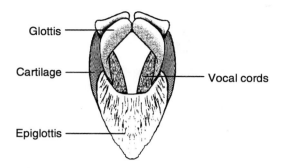

The **larynx**, or **voice box**, is situated at the top of the trachea. This is a tube of cartilage plates held together by membranes and muscle fibres, all covered by a mucous lining.

The larynx has three main functions:

1. Acts as a valve, regulating the air flow

    When the horse is resting the respiration is relatively shallow but, as the horse needs more air, for instance during exercise, the larynx widens. During hard, fast work the larynx is fully opened to allow a maximum amount of air into the respiratory system.

2. Protection of respiratory system

    Prevents food or foreign particles entering the respiratory system. The **trachea** in the neck lies below, or in front of, the **oesophagus.** The food being swallowed from the mouth has to cross over the top of the trachea into the oesophagus. To prevent food or other particles entering the respiratory system, a co-ordinated action by the **epiglottis** and the **larynx** and effectively blocks off the top of the trachea. The epiglottis is a flap of cartilage at the top of the larynx.

    When the horse swallows the soft palate moves upwards to the roof of the mouth cutting off the nasal passages. The **epiglottis closes over the larynx.** The larynx itself moves upwards and forwards towards the epiglottis shutting off the trachea and allowing the oesophagus to open.

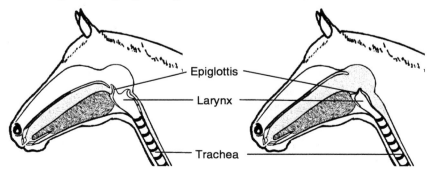

When air is inhaled the **soft palate at the back of the throat is lowered** and the **epiglottis slightly overlaps it.** Air is taken in and passes through the larynx into the trachea.

In humans this movement of the larynx can be seen when the Adam's apple moves up and down. This all takes place within a few seconds.

3.   Sound production

Some of the fibres within the larynx act as vocal cords creating sounds when air is exhaled.

When the horse breathes in, the air passes through the larynx into the windpipe or trachea. The trachea, which can be felt quite easily down the underside of the horse's neck, is also lined with cilia that filter the air passing into the lungs.

The Lower Respiratory Tract

The lungs are two large, elastic organs taking up most of the chest cavity apart from the space occupied by the heart, major blood vessels, the oesophagus, lymph tubes and glands.

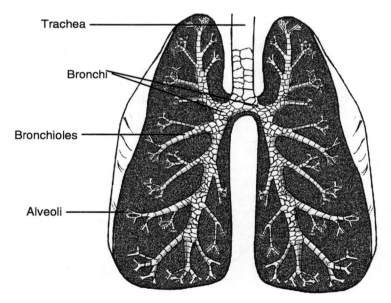

In the chest the trachea splits into two branches called **bronchi.** These tubes are kept permanently open by rings of cartilage. One branch goes to each lung where they divide again into narrower branches called **bronchioles.** These are not supported by cartilage. The bronchioles divide again into tiny ducts called **alveoli** which, in turn, terminate as **air sacs.**

The **alveolar sacs** have the appearance of bunches of grapes. These thin-walled sacs are covered with narrow blood vessels, the capillaries. This design gives a much larger surface area for the exchange of gases.

All the airways within the respiration system contain the tiny, hair-like cilia. On top of the cilia is a thin film of mucus. Dust and other foreign particles collected in this mucus are carried by the cilia in a wavelike motion through the airways to the throat. The horse then swallows the mucus.

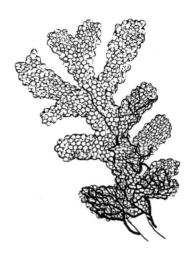

Situated behind the lungs and assisting with respiration, is a sheet of muscle called the **diaphragm**. This stretches from the loins under the spine, sloping downwards and forwards to the breastbone (sternum). It is cone or dome shaped when relaxed, like an open umbrella. The main artery of the body (the aorta), the main vein (the vena cava) and the oesophagus pass through it. The ribcage encloses and protects the lungs and the diaphragm.

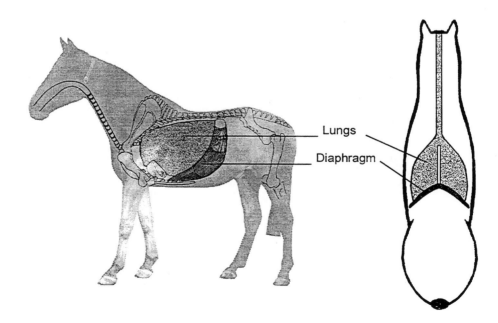

Lungs

Diaphragm

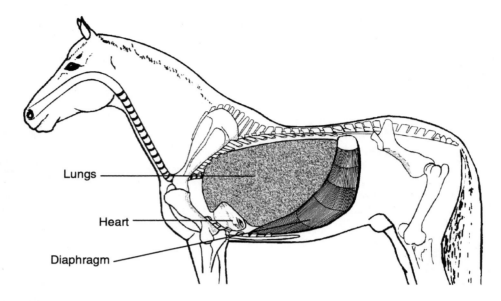

Respiration

At rest the horse takes 8 to 16 breaths per minute. The respiration rate increases at certain times, for instance after work or when the horse is stressed, nervous or ill. After fast exercise the rate can increase up to 120 breaths per minute.

The act of breathing starts within the respiratory centre of the brain. This controls breathing so that no conscious effort need be made; though the rapidity or depth of breathing can, to some degree, be consciously controlled.

The intercostal muscles between the ribs, together with the diaphragm, contract. This has the effect of bringing the ribs outwards and expanding the size of the lungs. The increased chest cavity creates a lower air pressure in the lungs than in the atmosphere and air is drawn into the lungs. When the muscles relax, the chest cavity reduces in size and air is exhaled.

The chest cavity and the lungs are covered with a smooth, moist membrane called the **pleura**. This allows the lungs to slide smoothly against each other and within the chest, preventing friction during expansion and contraction.

Air is sucked in and travels through the airways to the alveolar sacs. The blood vessels (capillaries) that cover the sacs have extremely thin walls so that oxygen is able to pass into (diffuse) the blood stream.

Carbon dioxide and water vapour diffuse from the blood stream into the alveoli and are excreted through the nostrils. The water vapour acts to keep the air in the respiratory tubes moist.

When the horse is resting, only a percentage of the lung capacity is used. The harder the horse works, the more oxygen is needed for muscle activity. The respiratory rate increases and the breathing becomes deeper. More of the lung capacity, that is, a greater number of alveoli, is put into use to pass this oxygen into the blood stream.

Heat Regulation

When the body is hot and needs to lose heat, one method is through the respiration. Breathing is increased in speed and depth so that cool air is inhaled. This cools the blood in the capillaries of the lungs. Warm air is exhaled and heat is lost from the body. During cold weather air is warmed up slightly as it enters the body to prevent the chill striking the lungs. The air being exhaled is warmer and this is visible as 'steam'.

Sound Production

The horse can give a variety of sounds, from a soft whinny to a bellow or a squeal, using the vocal cords within the larynx. Air is exhaled and the fibres in the larynx vibrated to produce the desired sounds.

Sense of Smell

In the nasal passages there are delicate bones (**turbinates**). The mucous membrane covering these bones has a rich blood supply and contains the nerve cells concerned with smell (olfactory). From this membrane tiny hairs (sensory cilia) grow. As the air passes over and touches the membrane it stimulates the cilia. The cilia pass the message onto the nerve cells and then, through nervous impulses, to the brain.

The nostrils can indicate the horse's emotions by contracting tightly, blowing out or strong sniffing.

External and Internal Respiration

External respiration is the inhalation of oxygen to the lungs and the eventual exhalation of the waste products, carbon dioxide and water.

Internal respiration is the exchange of oxygen for carbon dioxide throughout the body. Oxygen is vital for the functioning of the body tissues; these also need to excrete their waste products.

The respiratory system is dependent on the circulatory system. Transporting oxygen to where it is needed and returning carbon dioxide to the lungs for expiration is one function of the circulatory system.

The Circulatory System

Circulation is the body's transport system whereby blood, pumped by the heart through tubes, carries substances to and from all parts of the body.

Functions

In its role as a transportation network, the circulatory system helps the body to perform some of its essential tasks.

1.   Carries oxygen from the lungs to parts of the body where it is needed.

2.   Returns carbon dioxide and water to the lungs for excretion.

3.   Carries nutrients from the digestive system to the liver.

4.   Carries nutrients from the liver to other parts of the body.

5.   Carries waste material to the liver and kidneys for excretion.

6.   Excretes waste through sweating.

7.   Regulates body temperature.

8.   Mobilises the body's defence mechanism, transporting cells to areas of injury or disease.

9.   Carries hormones from the glands to various organs.

10. Carries water to the cells of the body.

A network of blood vessels spreads throughout the body, channelling blood and the substances it carries to and from every part.

The Blood

This is a fluid consisting of plasma, platelets and cells.

Plasma	thin, yellowish, transparent fluid in which platelets and cells are suspended. Plasma contains fibrinogen used in the clotting of blood.
Platelets	minute particles involved in the clotting of blood.
Cells (corpuscles)	two types; **red blood cells** that **transport oxygen** and **carbon dioxide**, and **white blood cells** that form part of the body's **immune system**.

Red Blood Cells

These cells are **round** in shape and **concave on both sides**, a dumbbell shape in profile. They are **flexible** and have the ability to change shape when passing through small blood vessels. Though the cells are extremely small, their large numbers (millions) give the blood its red colour.

Red blood cells are **manufactured** within the **marrow** of some of the larger **bones** and have a life of around thirty days, after which they are destroyed in the liver and spleen. In a healthy horse this creation and destruction of red blood cells is in balance.

Each cell contains **haemoglobin**, a red, iron-rich protein, which has the ability of binding with oxygen and carbon dioxide. When oxygen combines with haemoglobin this becomes **oxyhaemoglobin;** the blood becomes a bright red colour. The muscles, various organs and tissues need oxygen to work. When the **oxyhaemoglobin** reaches these parts the oxygen is released.

Carbon dioxide is then passed back into the blood stream; some of which is carried in the plasma and some binds with the haemoglobin to form **carboxyhaemoglobin**.

Once the blood has released its oxygen content and taken on carbon dioxide its colour changes. The blood in the veins becomes a characteristic blue or dark purple. This colour changes again to bright red as the blood passes through the lungs and is enriched with oxygen.

If a vein is cut, the red blood cells readily mix with some of the oxygen in the air causing the blue or dark purple blood to become a dark red. Blood from an artery, already carrying oxygen, is a bright red.

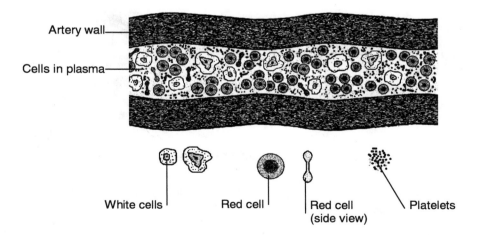

Artery wall

Cells in plasma

White cells   Red cell   Red cell (side view)   Platelets

Diagrammatic view of the blood in an artery showing white cells, red cells and platelets suspended in a plasma solution (not to scale).

White Blood Cells

These play an important part in the body's defence system, fighting infection. They flock to an area of injury or infection and can engulf foreign particles or microbes. They also release histamine to control inflammation.

Blood Clotting

As the blood is fluid, any opening in a blood vessel causes leakage which, in severe cases, can be fatal. The body deals with this problem by uniting substances in the blood stream to form a jelly-like clot to block the leak.

The two important constituents of a clot are the protein **fibrinogen** and the **platelets.** Basically the fibrinogen and the platelets unite to form a clot. To prevent the blood clotting other than at a break, (the blood within the vessels must remain fluid), the fibrinogen and platelets remain in an inert form until combined with other substances when a blood vessel is torn.

Blood Vessels

These are basically tubes of different sizes that carry the blood around and to all parts of the body.

The **arteries** these thick-walled muscular tubes carry blood **away** from the heart. The main artery carry blood from the heart to the body is the **aorta**. The main artery carrying blood to the lungs is the **pulmonary artery**. These large main arteries split into smaller arteries and then into arterioles.

The **arterioles** theses smaller tubes have quite thick walls.

The **capillaries** the arterioles split into even smaller tubes. These spread throughout every part of the body and have thin walls through which fluids can pass. Oxygen passes into the areas where it is needed and carbon dioxide is returned into the capillaries to be taken away.

The **venules** blood passes from the capillaries into the venules, which carry the de-oxygenated blood to the small veins and into the larger main veins.

The **veins** thin walled tubes carrying blood towards the heart. The main vein carrying blood into the heart is the vena cava. The main vein carrying blood from the lungs into the heart is the pulmonary vein. Most veins have valves. These act by opening to let blood through and then by shutting to prevent blood flowing back, rather like lock gates on a canal.

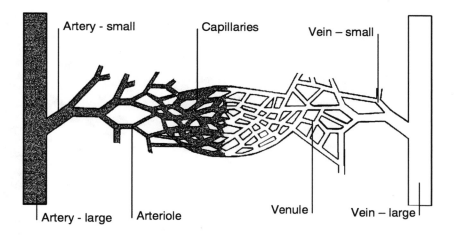

Diagram to show how the arteries and veins split into smaller vessels, into arterioles or venules and finally the capillary network. (Not to scale).

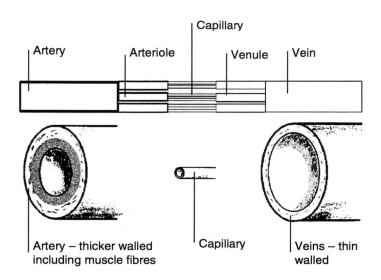

Diagram to show the relative sizes of the blood vessels. (Not to scale.)

The Heart

This organ, a hollow mass of muscle served by blood vessels and nerves, acts as a pump pushing the blood around the body.

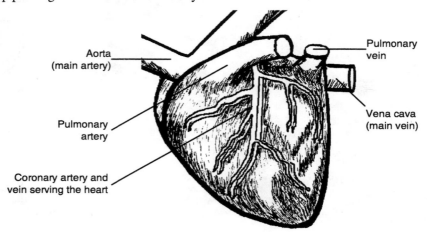

The pumping action of the heart can be heard or felt and counted in beats. When at rest the horse's heart beats about 35 to 42 times per minute. For situations when the blood needs to travel more quickly around the body, the heart will pump faster. The heart rate can rise to about 200 beats per minute when necessary, for instance, during fast work.

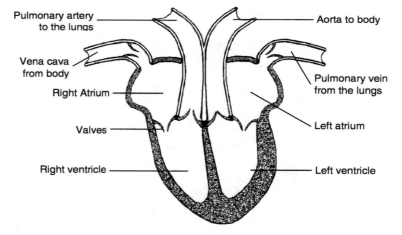

The heart is divided into four chambers, two upper chambers and two lower chambers. The two chambers at the top are called the right atrium and the left atrium (plural atria). Another term often used is auricles. The two lower chambers are the right and left ventricles.

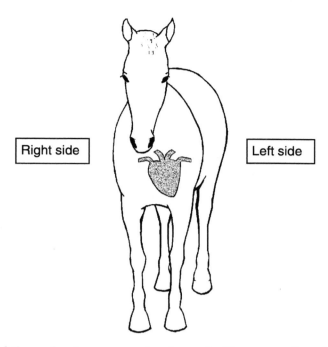

Right side | Left side

The walls of these chambers are made of muscle (the myocardium layer) with a watertight inner lining (the endocardium layer) which, being smooth, reduces friction to ease the blood flow.

Blood enters the heart through the veins into the two atria at the same time. Once the atria have contracted and pumped the blood through, they relax. The ventricles then contract and pump the blood through to the arteries. This produces a wave-like motion, atria contract and pump, then relax and fill up, ventricles contract and pump, relax and receive blood from the atria.

The muscular walls of the atria are relatively thin because they are only required to pump blood through to the ventricles. The walls of the ventricles are thicker. The right ventricle pumps blood towards the lungs and the left ventricle to the rest of the body. The left ventricle, because of the harder job it performs, has the thickest wall. This, and the positioning of the heart to the left of the chest, are the reasons why the heartbeat is more easily detected on the left side of the horse.

The blood passes from the atria into the ventricles through **one way valves**. The one way valves, because they prevent the backward flow of blood, are important to the pumping action of the heart; they maintain the pressure that takes the blood around the body. Once the blood has passed from the atria to the ventricles the valves shut preventing any return of blood. There are also valves between the ventricles and the arteries, which prevent a backward flow. The blood is then compelled to pass into the arteries through the pumping and blocking action of heart and valves.

1. Blood enters from the veins through the valves into the atria. Artery valves close to prevent backward flow.	2. Atria contract, push blood through to ventricles. Valves in veins close to prevent any blood being pushed back into veins.

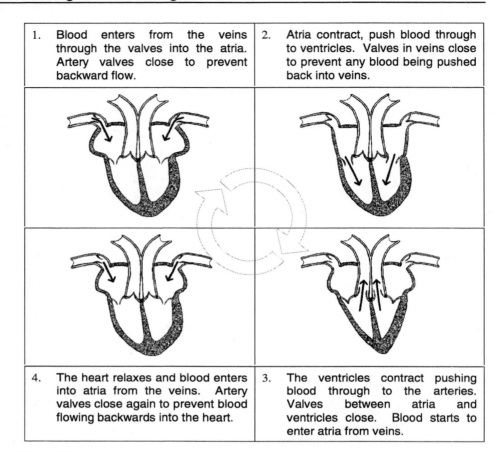

4. The heart relaxes and blood enters into atria from the veins. Artery valves close again to prevent blood flowing backwards into the heart.	3. The ventricles contract pushing blood through to the arteries. Valves between atria and ventricles close. Blood starts to enter atria from veins.

The Circulation

To distinguish between its two functional duties, the circulatory system is divided into two:

* Pulmonary system carries blood to and from the lungs.

* Systemic (pronounced sis-<u>stem</u>-ik) system carries blood to and from the rest of the body.

The Pulmonary System

This involves the heart and lungs.

Deoxygenated blood enters through the **vena cava** (the main vein) into the right atrium of the heart. The blood is pumped into the **right ventricle**. The ventricle contracts and the blood is pushed through into the **pulmonary artery** and so to the **lungs**.

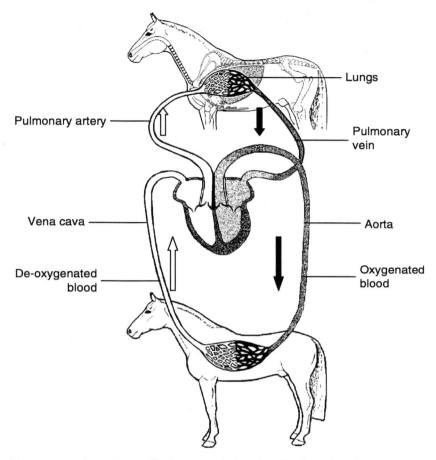

Pulmonary artery

Lungs

Pulmonary vein

Vena cava

Aorta

De-oxygenated blood

Oxygenated blood

The blood passes into the capillaries around the alveoli where it collects oxygen and gives up its waste. The **oxygenated blood** then travels through the **pulmonary vein** to the **left atrium** of the heart where it enters the systemic system.

The Systemic System

This consists of the heart and the rest of the body *apart from the lungs*.

Oxygenated blood enters the **left ventricle** from the left atrium and is pumped to the main artery **the aorta**. This artery divides, at intervals, into branches of arteries taking oxygenated blood around the body. These branches are named after the respective regions they serve.

The oxygenated blood from the lungs is first transported by the cardiac branch to the coronary arteries. These supply oxygen to the vital heart muscles.

Cardiac	coronary arteries take blood to the heart.
Brachiocephalic	takes blood to the forelegs and head.
Coeliac (pronounced seelyak)	supplies stomach, liver and spleen.
Mesenteric	supplies intestines.
Renal	serves the kidneys.
Iliac	serves hindquarters.

The blood passes to the arterioles, the capillaries, the venules and the veins. The **veins** join the main vein, the **vena cava**, which enters the **right atrium** of the heart. The blood passes to the **right ventricle** and into the pulmonary system.

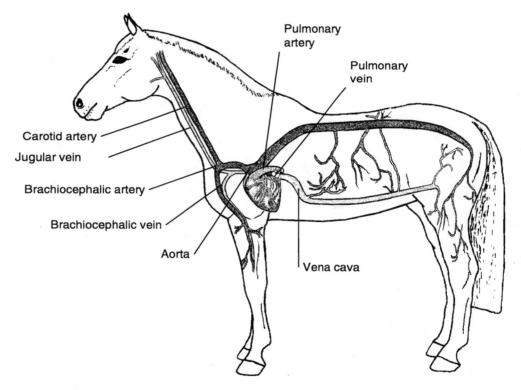

As the blood, pulsing through the blood vessels, takes nutrients to and collects waste products from every part of the body, it is vital that this transport system works efficiently and correctly. Any breakdown through obstruction of a vessel or loss of blood for any reason can have serious and even fatal results.

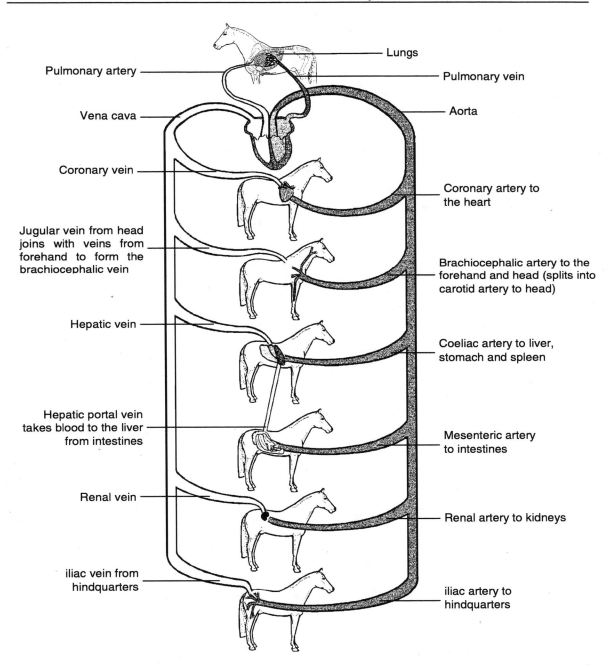

Lungs

Pulmonary artery

Pulmonary vein

Vena cava

Aorta

Coronary vein

Coronary artery to the heart

Jugular vein from head joins with veins from forehand to form the brachiocephalic vein

Brachiocephalic artery to the forehand and head (splits into carotid artery to head)

Hepatic vein

Coeliac artery to liver, stomach and spleen

Hepatic portal vein takes blood to the liver from intestines

Mesenteric artery to intestines

Renal vein

Renal artery to kidneys

iliac vein from hindquarters

iliac artery to hindquarters

Blood Analysis

The substances within the blood often help the diagnosis of illness or disease. Plasma contains various substances, hormones, antibodies, salts, and enzymes, as well as the red and white blood cells.

When blood samples are taken and analysed the proportion of substances present in the blood can often give a good indication of health or illness. For instance a reduction in the number of red blood cells can be an indication of anaemia. An increase in white blood cells could show infection.

The Three Systems

The respiratory, circulatory and muscular systems work closely together. The respiratory system extracts oxygen from the air and transfers this to the blood stream. The circulatory system transports and distributes the oxygen throughout the body where it is needed. The muscles need oxygen to work. The more work the muscles are required to do, the more oxygen is demanded. The circulatory system speeds up and demands more oxygen from the respiratory system. Breathing becomes faster and deeper as the fuel is used up more quickly.

As the circulatory system speeds up, the heart needs to work faster and for this the heart muscles need more oxygen. The muscles working the lungs, the intercostal muscles, and the diaphragm also needs more oxygen. Thus all three systems are dependent on each other for efficiency.

Exam Tips

Anatomy and physiology are fascinating subjects. How the body works is an absolute miracle when you realise how finely balanced each system has to be and how they all relate to one another. The heart itself is an organ that pumps millions of times in a lifetime, normally without replacement parts or constant repairs.

If you can develop an interest, a fascination in the subject of anatomy the study of it becomes so much easier. However not everyone is so inclined and for many the different anatomical terms, their position in the body and their relation to each other always remains a mystery. In this case the student needs to devise a method to memorise different parts. Something as simple as **Artery Always Away** from the heart may be helpful.

Try not to learn too much at a time. It is easy to overload with information and become totally confused. The knowledge needed at Stage III is not deep or expansive. You need to know the basics of the three systems, the names of the important parts and how they work. You will not need vast amounts of information, but you will need to know and understand the relation between the systems.

C H A P T E R   8
Minor Ailments

In the following section on minor ailments the descriptions are given as briefly as possible to facilitate learning and recognition. The definition of the particular ailment is followed by a description of the symptoms, which in most cases, are the first indications that something is wrong. So the order is definition, symptoms, causes, treatment and prevention.

Every groom, handler and owner should have a basic knowledge of diseases, infections and injuries that horses can, and do, suffer during their lives. This does not need to be a thorough medical knowledge, but the groom needs to distinguish between illnesses to decide on the appropriate course of action. Many conditions can be treated quickly and successfully in the yard; some illnesses need professional help either from the Vet or the Farrier. Contagious and infectious diseases need a quick diagnosis if the rest of the horses and ponies within the yard are to avoid contamination.

Whilst many ailments are detected by their specific symptoms, in a number of conditions the signs are often similar. This can make the groom's job of detecting ailments quite difficult especially as the horse can only indicate his state of health by his behaviour. If the groom, though, can recognise that certain symptoms relate to a particular type of illness (for instance colic), then the necessary action can be taken quickly to prevent deterioration in the horse's health.

Digestive Problems

Choke

Definition: **obstruction** within the **gullet** or **oesophagus**.

Symptoms: **coughing**, **discharge** from the **nostrils**, **difficulty in swallowing**. The **horse may extend his neck** and **show distress**. There may be a **visible lump in the gullet**.

Causes: **food obstruction: eating too fast, food not chewed properly** because of **teeth problems** or through **tiredness**. **Food incorrectly prepared: dry food** and **no water, carrots incorrectly cut, sugar beet that is not soaked thoroughly** may swell and lodge in the throat.

Treatment: **gently massage area around obstruction. Smear vegetable oil, butter or margarine** on the **back of the tongue** to try and make the obstruction slip down. **Do not give food and water,** may aggravate condition. If the **obstruction will not dislodge** within **five to ten minutes,** or the **horse has difficulty breathing,** *call the Vet immediately.* The Vet may administer a tranquilliser to help the gullet relax.

Prevention: **dampen feed and hay, prepare food properly,** cut carrots and apples into small pieces. Add chaff to food to prevent the horse bolting his feeds. **Do not feed when the horse is tired.** Change bed to shavings instead of straw if he tends to eat his bed. His teeth should be checked.

Colic

Definition: **problem** within the **digestive system** causing abdominal pain.

Symptoms: **difficulty passing droppings; fewer** or **no droppings; hard, dry droppings,** signs of **diarrhoea down hind legs. Refusal** or **disinterest in food.** The horse **appears tired, distressed, sweating, looking** at **flank, kicking** at **stomach** or **pawing the ground. Lying down** and **rising; constant or violent rolling. Respiration** may be **shallow** and **fast, stomach and abdomen swollen, distended. Restlessness, walking around box.**

There are **five main types of colic** – gastric, spasmodic, impaction, tympanitic, twisted gut.

1. **Gastric colic**: distension or abnormal swelling of the horse's stomach.
2. **Spasmodic colic**: spasms of the gut wall, excessive and irregular gut movement (peristalsis): build up of gas. Symptoms fluctuate.
3. **Impaction**: blockage of undigested food within the digestive tract usually around the pelvic flexure.
4. **Tympanitic colic (tympany or bloat)**: distension in the horse's intestines through fermentation of food creating gases.
5. **Twisted gut**: the gut twists on itself, restricting and possibly cutting off the blood supply to that area.

Causes: **damage to gut** through **worm infestation. Lack of water** or **watering before a large, dry feed, ingesting sand from a stream or with grass. Incorrect feeding; sudden changes** of diet, feeding **poor quality, stale or badly prepared food, working a horse too soon after a large feed. Change of grazing** may upset the delicate digestive process. **Bad habits; wind sucking, crib biting** or **eating the bedding.** If the **horse's teeth** are uneven he may **not masticate (chew)** his food properly.

Treatment: **put the horse** in a stable in a **quiet area** with a **thick deep bed** and **high thick banks. Remove all buckets, mangers** or **other fixtures** to prevent injury. If he is **lying down quietly let him remain.** If he is **restless, walk** him in hand for a **couple of minutes.** If he starts to **roll violently**, try and walk him round, if he persists then move him to an **indoor school** for safety. Put the **summer sheet** or **sweat rug** on him if he appears **cold** and **shivery. Observe horse constantly. Give NO food or water** unless he shows an interest in food, in which case, **offer grass. Most cases of colic improve within 30 minutes.**

Call the Vet immediately if:

• the horse is **severely ill**,

• the horse has been **ill during the night** and is still suffering in the morning,

• the horse is still **not recovering** from a mild colic **after 30 minutes**,

Vet may administer **sedatives (relaxants)** and **analgesics (painkillers)**.

Prevention: make any **change of diet gradual**, observe the **rules of feeding and watering. Worm** the horse **regularly** and have his **teeth inspected every 6 months. Good stable** and **grassland management** should prevent most cases of colic.

Respiratory Problems

Cold

Definition: a disease caused by a virus in the upper respiratory tract.

A virus is a microscopic entity capable of replication only within the cells of plants and animals.

Symptoms: nasal discharge, sneezing, coughing, lethargy and a rise in temperature.

Cause: infection from another horse.

Treatment: take the horse off work. Keep him warm and quiet. Put isolation and disinfectant routines into operation. Clean up nostrils regularly and give inhalations[*] of Friar's Balsam in hot water. Dampen food and hay, and change gradually to a convalescent and laxative diet. Place all food on floor to help drain nostrils. Use dust-free bedding. Record respiration, pulse and temperature regularly. If the weather is suitable a few hours out in a grass paddock will help him to improve.

Prevention: avoid contact with infected horses and ponies.

Cough

Definition: irritation in the respiratory tract.

Symptoms: coughs vary from a dry husky cough to a wet deep cough accompanied by laboured breathing. The horse may also have a nasal discharge.

Many horses do cough when working to clear the tubes. This is frequently followed by a snort and is nothing to worry about. If the cough becomes persistent then it needs attention.

Causes: a viral infection, in combination with a cold, an allergy to substances such as dust or spores, obstruction in the upper or lower respiratory tract. Bringing a horse up from grass into the dry, possibly dustier, atmosphere of a stable. Excessive work, especially in a dusty or sandy indoor or outdoor school.

---

[*] Inhalations consist of hot water in a bowl with a little Friar's Balsam or Menthol and Eucalyptus. The horse's head is held over the bowl for about ten minutes.

Treatment: for persistent coughs **stop work**. A horse should **never be worked when coughing**; this could damage the respiratory system. **Call the Vet**. **Remove any bedding, feed and hay** that could be the **cause of dust or spores**. **Dampen feed and hay**. A **period at grass**: *unless* this is a cough due to a cold in which case the horse needs to be isolated and kept warm and quiet.

Prevention: the horse should be kept in as **dust-free** an **environment** as possible. **Dampen feed** and **hay**.

C.O.P.D - Chronic Obstructive Pulmonary Disease

(Also called broken wind or heaves.)

Definition: an **allergy** of the **respiratory tract** causing a reaction similar to asthma.

Symptoms: the respiration rate **increases as the condition worsens, expiration becomes difficult**. The horse tries to use the abdominal muscles to push the air out of the lungs, this causes a **'heave line'** along the abdomen. **Coughing**, a **milky white nasal discharge**, the horse may even **cough up mucus**. As the **condition worsens** the **coughing increases** and the nasal **discharge becomes yellow. Reduction in performance**. Wheezing in severe cases.

Causes: **exposure** to **dust and fungal spores**. These invade the bronchioles, which become inflamed. The tubes go into spasm and there is an increased production of mucus, which reduces the diameter of the airways. The horse finds it **difficult to exhale** air, which in turn makes it **difficult** to **inhale fresh air**.

Treatment: *call the Vet* who may prescribe medication such as antibiotics and mucolytic drugs. **Increase stable ventilation, dampen all feed and hay,** or **feed dust-free vacuum-packed forage. Provide dust-free bedding, shavings** or **paper,** keep **scrupulously clean**. The bed should be completely removed regularly; even shavings develop fungal spores after a few months. If at all possible **turn the horse out for a few hours each day** or **walk out in hand**. Once the condition has settled **turn the horse out for a few weeks,** keep warm with rugs if necessary.

Prevention: once sensitive, the horse will always be prone to this condition. **Good stable management** is essential. **Bedding** should be **dust-free** and **kept** clean. **Feed and hay dampened**. The horse should be kept away from any dust or spores. **Work should never be excessive**. The horse should be **kept out** or turned out for as long as possible during the day. The **hay store** and the **muck heap** should be **positioned away** from the **stables** to limit air borne spores reaching the horse.

Influenza

Definition:	a **virus affecting the respiratory tract**.
Symptoms:	**rise in temperature: up to 41°C (106 °F)**. **Shivering, lethargy, inflamed throat, red watery eyes**. **Dry cough, watery nasal discharge** becoming **thick and yellow, enlarged glands** under the jaw, **loss of appetite**.
Causes:	exposure to **virus** either by:

- **Contact** with an infected horse directly or indirectly via his tack or handler;

- **Inhaling** spray from an infected horse coughing.

Treatment:	*call the Vet*. Follow the **isolation/disinfectant procedures** immediately. **Increase ventilation**, the horse needs plenty of fresh air. He may be turned out once the temperature is normal. **Keep box clean, minimise dust** and **spores**. This illness normally **lasts from 1 to 3 weeks**, rest the horse for at least two weeks after.
Prevention:	**keep equine flu' vaccination up to date**. Keep the horse away from any **infected animals**. When there is **an epidemic do not move horses** or travel to crowded events.

Pneumonia

Definition:	**bacterial infection** resulting in inflammation of the lungs. Young and older horses are more susceptible.
Symptoms:	**high temperature up to 41°C (106°F), shivering, 'tucked up'** appearance, **coughing, fast shallow respiration**, sometimes **nasal discharge** and **abnormal breathing sounds. Loss of appetite** and **condition**, the horse appears **miserable**.
Causes:	**inhaling bacteria; complications** after **viral infections** and other illnesses of the respiratory tract such as influenza. **Stress, over work, over exposure** to bad weather conditions.
Treatment:	*call the Vet*. Follow the **isolation/disinfectant procedures**. Keep the horse in a **ventilated box** with a **clean, deep bed**. **Soft, palatable (possibly cooked) food; constant supply of clean water**. May need **rugs** and blankets to **keep him warm**.
	The Vet may give **antibiotics, anti-inflammatory** drugs, **intravenous fluids**.

Prevention: treatment of other **respiratory diseases** and **sufficient recuperation time**. **Efficient management** of **horses** and **ponies**, especially those **who live out during the winter**.

Difference between contagious diseases and infectious diseases:

Contagious diseases are passed on by **direct contact** either by one horse to another or via the handler, tack or clothing.

Infectious diseases are spread both by **contact with an infected animal** and at a distance by **organisms transported by air** (air-borne micro-organisms).

Whistling or Roaring (Laryngeal Hemiplegia)

Definition: **damage** to the **nerve** serving the left side of **larynx**, which, being paralysed, cannot open in exercise to allow airflow. The obstructed air makes a noise.

Symptoms: a **whistle** or **harsh roar** as the horse **breathes in (inhales)** during canter or gallop. In extreme cases can occur at trot. Can affect performance.

Causes: may **follow a respiratory illness**, could be **hereditary**, or through **excessive work** when unfit. The causes are not definitely known. **More usual in horses over 16 hands**.

Treatment: if **performance not affected**, *no treatment*.

If horse's physical health is affected:
1. **Hobday operation: tissue** is **removed** from **the left side of the larynx**, helps with breathing difficulties and totally or partially cures the noise.
2. An **operation** where the left side of the **larynx is tied open**. This may lead to complications. As part of the larynx is permanently open, food may enter the trachea.

Prevention: efficient **treatment** and **recuperation** after respiratory illnesses. **Correct fittening programme**. **Avoid breeding** from a horse with this condition.

Strangles

Definition: **highly infectious disease** of the **upper respiratory tract**.

Symptoms: **coughing, watery nasal discharge, turning thick** and **yellow; rise in temperature, lethargy**. **Abscesses** in the **lymph glands** under the **throat, hard** and **hot** then **swelling** and **softening**. After about **two weeks**, these **burst**. The horse has **difficulty swallowing**.

Cause: **bacterium**, *Streptococcus equi*, **invading the respiratory tract**.

Treatment: *call the Vet.*   Follow **isolation/disinfectant procedures** immediately.   **Poultices** can be applied to the abscesses **to encourage their bursting. Nasal discharge** can be **cleaned away** with cotton wool. **Food** should be **dampened** to help swallowing. **Water buckets** should be **cleaned** out several times a day as pus from the horse's nostrils can be left in the water.

The Vet may use **anti-inflammatory** drugs to reduce the initial pain and lower the temperature. **Antibiotics** may be prescribed **once the abscesses have ruptured**, not usually before as these slow down the time it takes them to burst.

Prevention: At the start of an outbreak **keep all horses confined to the yard. Isolate** those affected. Avoid yards where strangles is present.

Muscular Problems (Dietary or Nervous Problems)

Azoturia

Definition: a condition **affecting certain muscle groups** resulting in **loss of movement, cramp**, possible **muscle wastage**. This illness **can be fatal**.

Symptoms: normally occurs **10 to 15 minutes** after **start of exercise. Reluctance to move, pain and sweating. Back muscles tense, stiffen** and **feel hard. Respiration rate increases**, the horse may **blow. Strained, anxious expression** on face, **pawing ground, restlessness. Attempts to urinate** and, when water is passed, it is **discoloured, reddish to dark brown with a sweet smell.**

Causes: traditionally considered the **result of too rich a feed** with **too little exercise**, perhaps after a period off work on full feed. **Excess carbohydrate** is **stored** in the **muscles** as **glycogen.** When the horse is worked **lactic acid** is produced, which normally passes into the blood stream. An over abundance of glycogen in the muscles creates lactic acid faster than the blood stream can cope with it. **The lactic acid builds up in the muscles damaging the fibres, causing severe cramps and pain.**

Research is still being done on this condition. Other possible causes are **Vitamin E and selenium deficiency; imbalance of calcium, sodium and potassium (electrolytes); hereditary, poor blood supply to affected areas.** Azoturia can lead to **kidney damage** and **failure, resulting in death.**

Treatment: immediately stop work. *Call the Vet.* **Stable the horse.** If out, arrange **transport; move the horse physically as little as possible,** unnecessary movement **can further damage the muscles. Cover** the horse's **hindquarters** with **rug, blanket** or **coat. Reduce feed** to a **minimum,** give **water** and **hay.** Offer a **salt lick** or an **extra bucket** of **water** with **electrolytes. Supplements** of **Vitamin E** and **selenium** may help. The Vet may prescribe **analgesics, anti-inflammatory drugs.** Light in-hand exercise may be introduced as the horse recovers.

Prevention: **good stable management,** a **balanced diet, reduced** when **the horse is off work.** Any **change of diet** or **exercise** should be **introduced gradually. Correct fitness programme.**

       This illness could be classed as a muscular, dietary or circulatory problem.

Tetanus (Lock Jaw)

Definition: **poisons,** introduced into the body by **bacteria,** attack the **central nervous system.**

Symptoms: **stiffness, rigid limbs and rigid neck. Jaw locks** because of **muscular spasms** of the **masseter muscles. Third eyelid covers eye, nostrils flared, tail raised. Muscle spasms** through body triggered by **light, noise and touch. Rise in temperature** and **respiration rates.** If left untreated this condition is **fatal.**

Cause: **injuries** that become **infected particularly puncture wounds.**

Treatment: *call the Vet.* **Isolate** the horse in a **dark, quiet box. Thoroughly clean wound with antiseptic.** Offer **clean water** at a height that horse can reach easily because his movement will be limited. Feed on **moist palatable feed,** which the horse may be able to suck down. The Vet will give **sedatives, anti-toxin and antibiotics.** *If this condition is caught early the horse has a chance of recovery.*

Prevention: **regular immunisation against tetanus. Treat wounds promptly.** Unvaccinated horses should be given a tetanus anti-toxin when wounded.

Skin Problems

Sweet Itch

Definition: **allergic skin reaction**.

Symptoms: **rubbing** the **mane** and **tail**, sometimes the **back** and **hindquarters**. **Irritation** and **rubbing varies** from **broken hairs** to **weeping raw patches**, which may become **infected**. **Thickening** and **ridging** of the **skin** along the **horse's crest**.

Causes: **sensitivity** to the **saliva** of **midges**, causing **irritation**. Usually occurs from **April through to November**. This condition is **hereditary**.

Treatment: the **midge** is **active mostly at dawn and dusk; stable** the **horse** at **these times** or **overnight. Apply** a **soothing lotion** or **cream** such as **Calamine**. **Wash mane** and **tail** with an **antibacterial shampoo. Hogging** the **mane helps** to **treat the sores**.

Prevention: restrict pasture time; put horse out either during the day or at night. **Avoid grazing** on **wet** and **marshy land** where the midges breed. Apply **fly repellent**, special repellents on the market are excellent, and add **garlic** to his feed. This condition cannot be cured only checked.

Ringworm

Definition: **fungal infection** of the **skin**.

Symptoms: **round patches** on the **skin**. The **hair falls out** in tufts; the **skin is dry and scaly**.

Causes: a **fungus** that is **highly contagious**. **Spread by contact** with infected animals, humans, tack, clothing, grooming kit, feed buckets, clippers, trailers, stables. The fungi release **numerous spores** into the environment and these are able live for years in woodwork, on tack and clothing. *Humans can also be infected.*

Treatment: follow **isolation/disinfectant procedure immediately**. **Stop grooming, do not clip horse, do not ride if saddle and girth areas infected. Apply a fungicidal dressing** for at least a week. **Iodine** may be used to kill the ringworm though use with care on thin-skinned animals, and never near the eyes. **Keep all utensils coming into contact with the infected horse away from other horses.**

Prevention: disinfect *everything* that comes into contact with the contaminated horse. **Remove** and **burn** all the **bedding, creosote woodwork, wash stone** or **brick walls** with **fungicide. Check all the other horses in the yard daily. Do not remove the horse from the yard. Isolate** all horses and ponies new to the yard particularly if they have travelled some distance.

Urticaria (Nettle Rash)

Definition: **allergic reaction** of the **skin**.

Symptoms: **lumps**, varying in size, appear on the **neck, chest, stomach**, sometimes on **eyelids** and **muzzle**. Though **painless**, the lumps may **irritate** causing the horse to **rub** or **bite** them.

Causes: **fly bites, nettle stings, allergies** to food such as barley or a **reaction** to some **drugs**.

Treatment: the lumps can **disappear** within a few hours or remain for a **few days**. If they persist or the horse is distressed, *call the Vet*. **Find the cause**. Feed the horse a laxative, light diet.

The vet may prescribe an **anti-inflammatory drug** or **antihistamine**.

Prevention: use a fly repellent as protection from flies. Do not ride through nettles, remove or spray nettles in the field. **Change diet** if that is the problem.

Consult the Vet if the horse is on drugs. It may be something so simple as the type of **washing powder** used for his numnah, girth or rugs. Use a **non-biological powder**. The key is to find the cause of the problem.

Warble Fly

Definition: attack by a **parasite**.

Symptoms: **lump on the horse's back,** occasionally under the saddle. This may be a **painful swelling** possibly turning into an **abscess**.

Causes: **the larva of the warble fly**. During late summer this fly lays its egg onto the horse. The egg hatches and the larva buries into the horse. Through the winter months the larva migrates through the horse's body emerging through the horse's back during the months of February to April.

Treatment: if the lump is not painful it may be left so that the larva can emerge naturally. The process can be speeded up by applying **warm fomentations** to the affected area. If possible the larva should not be killed; do not squeeze the area, this will cause an abscess. If an **abscess** does form, **poultice with warm kaolin** or use hot fomentations three times a day. The poultice can be covered with a piece of brown paper. Treat then with an antiseptic lotion until healed.

Prevention: use a **fly repellent** whilst the horse is at pasture. This is an unusual condition normally more prevalent where there are deer.

Mud Fever (and Cracked Heels)

Definition: **skin infection** caused by a **soil organism** (*Dermatophilus congolensis*).

Symptoms: **skin around pastern and heel becomes scabby, inflamed** and weeping. The **legs** may become **inflamed** and **swollen**. **Eventually leads to lameness**.

Causes: **constant damp, wet and muddy conditions** on the skin allow the invasion of this organism. Sometimes caused by **negligence, bad stable or grassland management**.

Treatment: **remove horse from cause**, bring him into a dry stable. **Clip the hair away from the area** and wash gently to remove the scabs. Apply an **antibiotic ointment** or **zinc and caster oil ointment**. **Bandage legs** to keep them warm, dry and clean.

In **severe cases** the legs may need a **poultice to draw out dirt and infection**. *Call the Vet* for serious mud fever, he or she may give antibiotics.

Prevention: **good stable and pasture management**. Apply **Vaseline, or zinc and castor oil ointment to heels and legs before riding or turning out; reduces the chances of infection. Clean the feet, heels and legs** on return from the field or exercise and dry legs thoroughly.

Rain Scald

Mud fever in other areas, affecting the shoulders, back, loins and quarters. The horse's body becomes wet and the organism is able to penetrate the skin. The hair clumps and falls out in tufts. Treatment as for mud fever. Often occurs to horses left out in a field with a damp New Zealand rug.

Lice

Definition: **infestation by a parasite**.

Symptoms: **irritation**; the **horse rubs and bites himself. Bald, sore patches; coat scurfy and dull, loss of condition**. The horse is **restless, distressed. Lice** and their **cream coloured eggs** can be seen in the **coat, the mane and forelock**.

Causes: **two types of louse** – the **sucking louse** (*Haematopinus asini*), feeds on blood and tissue and the **biting louse** (*Damilinia equi*), feeds on scurf from the coat. Infestation usually occurs during the winter when the coat is long.

Treatment: an **anti-parasitic wash** or **a liberal dusting of louse powder**. The treatment needs **repeating 14 days** later to dispose of lice that have hatched from the eggs. In **severe infestations** the horse can be **clipped** and then treated.

Prevention: **good stable management**. Lice are spread by **direct contact** or through **grooming kits and clothing**. Follow the **isolation/disinfectant procedures**. If the horse was out at grass treat all the other horses.

Tack Sores (Girth Galls, Saddle and Bridle Sores)

Definition: **injuries from the horse's tack**.

Symptoms: **lumps, pressure points, tenderness** under the saddle, girth or bridle. **Bare, sore patches developing into open wounds**. Galls and tack sores may even develop into ulcers.

Causes: **badly fitting or dirty tack**. Saddle needs re-stuffing. Dirty numnahs. **Bad riding, rider too heavy in the saddle, incorrect position.**

Treatment: **stop using tack** on the affected area, exercise by lungeing, ride and lead or rest the horse. For **unopened wounds, clean** area and **apply surgical spirits** to harden the skin. For **open wounds, clean** area and **apply antiseptic ointment or wound powder. Do not use the tack** until the wounds, sores and galls have completely healed. **Prevent bad rider from riding horse.**

Prevention: **find the cause** and rectify it so that the problems do not reoccur. Use **clean numnahs and girth sleeves** for horse with a sensitive skin. **Keep all tack scrupulously clean**, groom the horse thoroughly.

Sunburn

Definition: **reaction to sunlight.**

Symptoms: **skin** becomes **pink or red** and **may develop small scabs**.

Cause: pink, sensitive skin **exposed to sunlight**; normally around the muzzle.

Treatment: **keep the horse away from the sunlight**. Apply a **soothing cool ointment or lotion, such as Calamine.**

Prevention   **keep horse in stable or shelter when hot and sunny**. Use **sunblock cream around affected areas**.

Foot Problems

Bruised Sole and Corns

Definition: **injury causing bruising** on the **sole of the foot. Corns** occur between the hoof wall and the bars of the foot, in the **seat of corn**.

Symptoms: **increasing and acute lameness** especially on hard ground. **Red areas** on the sole of the foot and **pain** when pressure is applied to the area.

Causes: **concussion** from work on hard ground, **treading on a object** such as a stone. **Incorrect and irregular shoeing**. A horse with **flat soles** is more prone to bruising.

Treatment: **box rest** with a deep, clean bed. **Call the Farrier,** he may remove the shoe and cut out the bruised area (for corns). In the case of **severe pain** and discomfort *call the Vet*. The Vet may **prescribe anti-inflammatory drugs.** If the corn becomes infected, **poultice** for 48 hours, then continue **tubbing** until the horse is sound.

Prevention: the **Farrier** can fit a **pad** under the shoe to protect the foot, or fit **a wide-webbed, seated-out shoe** to protect the corn area. **Do not work horses** on **hard or stony ground.** Horses should be **shod regularly** at least every six weeks.

Seedy Toe

Definition: the **insensitive and sensitive laminae separate** creating **a cavity within the white line.** This **fills up with crumbling horn. If soil and debris** enter the cavity this **causes infection.** The cavity can be of varying depths.

Symptoms: **often** there are **no symptoms;** the **Farrier** often **discovers** this **condition when shoeing.** If there is inflammation of the laminae or an infection in the cavity, the horse will be lame.

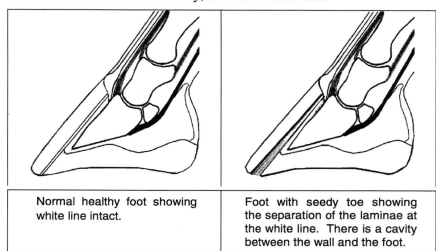

Normal healthy foot showing white line intact.	Foot with seedy toe showing the separation of the laminae at the white line. There is a cavity between the wall and the foot.

Causes: **concussion** to the toe area. Complication **after laminitis. Irregular shoeing** allowing the toe to grow long.

Treatment: **remove crumbly horn, clean out cavity, pack with Stockholm tar.** For deep cavities **the Farrier may remove some of the hoof wall** for proper cleaning. May pack cavity with plastic putty. If **infected, poultice** for **48 hours** then **tub the foot daily.** The foot is left **unshod** until the infection has disappeared.

Prevention: **regular shoeing**, keep the **feet dry and clean**. A **balanced diet** and **limited pasture to prevent laminitis**. For **poor foot growth**, supplements of **Biotin or similar**. Use **grass tips** if the horse is on holiday at pasture in hard, dry conditions.

Thrush

Definition: **bacterial infection** of the **frog**. May penetrate to the sensitive tissues of the foot.

Symptoms: **black debris** in the **grooves of the frog**. A **characteristic foul smell** from the foot. In severe cases the horse will be lame.

Causes: **bad stable/grassland management and hygiene**. **Neglect**, a lack of attention to the horse's feet. **Wet, dirty bedding**. **Wet, muddy fields**.

Treatment: **clean** the **foot thoroughly** daily with water and a stiff brush to remove the debris. Treat with an antibiotic spray, various available for purchase or apply a dressing such as **Stockholm tar**, or **diluted iodine**. If the **infection** has spread inside the foot, **poultice and tub the foot**. The **Farrier** may **trim** away some of the **frog**. **Find the cause** and rectify, bed on **clean, dry bedding** or put the horse out in a **dry field**.

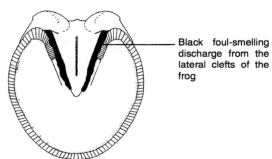

Black foul-smelling discharge from the lateral clefts of the frog

Prevention: **good stable/grassland management, hygiene, clean, dry bedding**. Daily attention to the horse's feet.

Canker

This disease of the foot is caused by untreated or neglected thrush. The infection spreads deeper into the foot affecting the sensitive layers. Symptoms will include a foul smell, swelling around the frog and a whitish discharge like cream cheese. Call the Vet. The horse will need antibiotics. This is a sign of bad stable management and negligence.

Sandcrack and Grasscrack

Definition: **splitting of the hoof wall. Sandcrack** splits from the **coronet band downwards**, grasscrack from the **ground upwards.** (Memorise the difference by 'grass on the ground grows up'.)

Symptoms: **splits or cracks in the hoof wall.** Lameness if the crack is deep and affects the sensitive laminae.

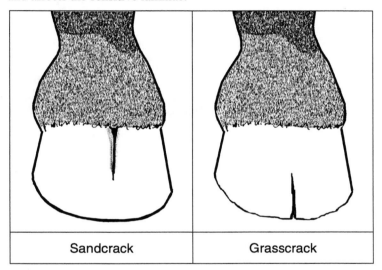

| Sandcrack | Grasscrack |

Causes: **poor foot condition; bad conformation; thin, weak hoof wall; long toes with low heels. Bad shoeing; irregular trimming.** Working an unshod horse or putting him out to pasture on hard ground. **Injury; a direct blow, to the wall or coronary band.**

Treatment: *call the Farrier*, he will trim the hoof.

Grasscrack: the **Farrier** may cut a **groove** into the **upper end of the crack** to prevent it climbing any further.

Sandcrack: for superficial sandcrack, the **Farrier** may place a **toe clip either side** of the crack to stabilise it. If **crack is deep** it can be **riveted** to prevent spreading. If the crack is **infected poultice the foot.** The **Farrier** may **fill the** crack with an **acrylic substance** to keep the internal parts of the foot clean.

Prevention: **good, regular foot care** and **shoeing. A supplement of Biotin** to improve the hoof condition. Fit **Grass Tips** for a horse out at pasture.

Laminitis

Definition: **inflammation** within the **sensitive laminae of the foot**.

Symptoms: the **horse rests his weight on hind feet** and **stretches forelegs forwards** taking pressure off the front feet. A **reluctance to move**; **heat in the feet** and **may show intense pain**. **TPR** rates **rise**. (Normally front feet affected but can affect hind feet as well.)

Causes: **excess lush grass, rich feed, excess carbohydrate. Concussion**, excessive weight or stress on the legs. **Irregular shoeing**.

Any of these factors causes an increased flow of blood to the foot. The veins, unable to return the supply quickly enough, cause a bottleneck to form. The capillaries become congested preventing oxygenated blood from reaching the sensitive laminae.

Treatment: *call the Vet immediately.* **The Farrier may remove the shoes. Remove the horse from pasture** and **reduce feed** to a minimum. Bed on shavings or other non-edible bedding. **Bathe the feet in warm water**, this encourages the blood vessels to expand. (Cold water relieves the pain at first, but does not help as it contracts the blood vessels restricting the blood flow further.) **Light in hand exercise** (except where the pedal bone has started to rotate) will encourage the blood supply to improve.

The Vet may prescribe painkillers and drugs to improve the circulation.

In extreme cases the **Farrier** can remove the front of the hoof wall to relieve the pressure.

Prevention: **restrict grazing** when the grass is rich. **Stable the horse** or pony or put into a **bare paddock** during the spring, summer and autumn. Laminitis can occur as early as March if the spring grass comes through at that time. Do **not over feed** horses or ponies. **Regular attention to the horse's feet. Avoid work on hard ground**.

Once a horse or pony has suffered from laminitis they will be prone to it again. Extra care is needed. Rings on the hoof can be an indication of laminitis, the rings will be narrow around the toe, widening towards the heels. (Rings that go straight round the hoof are an indication of a change of food or pasture.)

Stop Press: new research is now suggesting that ponies and horses susceptible to laminitis should graze on pasture with longer, poor quality grasses rather than a starvation paddock. It also advises than these animals should graze in the afternoon and evenings rather than in the mornings. Research is suggesting that the concentration of certain nutrients in the grass in the mornings may make animals more prone to laminitis.

Rotation of the Pedal Bone

Definition: **result of laminitis:** the **pedal bone rotates** in the foot.

Symptoms: **severe lameness, pain when trying to move.** The **sole becomes flattened** even convex as the pedal bone pushes against it. The **pedal bone may emerge from the sole** of the foot.

Causes: **severe laminitis.** If laminitis is not treated in time, the sensitive laminae die. The interlocking with the insensitive laminae breaks down and the laminae separate. **The flexor tendon**, attached to the back of the pedal bone, **exerts an upwards pull bringing the toe of the bone down towards the sole.**

Treatment: *call the Vet and the Farrier.* **Corrective trimming and shoeing** of the foot. A heart bar shoe may provide support to the pedal bone whilst treatment is in progress. Do not exercise the horse, as this will cause further damage.

Prevention: **treat laminitis immediately**.

Navicular Disease

Definition: **disintegration** or **degeneration** of the **navicular bone.**

Symptoms: **intermittent lameness**; the horse is lame then sound. Lameness may improve with exercise. The horse's **stride becomes short and pottery**, he will place the toe down first. He may **shift his weight from one foot to another, point a toe at rest.** This condition begins slowly and is often not apparent until the later stages, particularly if both the fore feet are affected as this makes the horse look sound even though the stride is short.

Causes: **concussion, poor foot conformation.** A **direct injury. Irregular or bad shoeing causing** a long toe and low heels. It is possibly **hereditary**.

The blood flow to the foot is reduced, possibly through blood clots in the arteries. There is a lack of nutrition to the navicular bone and the bone degenerates. The cartilage of the navicular bone becomes ulcerated and rough, affecting the deep digital flexor tendon that passes over the cartilage.

Treatment: *call the Vet.* **Confirmation of the disease is by nerve block or radiography. Continuous, gentle exercise** to promote circulation, if possible **turn out into a field.** The Farrier will give **corrective trimming and shoeing.** *Eggbar shoes* or shoes with raised heels relieve pressure on heels and flexor tendons. The Vet may prescribe drugs to improve the blood flow and painkillers.

Navicular is not curable at present. The treatment is designed to slow down the degenerative process and give comfort to the horse.

Prevention: **avoid work on hard ground. Regular shoeing and attention from the Farrier.**

Nail Bind and Nail Prick

Definition: **nail bind** - the Farrier drives a nail too close to the sensitive part of the foot causing a pressure point.

nail prick - the Farrier drives a nail into the sensitive part of the foot.

Symptoms: **lameness**, immediately after shoeing for **nail prick** and up to **72 hours** with **nail bind**. With nail prick, blood may be visible as the nail is removed.

Causes: the Farrier. The horse may be awkward and restless. Normally the Farrier will know if he has pricked the foot as the horse will show pain.

Treatment: *call the Farrier* who may remove the shoe. **Clean the foot** with an **antiseptic solution** and then **poultice**. Box rest until the horse is sound. **Check tetanus vaccination up to date.**

Prevention: a good Farrier. Warn the Farrier if the horse tends to be difficult to shoe.

Puncture Wounds

Definition: **penetration of the sole or frog by a sharp object.**

Symptoms: **lameness, heat** in the foot, a **puncture hole** in the sole or frog (not always visible). The **leg may be swollen**; the horse may refuse to put weight on the foot.

Causes: **sharp object penetrates the sole or frog** into the sensitive areas of the foot. If **dirt enters the wound** this will lead to **infection. Horses with flat feet and soles are more prone to injury**.

Treatment: *call the Vet and Farrier.* **Thoroughly clean the foot** and wound if visible. **Poultice for 48 hours** and then **hot tub the foot**. The Farrier may cut away some of the sole or frog to allow for drainage of pus. Keep the foot clean. **Check tetanus vaccination**.

Prevention: **avoid riding over areas where there are sharp objects. Inspect fields regularly. Regular attention from the Farrier.**

Quittor

Definition: an **abscess** in the foot emerging from the **coronary band**.

Symptoms: lameness. **Swelling, heat, pain** and a **discharge of pus** from the **coronary band**.

Causes: an **injury to the foot** causing the formation of an abscess. A wound in the foot that has healed, trapping the infection and pus inside. The pus will travel through the foot until it finds a soft place from which to erupt.

Treatment: *call the Vet*. **Poultice for 48 hours** or until the infection has been drawn out. Keep the foot clean.

Prevention: **treat puncture wounds correctly. Puncture wounds need to heal from the inside out.**

Pedal Ostitis

Definition: **inflammation** of the **pedal bone**. Normally affects the fore feet.

Symptoms: lameness that improves with rest but reappears when worked. The **stride shortens**, especially on hard ground.

Causes: **constant concussion** and **bruising especially for horses with flat feet. Develops from other foot conditions** such as **laminitis, corns, puncture wounds.**

Treatment: *call the Vet* who will confirm this condition with X-rays. The Farrier will give **corrective shoeing**, wide webbed shoes protecting the sole. Box rest.

Prevention: **avoid working the horse on hard ground. Regular attention by the Farrier.**

Long Toes, Collapsed and Contracted Heels

Definition: **abnormal conditions of the horse's feet.**

Symptoms: the **toe is too long** and the **heel too low**. The foot pastern angle (FPA) becomes incorrect as the foot spreads out and the heels collapse. In severe cases the hoof wall becomes concave.

Causes: **irregular or faulty shoeing. Poor foot conformation and neglect in correcting this fault.**

Treatment:	*call the Farrier*. **Corrective shoeing**; eggbar shoes or shoes with longer, wider heels to support the heels allowing growth and expansion. Depending on the severity can take six to nine months to correct.
Prevention:	**regular attention from the Farrier every 4 to 6 weeks**. This condition is mainly due to bad management.

Sidebone

Horse's foot showing extent of lateral cartilages around the pedal bone.

Definition:	the **lateral cartilages around the pedal bone become ossified (converted to bone)**.
Symptoms:	**lameness, pain** when the area is pressed. The area above the coronary band is normally springy to the touch, but hardens with sidebone.
Causes:	**concussion, poor conformation** such as toes pointing in or outwards; **direct blow or injury**.
Treatment:	**box rest at first**. May need **corrective shoeing**, *contact the Farrier*.
Prevention:	**care when exercising, avoid hard ground**.

Injuries to the Bones

Sore Shins

Definition:	the **front of the cannon bone is sore and inflamed**. Usually occurs in young horses, two and three year olds.
Symptoms:	**swelling** on the **front of the cannon bone, heat and pain** around the area. **Shortness of stride and possible lameness**.
Causes:	**excessive work when the horse's bones are immature**.
Treatment:	**cold hosing, ice packs to reduce the swelling. Box rest and anti-inflammatory drugs**.
Prevention:	**control and care of work when training the younger horse**.

Splints

Definition: **bony enlargement of the splint bone.**

Symptoms: **heat, swelling** and sometimes **pain**. Splints normally form on the inside of the forelimb but can be present on any leg inside or outside.

Lameness during formation of splint becoming **worse with harder work**.

The **swelling hardens into a lump once the splint has formed** and the horse normally then **becomes sound**, unless the **splint interferes with the knee/hock joint or the suspensory ligament**.

Causes: **poor conformation**; a **direct blow or injury from a kick** or by **speedicutting. Concussion.** The ligament attaching the splint bone to the cannon becomes damaged. The periosteum, the thick fibrous membrane covering the splint bone, is inflamed. Eventually this ossifies, that is converts to bone.

Treatment: **box rest, cold hosing, ice packs** and **support bandaging.** Anti-inflammatory drugs help to reduce the inflammation. If the new bone affects the knee or hock joint or the suspensory ligament surgery may be necessary.

Prevention: **normally occurs in young horse under six years old. Avoid working** on **hard ground. Use brushing/speedicut boots or bandages when exercising and boots when the horse is in the field.**

Carpitis

Definition: **inflammation of the knee.**

Symptoms: **lameness. Swelling on the front of the knee. Pain** when pressure is applied or the knee joint is flexed. **Shortening of stride,** may **stand with the knee slightly bent.**

Causes: **excessive work in younger horses.** A **direct blow or injury. Poor conformation** which leads to strain in the knee joint.

Treatment: **box rest. In hand exercise for short** periods to keep the joint working. **Cold hosing, ice packs. Anti-inflammatory drugs.**

Prevention: **control of work for the younger horse.** Use of skeleton knee boots when exercising especially when jumping.

Sesamoiditis

Definition:	**inflammation of the sesamoid bones.**
Symptoms:	**lameness. Heat and swelling** to the **back of the fetlock. Painful reaction to firm pressure.**
Causes:	the **suspensory ligament** around the sesamoids **is damaged or torn**, sometimes the bones can fracture. **Direct blow, an overreach injury. Working the horse when he is tired. Bad or irregular shoeing**, infrequent trimming and long toes can put stress and strain on this area.
Treatment:	**box rest for 4-6 weeks. Cold hosing and bandaging** for support. **Trimming to reduce the length of the toe**, *call the Farrier*. Anti-inflammatory drugs. This condition can take months to heal completely; the horse should be turned out to grass.
Prevention:	**regular attention to the feet. Control of work**, especially when horse is tired. **Use boots for protection when working.**

Problems of the Joints

Joint Infection

Definition:	**bacterial infection of the joint.**
Symptoms:	**acute lameness. Swelling to the joint area, heat and pain.** The horse may also show a loss of appetite and a rise in temperature.
Causes:	**entry of bacteria via a puncture wound.**
Treatment:	*call the Vet*. **Drainage of joint, antibiotics and analgesics.** Complete rest for a long period.
Prevention:	it is impossible to protect the horse all the time but prompt attention to injuries involving any joint may prevent this condition.

Joint sprain

Definition:	**damage to the ligaments** within or surrounding a joint or the joint capsule itself.
Symptoms:	**lameness, heat and swelling in the joint area. Pain** and **reluctance to bend the joint.**
Causes:	**twisting the joint** and wrenching the fibres through a **fall, stumble or slip.**
Treatment:	*call the Vet*. **Cold hosing, ice packs** and **support bandaging. Anti-inflammatory drugs. Box rest.**

Prevention: **careful riding over uneven or rough ground** and when the horse is tired. **Correct fittening programme. Use boots or bandages** when the horse is working.

Degenerative joint disease

Definition: **disease affecting the articular cartilage in a joint.**

Symptoms: depends which joint is affected: **swelling, heat, pain, lameness, reduced joint movement.**

Causes: **injuries, sprains, fractures, infected wounds.** A joint capsule becomes damaged or infected and causes deterioration of the cartilage, which becomes thin and ulcerated. New bone may develop that affects the working of the joint. Also resulting from **poor conformation** – upright, boxy feet and upright pasterns.

Treatment: **INCURABLE.** *Call the Vet.* **Box rest. Pain killing** and **anti-inflammatory drugs.** Light exercise only may be possible for the rest of the horse's life.

Prevention: **care when working, support and protective boots or bandages. Efficient treatment of wounds.**

Bone spavin

Definition: **degeneration of the hock** affecting the joints between the tarsal bones.

Symptoms: **stiffness in the hind limb** at first. A **shorter stride, dragging the toe** and an **irregular sound to the footfall. Swellings** appear on the **inner, lower part of the hock. Heat and pain. Lameness or unlevelness.**

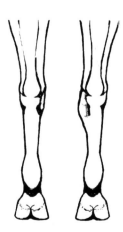

Causes: **general wear and tear to the hock joint, twisting, turning actions,** predominantly in jumpers and polo ponies, particularly horses with poor conformation, sickle hocks or cow hocks. The **tarsal bones gradually fuse** together at the joints.

Treatment: **INCURABLE.** Treatment mainly concerned with keeping the horse working until the joints fuse, then the horse can be sound enough for light work. **Corrective shoeing**; shoes with rolled toes and raised heels. Shortening the toe on the hind feet helps improve the horse's action. **Pain killing drugs** allow the horse to continue working through the lameness.

Prevention: **care when working and jumping** the horse, **preventing strain on the hocks**. **Regular attention from the Farrier** especially with horses who have a poor hind leg conformation.

Bog Spavin

Definition: **a swelling in the joint capsule around the hock**.

Symptoms: swellings around the hock, a **large one** at the **front inside** the **hock**, a **smaller one outside** the **joint just below** the **point of the hock**. If one side is pressed the other enlarges.

Causes: after an **injury or blow to the joint**, the synovial membrane produces synovial fluid to protect the area. When an abnormal amount of synovial fluid is produced, this causes swellings around the joint. Made more likely through **poor conformation** such as cow hocks or sickle hocks.

Treatment: **no treatment necessary**. The swellings may reduce of their own accord.

Prevention: **Protect the hock when possible with hock boots**.

Ringbone

Definition: A **degenerative joint disease** affecting the lower leg (normally a foreleg).

There are different types:5

True ringbone   involves a **joint**. **Inflammation** of the **joint capsule** breaks down the **articular cartilage**. New bone may be created eventually filling up the joint space, making it incapable of movement.

False ringbone   when **a joint** is **not involved**. New bone forms on the top or lower end of a bone but does **not affect a joint**.

High ringbone   affects the **pastern joint** or **bones**.

Low ringbone   affects the **coffin joint**, the **short pastern or pedal** bones.

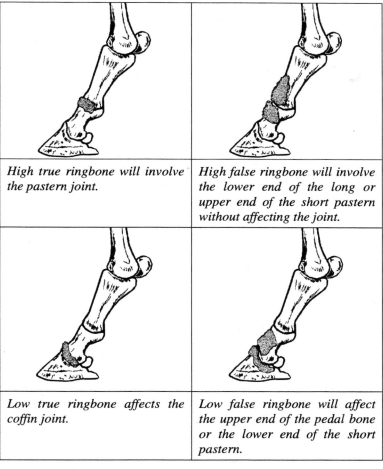

High true ringbone will involve the pastern joint.	*High false ringbone will involve the lower end of the long or upper end of the short pastern without affecting the joint.*
Low true ringbone affects the coffin joint.	*Low false ringbone will affect the upper end of the pedal bone or the lower end of the short pastern.*

Symptoms: True ringbone (affecting the joint): lameness, heat, hard swelling in the pastern area. Pain when the joint is flexed or manipulated.

False ringbone (affecting bone): **initial lameness** then the horse **becomes sound. Hard swelling** in the **pastern region.**

Causes: **poor conformation**, *'toes in' or 'toes out'*. A **direct blow** or **injury, damage to a joint capsule**, a **torn ligament** or tendon in the joints. **Stress on the joints** by quick, sharp movements, as with polo ponies.

Treatment: **INCURABLE, no treatment.** It may be possible to work the horse with administration of a pain-killing drug.

Prevention: **protection during work. Remedial shoeing** may improve the horse's conformational problems.

Windgalls

Definition: swollen areas around the fetlock joint.

Two types of windgalls

- **Articular windgalls** are swellings of the **fetlock joint capsule**.

- **Tendinous windgalls** swellings of the **flexor tendon sheath**. The tendon has a sheath of synovial fluid to protect it over joints. Overproduction of fluid causes swelling.

Thoroughpin - **Tendinous windgall** of the **tendon** passing over the **hock**. Swelling occurs just above point of hock.

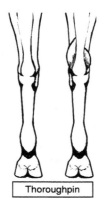

Thoroughpin

Symptoms: **soft swellings** around the joint. Possibly, but not usually, heat and lameness.

Causes: **concussion, injury or blow. Poor conformation.**

Treatment: **bandage** the legs to contain the swellings may help. There are no real problems and the horse is not usually lame so **no particular treatment is given.**

Prevention: **Avoid working** on **hard, rough ground. Protect fetlock joints** when possible.

Bursal Enlargments, Capped Hock, Capped Elbow, Swollen Knee

Definition: **enlargements** and **swellings around the joints**.

Symptoms: **swollen areas** in the **hock, elbow and knee** areas.

Comparison to show difference between normal hock and capped hock

Causes:	a bursa is a small sac filled with synovial fluid. Its function is to protect and reduce friction especially at joints. **Blows, injuries, kicks, insufficient bedding** in the box, **banging the stable door, leaning against stable wall. Injuries from travelling in box or trailer.** These types of trauma to the joints will cause the bursa to swell as a reaction.
Treatment:	**find, and if possible, remedy the cause.** The swellings may reduce on their own.
Prevention:	**care** when **exercising and travelling, adequate support and protection** by boots and bandages. **Thick bedding. Rubber matting on stable door**.

Tendon and Ligament Problems

Tendons and ligaments are prone to strains and sprains particularly in the lower legs.

A **strain** is a partial tearing of a **tendon or muscle**.

A **sprain** is **damage to a ligament** at or near a joint.

(Memorise by strain has a 't' for tearing tendons.)

Tendon Strain

The tendon most likely to strain is the **superficial flexor tendon** at the **back of the foreleg**.

Symptoms:	lameness, **heat and swelling** around the tendon, **fetlock may sink lower** to the ground. Mild cases: the horse may be sound but warmth and slight swelling around the tendon.
Causes:	**poor conformation**, particularly **long toes** and **collapsed heels**, which extend the tendon. **Fast work** especially if the horse is **unfit** or **tired**.
Treatment:	**treat immediately** before exercise aggravates the problem. **Cold hose, ice packs, bandaging for support. Box rest** for up to **2 months** depending on severity. **Light in-hand exercise** when possible.
Prevention:	**care** when **working, good fittening programme. Protect** with boots and bandages. **Regular attention** from the **Farrier**.

Ligament Sprain

Definition:	**damage to ligaments**. The ligament most likely to suffer is the **suspensory ligament** at the back of the foreleg.
Symptoms:	lameness, **heat** and **swelling** in area of injury. **Pain** on touch.

Causes: **fast work**, eventing, hunting. **Injuries** to **splint bones** or **sesamoids**.

Treatment: *call the Vet*. **Box rest, cold hosing, ice packs, support bandaging. Analgesic** and **anti- inflammatory** drugs. **Recuperation** in field for **several months**.

Prevention: **care when working** especially during fast work. Good fittening programme.

Curb

Sprain to **ligament at back of hock**. Swelling below hock joint, possible heat and pain. Causes include **poor hock conformation, hard, fast work, sudden movement** as in bucking and kicking. Most horses developing curb are sound. Treatment and prevention are as for ligament sprains.

Exam Tips

There are other ailments and injuries that may affect a horse during his lifetime and many Veterinary books that give descriptions of these. Those mentioned in these chapters are the more common ailments that are needed for the Stage III Examination.

You are not expected to have the knowledge of a Veterinary surgeon, but you will be expected to recognise certain symptoms and to know when to call the Vet and when to put the isolation/disinfectant routine into operation. You should try and think about minor ailments in practical terms, what would you do if the horse started coughing, had a discharge from his nose, looked lethargic and ill? The symptoms are often the only signs you will have of any illness. Think about what you would do in real life, probably alert a more senior member of staff. Certainly keep everyone away, keep the horse quiet, take him off work definitely if he is coughing. Discharges can mean infection, so probably isolate the sick animal. You would possibly take the horse's temperature, respiration rate and pulse, and if there is any doubt as to the horse's welfare, call the Vet. The horse would need a dust free environment, dampened food as part of his after care.

To learn these ailments, of which there are quite a number, break them up into groups. First learn the ailments you have personally experienced with your own horse, in your yard or through friends. Then learn the serious illnesses, those that need the Vet and the isolation programme. Then learn the ailments of the foot, the leg and so on. In this way, over a period of time, it will be easier to assimilate the information. You will not need to know every detail, but a broad idea of the symptoms, causes and treatments will suffice.

CHAPTER 9
Medical Treatment

The ultimate aim of every horse owner, yard manager and proprietor is to keep the horses in their care as healthy as possible. As can be seen from the previous chapter many injuries and illnesses can be prevented by good stable and grassland management, a balanced diet regulated to the horse's needs, care when working the horse and by regular attention from the Farrier. There will always be the unavoidable accident or illness but if these are dealt with promptly and the horse is given the appropriate treatment he will normally recover quickly.

Preventative treatment such as inoculations and a worming programme further increase the probability of the horse staying in good health for most of his life. This chapter describes the methods of taking the temperature, pulse and respiration of the horse, methods of administering medicines and dressings, equine vaccinations, worms and worming control.

General Health

Every efficient yard manager and horse owner will keep a record of each horse's general health. This includes normal temperature, pulse and respiration rates, previous illnesses and injuries, dates of shoeing, worming, annual inoculations and any other relevant details such as allergies. Even for the owner with one horse it is sometimes difficult to remember exact dates for shoeing, worming or inoculations. In a yard with a large number of horses and ponies this is impossible without records.

If illnesses are to be recognised quickly and treated effectively, the person caring for the horse needs to know his normal general behaviour so that any deviation, however subtle, is noticed.

Temperature, Pulse and Respiration (TPR)

Temperature is the horse's natural body warmth, the pulse his heart rate and respiration the number of times he inhales and exhales. Under normal circumstances horses will exhibit similar rates that can be taken as a guideline for the horse's health at any time. To make an accurate comparison possible, so that any deviation can be recognised, TPR should be taken when the horse is known to be healthy. He should also be calm and at rest in his normal surroundings.

The average readings are:

Temperature	**100.5 °F or 38 °C**
Pulse	**36 to 42 beats per minute**
Respiration	**8 to 15 breaths per minute**

A number of readings should be taken over a few days and at different times of the day. TPR rates do vary slightly at different times of the day, weather conditions and in different circumstances, for instance if the yard is busy or noisy that day.

Readings also vary between individual horses. For instance, some horses can have a temperature as low as 98.5°F or 37°C but, as long as this rate is known to be normal, any rise or drop can be recognised immediately.

Method

The horse's respiration rate is recorded first. If the temperature and pulse are taken first, this may make him anxious and quicken the respiratory rate.

Respiration

The horse's rate of respiration is taken simply by watching the flanks as they rise and fall. Stand just in front of the horse's shoulder or to one side, whichever is the clearest view, and watch the horse's flank. His ribcage will expand and contract; this counts as one breath. There are three phases; breathing in (inspiration), breathing out (expiration) and a pause. One breath in and one breath out count as one. On a cold day the respiration can be counted by the vapour from the horse's nostrils.

Pulse

The pulse is detected wherever an artery passes over a bone. It is normally taken from one of two points:

❖ under the lower jaw where the facial artery crosses the inner surface of the jaw.

❖ on the inside of the foreleg, level with the knee joint, again where an artery crosses the bone.

To check the facial artery pulse, place two fingers in the region of the artery and gently feel until the pulse is found. This can sometimes be a little awkward, if so, press a little more firmly until the beat is evident. Count the number of beats for 15 seconds, timed by a watch, and then multiply by four to obtain the reading per minute.

Temperature

❖ Prepare the thermometer first. Clean it with a mild antiseptic wipe and then shake to lower the mercury level. Check that the level has dropped.

❖ Grease the bulb lightly with Vaseline.

❖ Prepare the horse; restrain with headcollar and leadrope or bridle, preferably with an assistant holding him.

❖ Approach the horse as normal from the neck and, running a hand over his neck, shoulders and back, proceed to the hindquarters. (Approaching the horse from the back without warning and taking his temperature will do nothing for his nerves!)

❖ Standing to one side, lift the tail and insert the thermometer into the anus and rectum rotating it so it inserts easily.

❖ Tilt the thermometer so that it lies in contact with the rectum wall, otherwise the reading could be inaccurate.

❖ Hold the thermometer firmly so that it does not slip inside. Thermometers have been known to disappear!

❖ Wait for one full minute before removing the thermometer.

❖ Gently remove and clean to read the temperature.

❖ Clean the thermometer with disinfectant and shake to return the mercury for the next reading. Put the thermometer away in its usual place.

All new horses to the stable should have their TPR taken over a period of several days to obtain an accurate reading. Commence taking these readings one week after the horse arrives; he may be nervous for the first few days in a new home.

Equine Vaccination

Horses are vaccinated against two specific diseases - equine influenza and tetanus. The programme starts with a course of two combined primary injections with the second primary injection being administered between 21 – 90 days after the first primary. Maximum immunity is attained 2 weeks after the second injection.

A further influenza booster is given approximately six months after the second injection. An influenza and tetanus booster is required six months later (one year after initial vaccination). After that boosters are needed for influenza no later than 12 months and for tetanus no later than 18 to 30 months. If an outbreak of influenza occurs or if the horse regularly competes, an influenza vaccination is recommended every 6 months.

Only healthy horses should be vaccinated. If the horse is unwell, even suffering from a slight cold or cough, contact the Vet. After inoculation the horse is kept under surveillance and rested for one or two days. (Some vaccines now do not require rest afterwards.) Do not travel or tire the horse directly after vaccination. If there are side effects do not work. Call the Vet.

It is imperative that the immunisation programme is maintained, primarily to protect the horse. It is also a condition at many shows that the Vaccination Certificate is shown to be up to date. The Vet will sign and stamp the Certificate. If one vaccination is overlooked and the immunisation period has expired, the whole programme has to be started again.

When buying a new horse, or if a new horse arrives at the stable, always enquire about vaccination. Request to see the Vaccination Certificate. If there is no information as to when, or if, the horse has been vaccinated, a new programme will need to be started to ensure his full immunity.

Worms and Worming Procedures

For economic and health reasons a strict worming programme should be practised in all yards and centres. Every horse and pony should be wormed regularly. The owner who neglects this vital part of stable management will be condemning the horse or pony to ill health and possibly death.

There are a number of worms and parasites that cause infestation in the horse. The main types are the **small redworm, large redworm, threadworm, large white roundworm, lungworm, pin, whip or seat worm, tapeworm and the larvae of bot flies**.

Worming Programme

All horses are infected by parasites; the vital point is to keep infestation to a minimum. If a regular worming programme (anthelmintic strategy) is not adhered to strictly the horse will suffer, sometimes with fatal consequences.

Each horse and pony should be wormed, as a rule, at least every 6 weeks. The eggs are usually immune to Wormers, as are some of the larvae, so the dose needs to be repeated. The horse will also be re-infected from his environment. The frequency may be altered to accommodate weather conditions. If the weather has been mild during the winter or is warm and damp in summer the worming programme can be increased to every 4 weeks. If the winter is cold the frequency may be decreased to 8 weeks and then increased to 4 to 6 weeks during the spring, summer and autumn. Worms and larvae thrive in warm, moist conditions whereas during cold spells their numbers can be depleted.

To prevent omission some owners prefer to worm their horses on a specific date. The first of every month for instance, or when the Farrier makes his visit every six weeks.

All new horses coming into the yard should be wormed. In most establishments new horses are put in the isolation box for a few weeks to prevent any possible infectious diseases spreading onto the whole yard. The horse can then be wormed after he has arrived without the problem of infesting the fields.

All horses in the establishment should ideally be wormed at the same time. This is easier in a Riding School or Equitation Centre where most of the horses are managed by the yard. It is not so simple in a livery or DIY yard where each horse is cared for individually. The yard owners will need to keep control and ensure that worming is still carried out strictly.

If at all possible the horses should be kept in the stables for 24-48 hours after worming. Any surviving larvae in the droppings will then be prevented from contaminating the pasture. This is not normally practical though especially if the horses are accustomed to being out each day or live permanently at grass.

Fields and pastures should either be cleared of all droppings every few days or, where this is not feasible; the pastures can be harrowed. This is done on hot, dry days to prevent spreading the larvae.

Rotation of fields reduces worm larvae. The horses are moved periodically into other fields. If possible other animals, sheep or cows (not donkeys) can graze the fields. Apart from eating the grasses that horses refuse and thereby improving the pasture, these animals ingest the larvae which, in most cases, do not survive within another host.

A couple of days before changing to a new pasture, the horses and ponies can be wormed so contamination of the new fields is reduced. When fertilising the fields it is wiser not to use horse manure as this can spread worm contamination.

Any field should not be overstocked with horses and ponies. Horses are destructive to pasture, eating the grass in patches and leaving rough spots where they usually do their droppings. Any field that is stocked with too many horses and ponies will become heavily contaminated with worms, their eggs and larvae.

Horses and ponies should be kept in good condition. Those in poor condition are more prone to worm infestation and damage. In the stable the bedding should be kept scrupulously clean, droppings removed three or four times a day.

Feed from rubber skips or buckets rather than from the floor. The horse is still feeding from the floor in his 'natural' way but the skip or bucket will prevent larvae migrating from the bedding to the feed. Skips and buckets can also be cleaned after every feed.

Hay can be placed in a haynet. This also prevents hay being wasted in the bed, or the horse eating the bedding. In practice, feeding hay from haynets is ideal for one or two horses. In a large yard filling numerous haynets three times a day is not realistic. Many horses are fed hay from the floor with no ill effects providing the bed is kept thoroughly clean and skipped out regularly.

The horse should be inspected daily during the spring, summer and autumn for bot fly eggs, particularly if the horse is out at grass permanently. The eggs should be removed either with a bot egg remover or bot knife.

The horse's dock should be cleaned regularly to remove pinworm eggs. These appear as yellow wax under the tail. The cloth should then be burnt or disposed of hygienically.

Wormers

Wormers consist of specific chemicals that kill the worms within the horse's body. There are a number of commercial Wormers on the market and new types are introduced periodically. The Wormers come in paste form or as granules. The amount a horse or pony will need depends on his weight. The manufacturer's instructions on the side of the packet will indicate the amount to administer. When buying a Wormer from the Feed Merchant or Tack Shop, (which needs to be signed for in a book) the assistant will be able to advise on the amount necessary for the horse or pony.

The paste comes in a syringe, which has marks on the side corresponding to different weights of horse or pony. Generally a 16 hand medium horse is about 600 kg, and a 13 hand medium pony about 400 kg. The paste can either be given orally or mixed in with the feed.

To administer orally, with the horse restrained in a headcollar and lead rope, remove the top from the syringe and insert the nozzle into the side of the horse's mouth in the interdental space. The nozzle should be facing the back of the throat. Press the plunger in and squirt the paste as far back as possible into the horse's mouth. Hold the horse's head up and stroke his throat and neck to make sure the paste is swallowed. Do not give a titbit or feed until all the paste has been swallowed.

Some horses are experts at spitting the paste out. Hold the horse's mouth closed until the paste has been swallowed. Others will shake the head splattering everything in sight, walls, ceiling and handlers. Sometimes the nozzle of the syringe is small and it takes strength to push the plunger. If there is any difficulty try mixing the paste with the feed.

Granules are simply mixed with the feed. Some horses though will sift through the feed and, as if by magic, the granules will be left in the bucket when the feed has disappeared. In this case mix with some sugar beet, molasses or carrots. If the horse still rejects the granules, try paste.

Types of Wormers

Most Wormers are based on drugs such as Ivermectin, Pyrantel, Benzimidazole, Fenbendazole and Thiabendazole. There are some important points that need to be known about Wormers and their effectiveness.

* No one brand of Wormer deals with all types of worms.

In the worming programme one type of Wormer is used as a base Wormer throughout the year. Then at specific times a different Wormer is used to combat other worms, normally during spring and autumn. The two parasites that may need a different Wormer are the tapeworm and the bot fly larvae.

Some worms are dealt with by giving a larger dosage, perhaps double the normal amount or two doses within a few days of each other.

Redworms need a larger dose of Wormer. (The recommended times are late October or early November and again in February. In damp, warm summers it may be advisable to worm additionally for redworms in June and July.)

* Certain worms can build up a resistance to the drugs within some Wormers.

This is particularly so with small redworms and the drugs of the benzimidazole group. The base Wormer can be changed after every twelve months to counteract resistance and a different Wormer used at certain times of the year.

A worm count can be performed by the Vet, who will test samples of dung from the field or stable. This will show any resistance to Wormers or whether one particular type of worm has been missed.

The main brands of Wormer are:

Panacur, Strongid P, Eqvalan, Multiwormer, Telmin, Equisol and Equitac.

The horse should be rested for a day after worming as the impact on the gut may make the horse feel slightly unwell.

Importance of Worming

The importance of a regular planned worming programme cannot be overemphasised. Worm damage within the horse's gut or blood vessels can be irreparable, at the very least the horse will lose condition and his performance will suffer. Horses even suffer for years afterwards, and may possibly have a shortened life.

In the worst cases the infestation can cause the horse's death. This is compared with the ten minutes it takes to worm every 4 to 6 weeks and the small cost, which is saved in food bills and most likely Vet's bills.

Worming less than 8 times a year will not reduce the worm contamination. It is a false economy to reduce the number of times horses and ponies are wormed even when the cost of worming large numbers of horses is a consideration.

Feed bills will increase. Parasites take the nutrition from the horse, who then loses condition and needs more feed. The Vet's bills increase. Horses in poor condition are more likely to catch other diseases. Horses may be off work and any horse not in work, particularly for a commercial yard, will be a drain on the income.

Wounds

Revision

Minor wounds, treatment and basic nursing were covered fully in the Stage II book. Types of wounds, galls, grazes, bruises, lacerations (torn wounds), incised (clean cut wounds) and puncture wounds. GGBLIP. Basic procedures for treatment arrest bleeding, clean, dress and protect the wound. ABCDP. Methods of cleaning, poulticing, types of poultice, dressing and protecting the wound. Basic nursing.

All students are advised to revise this section from the Stage II Riding & Stable Management.

First Aid Box

Every riding establishment and horse owner should have an equine first aid box. Complete medical kits can be bought from tack shops. More usually the kit starts with the essentials first and is then built up by adding to these when necessary.

Some of the items included in the kit would be; antiseptic wound powder, ointment or cream and antiseptic lotion for cleaning wounds. Lint or cottonwool is used to clean wounds and injuries, sterile pads for dressing and protection. A poultice, normally Animalintex, which can be cut to shape, and a pair of blunt ended scissors, also used for cutting hair around a wound. Bandages are useful, Vetrap which sticks to itself, a crepe or leg bandage for covering poultices. A tubular bandage is extremely useful for covering wounds to keep them clean, and poultices to keep them in place. A thermometer will be needed and Vaseline.

Other useful products are fly repellent, especially in the summer, surgical spirits, Stockholm tar, hoof pick, plastic bag, clean towel, small plastic bowl, bone liniment, ice jelly or paste (used for bruising, very expensive). The telephone numbers of the Vet and Farrier.

Most of the items are for everyday use within the yard; some items are purchased for special occasions depending on what type of activity the horse is performing. For instance the ice jelly for bruises is useful for horses who show jump or event.

Administering medicines

Medicines are normally administered to the horse in his food, water, by oral syringe or by injections. The medicine given in the food is powder such as Phenylbutazone (Bute) or granules as in Wormers. These need mixing up with the feed quite thoroughly perhaps with the addition of a 'mixer' or 'opener' such as sugar beet or molasses. Alternatively the medicine can be mixed with some molasses, put onto a wooden spoon and then placed carefully on the back of the horse's tongue.

Medicines that are soluble such as electrolytes can be given with the water. This may not be as effective; the horse can refuse to drink. A bucket of clean water should also be offered so that the horse does not become dehydrated.

Medicines can be administered by oral syringe quite successfully. A clean Wormer syringe may be used.

Administering medicine by injection should only be performed by an experienced groom or the Vet. Injections can either by inserted into a muscle (intra-muscular) or a vein (intra-venous). The intra-venous injection should only be given by a qualified Vet.

Checking for Lameness

One of the more usual and important aspects of stable management is being able to recognise when a horse is lame. Lameness can vary from a slight stiffness in an older horse to a disease or injury that needs immediate medical attention.

Occasionally the horse will show signs of leg problems within his stable. He may be resting a leg. Horses often rest a hind leg but rarely a fore leg unless something is wrong. The horse may be pointing his foot, resting his toe on the ground with the heel raised.

Assess the horse in the box first. The source of most lameness, though not all, is the foot. Check for wounds, injury or tenderness by tapping the sole gently with a hoof pick. There may be signs of bruises or corns, which will show by a discoloration on the sole. If there is an infection any slight pressure will cause a reaction. If the feet appear sound, check the suspected leg for heat, swelling, pain, lumps, injuries, puncture wounds. If the horse is obviously lame, in pain and the source is known, treat or call the Vet.

Most of the time lameness becomes apparent when the horse is brought out of his box for work.

In hand Assessment

The horse is assessed first on firm, level ground at halt. If the horse is obviously in pain and cannot put weight on one foot then he should be returned to his stable and treated. Often though the horse needs to be walked and trotted in hand to check which limb is lame or to confirm the diagnosis.

On level firm ground, ask the handler to walk the horse away at a brisk walk. Assess the horse from a side view, from in front and from behind. The horse is walked on a free rein allowing his natural head movement. The horse is then assessed at trot. Lameness is more easily diagnosed in trot because it is more difficult for the horse to support his lame leg when using diagonal pairs.

Observations

- Look at the horse's body, his head movement, at each leg in comparison with the other, length of stride, any unusual action from any leg.

- Watch the way each foot is placed on the ground. Does the horse put his weight on each foot squarely or does he tenderly place one foot down and raise it quickly again?

- Note the strides of the forelegs and hindlegs in relation to each other. The affected leg may have a shorter length of stride so that it bears the horse's weight for less time.

- Observe the limb motion. Does the horse swing one limb outwards? Does the horse move with a jerky or stiff movement?

- Listen to the footfalls at walk and trot. Is the rhythm regular or is there an irregular pattern?

For lameness in foreleg

- The horse's head will rise and fall. His head will rise to take the weight off the injured leg, and will drop when the sound leg is on the ground.

- The horse will land more heavily on the sound leg.

- The length of stride on the lame leg will be shorter.

- If the horse is lame on both forelegs he will move with short, pottery strides.

For lameness in a hind leg

- The affected hind leg may have a shorter stride resulting in an irregular rhythm.

- The whole of the lame leg may move stiffly if the source of the problem is the stifle or hip joint. This will result in a lower arc of flight; the horse may drag the toe on the ground.

- From the rear view look at the hips; on the side of the injured leg the hip may rise higher than the other side or not drop as low, as the horse avoids putting his weight on the injured leg.

- Listen for the sound of the hooves on the ground. The rhythm of the footfall will not be constant.

If necessary turning the horse on small circles at walk, first on one rein then the other, will emphasise the lameness.

Calling the Vet

One of the most perplexing decisions the horse owner has to make is when to call the Vet. The call-out fee may be expensive and the owner may feel he has wasted the Vet's time if the horse's condition is not serious. If medical attention is delayed, however, the horse's condition may worsen.

Knowledge and experience of dealing with horse's injuries, illnesses and diseases makes the decision easier. An experienced groom or owner will know when a condition can be treated successfully without the Vet or if medical attention is necessary. This is one reason why studying about diseases and illnesses is important.

As a rule of thumb, **if in any doubt call the Vet**. It is wiser to be over cautious than to create a situation where the horse worsens and eventually needs more medical treatment.

On the practical side, if the horse is stabled at a livery yard, riding school or equestrian centre, ask the Stable Manager if a Vet is making a visit that day or the next. The Vet can be requested to assess the horse in question as part of a shared visit. This saves the Vet's time and reduces the call out fee, as a shared visit is cheaper.

If attention is required urgently, the Vet will need to be contacted as quickly as possible. When calling the Vet there are a number of facts he or she will need to know.

* Name and address of the owner.
* Address of the yard where the horse is kept.
* Symptoms of the illness, injury or disease. If the horse is eating and drinking normally and any other information possible, state of droppings, TPR if relevant.
* Origin of the problem, when it started, where it took place, how it happened.
* Age of the horse and approximate height.

The Vet or receptionist will then give an approximate time for the Vet to call. Preferably the owner should be present but if not, there should be someone who can assist the Vet at the time.

Exam Tips

The minor ailments section of the Stage III is a written paper consisting of five random questions about minor illnesses and injuries.

You will be given three quarters of an hour to answer these questions. Be concise, factual and logical in your answers. Do not write lengthy essays, the facts in note form, or very precise sentences will be sufficient. The Examiners do not have a lot of time to assess the answers and will appreciate a clear, concise sheet. Writing in a sequence – definition, symptoms, causes, treatment and preventative measures can often help you to remember relevant points.

The questions will cover the type of conditions that you may experience within the yard. If you can base your answer on personal experience this will show practical knowledge.

If possible assist the Vet whenever he or she visits the yard. If you explain that you are interested and that this will help in your Exam they are normally only too pleased to answer any questions or queries.

Examples of questions

❖ A horse in the yard has ringworm. What action would you take?

❖   A horse comes into the yard with a girth gall. Describe the causes, treatment and how to prevent galls in the future.

❖   Describe how to take the horse's temperature, pulse and respiration and what your findings should be in a healthy horse at rest.

❖   What is a tendon? Describe a strained tendon, symptoms, causes and treatment.

❖   Your horse, out at grass in spring, is looking unhappy and standing back on his heels. What is your diagnosis and how would you treat this ailment?

❖   Name three parasites of the horse and give the symptoms for one of them.

❖   What is fomentation, how would you do this and for what ailments?

❖   The horses in fields during the summer have small yellow eggs on their legs. What are these and what action would you take now and later in the year?

Some ailments have similar symptoms; a cold, influenza and strangles may show a resemblance to each other at the start. If one of the questions describes symptoms that may refer to two or three different illnesses, you can state that this could be either of these particular conditions. Then explain the causes of each briefly and what you would do for treatment. Try and relate this to practical actions. For instance if a horse did exhibit symptoms that could be construed as strangles you would certainly quarantine the horse and put the isolation/disinfectant routine into operation until proved otherwise. In a real life situation taking safe precautions would be the practical and wise option for the yard.

Note: as research into equine illness is progressing constantly, so causes and treatments are changing. Similarly equine medical technology is advancing; new drugs and treatments are being introduced. Students for the Stage III should be aware of new medical advances by reading articles and by questioning yard managers and Vets.

There may be a question about worms and worming on the ailments paper or the Examiner may ask general questions about this subject with the group in another session. You will not need to know the Latin names of every worm, but it is necessary to know the main types of worm that infect the horse. You should be able to describe the effect on the horse's health, how to institute a proper worming programme and how important this is to the health of the horse. At some tack shops or feed merchants there are videos available for hire, free of charge, which explain about worms and worming.

For the section about checking for lameness in a horse, each group of candidates will be asked to walk and trot a horse in hand and possibly asked to assess if he is sound or unlevel. Apart from obvious limping, sometimes lameness can be difficult to observe. You need to practise developing an 'eye' for unsoundness. Watch horses being assessed and try to diagnose which leg is lame. With experience you will be able to see and hear any abnormal action or movement. Remember, when checking for lameness an assessment should be performed first in the stable or outside on level ground with the horse standing still, before asking the horse to walk and trot.

C H A P T E R   10
Conformation

The conformation of a horse is his general shape. This is based on his skeleton, the shape and size of his bones. To a certain extent this is dependent on his breed or type, though even within breeds, horses do vary in conformation. The horse's shape is also influenced, to some degree, by his muscles; his fitness and age.

Good conformation in a horse is important because it affects his ability to work, his health, soundness, length of life, action, performance and quality as a ride.

The structure of the bones and the basic characteristics of a horse are described as *static conformation* and the way the horse moves *dynamic conformation*.

Static Conformation

The first general impression of the horse should include:

* Approximate size – height and build.

* Colour and markings.

* Gender.

* Possible breed or type.

* The horse's condition, whether he looks healthy, has a shiny coat.

* Temperament; whether or not he has a 'kind' eye. His reaction to people in his box.

* Check his mouth for approximate age and the state of the teeth.

All this can be evident from an inspection in the stable. To achieve a more detailed analysis, the horse needs to be viewed outside his box so that he can be seen in the light from all sides.

The horse should be stood squarely, if possible, and restrained either with a headcollar and lead rope or a bridle. The handler stands a little way in front, so that the horse can hold his head in a natural position. Information can be gained quickly by observing the horse and noting the characteristics.

In this example, even though a sketch, the following points can be seen. This is a mare, approximately 16 hands high (estimated from height of girl). The build suggests a **medium to heavy hunter type**, deep girth, well-rounded quarters, strong neck and shoulders. This could be an Irish Draught or a Cleveland Bay.

In appearance the mare is bright, alert and in good health. In this case the clip suggests that the mare is doing hard work probably hunting as the legs and saddle area remain unclipped, giving a hunter clip.

These observations can be made very quickly without being an equine Sherlock Holmes. A more detailed analysis can then be made taking each part of the horse separately.

Top Line

The top line runs from the poll, through the neck, withers, back and croup to the dock. Whilst the underlying structure is bone, the top line is influenced by muscle condition.

* This 'line' should form a smooth outline.

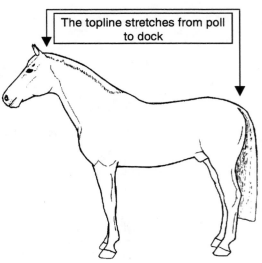

The topline stretches from poll to dock

Look out for:

• A dip in front of the withers: the *'ewe-neck'*.

This may be caused either by;

1. a skeletal defect in the cervical vertebrae. This defect can indicate a difficulty to work in a rounded outline. Often this type of horse will work with his head held high.

2. underdeveloped muscle in a young horse, a horse off work or not being worked correctly. This can be improved by proper exercise and schooling. Observe the muscle tone of the neck and the rest of the body.

This young horse has a slight ewe-neck. Evidently from the lack of musculature in the rest of his body he has not been in work for long and his shape will change and improve with correct training.

＊   The withers should be clearly defined but show a continuous line with the crest and the back.

＊   The withers should be slightly higher than the croup.

•   High or prominent withers. Often, but not always, coupled with a dipped back. Can be very difficult to fit a saddle on this type of horse. Watch out for white markings around the withers area indicating past saddle sores.

•   Low withers. May be coupled with a straight back; again difficult to fit a saddle.

∗ The back, from the withers to the croup, should be of medium length, in proportion with the rest of the top line.

• A short back, *'short coupled'*, is stronger than a long back but the horse will be less comfortable to ride. This type of horse will find it difficult to give good length of pace.

• Too long a back is liable to strain and weakness. The horse should be able to give a better length of stride but he may find it difficult to give true impulsion as his hindquarters will not be able to push up underneath.

*   The back arches upwards, a *'roach back'*, usually causes no problems but this can look unsightly.

•   A dipped or hollow back either through poor conformation or age may indicate weakness along the back.

The croup area lies between the point of croup and the dock, the top of the tail. The height of the point of croup can indicate whether a horse is likely to find flatwork or jumping easier.

∗   The point of croup should be fairly evident.

∗   The croup should be slightly lower than the withers.

∗   A slightly prominent point of croup, called the *'jumper's bump'*, is reputed to be the sign of a show jumper or eventer.

- Horse with a croup higher than the withers, is said to be *'croup high'*. This conformation will give a 'downhill' ride; the horse will tend to work 'on the forehand' that is, placing more weight on his front legs.

- Croup significantly lower than the withers; indicates weak hindquarters. The horse will find difficulty in giving impulsion.

- Short croup, length between point of croup to dock, tail usually set high. Weak hindquarters usually lacking muscle. Hind legs normally quite straight, liable to stress and strain.

- Long or sloping croup, tail usually set too low, a *'goose rump'*. Weakness in hindquarters normally linked with poor muscle development.

This analysis of the top line covers a number of points and will give an indication of the strengths and weaknesses to be discovered in the remainder of the body.

The Body

Once the top line has been assessed, the remainder of the body can be judged from the side, front and back views.

The Head

The size and shape of the head can vary depending on breed or type and will often give hints as to breeding. The head may also indicate temperament though this is never a hard and fast rule.

Though ideally the head should 'fit' the rest of the horse, without being too small or over large, any modest variation will not signify weakness.

 * *Dish face* – concave profile. Arab, Anglo-Arab, part Arab.

 * Small, fine head – gives lightness and mobility.

 • Small, thin face can indicate a lack of intelligence.

 * Large (coarse) head –a heavy or overlarge head.

   May be an indication of 'common breeding' that is a cold-blooded breed, a draught horse.

 • The horse may work on the forehand and have a tendency to 'lean' on the bit.

 * *Roman nose* or *arched face* – convex profile: good temperament and nature.

A roman nose

An arched face

The Eyes

✳ Large, shining, bold, clear with a 'kind' expression. Blue eyes, or pink eyes in albinos, look strange but do not usually denote any inferior trait.

• Small mean eyes show a mean spirited animal with a bad temper.

• Eyes showing a fair amount of white show a nervous or possibly vicious horse.

Nostrils

✳ Need to be large and mobile so that the horse can breathe easily and fully.

• Tight, small nostrils will limit breathing capacity.

The Ears

The size and shape of the ears can add or detract from the beauty of the head, depending on personal preference. Ideally ears should be medium length and width, mobile, slender, set well on the head.

Short or over long ears may look odd against the general proportion of the horse.

The appearance of the ears can indicate the horse's state of health or behaviour.

- Ears flat back show anger or aggression.

- Limp, static, drooping ears show tiredness, ill health, boredom, a sluggish horse.

Jowl

This is an important point in conformation as the set of the head onto the neck does affect the horse's breathing, his head carriage and performance in work.

* The angle at the jaw should meet the neck in a smooth curve. The division between the cheekbone and the neck should be clearly defined by the groove extending from below the ear to the throat.

* There should be a space for two fingers to fit in this groove.

- *'Too loose'* – the head looks as if it has been stuck on as an afterthought. The neck is thin and narrow where it meets the head and the groove around the cheekbone and throat is wide, more than two fingers' width. Normally associated with a long narrow neck and poor muscular development.

- *'Too close'* or *'close coupling'* – the head has the appearance of being stuck on the neck *'too soon'*. The neck is normally short and thick. The head will not have the mobility of action or flexion. The groove around the cheekbone is narrow and shallow. The head looks too close to the neck

✳ Look at the space between the cheekbones under the horse's jaw. There should be a good space, room to fit a fist. This will indicate sufficient room for the windpipe.

Neck

✳ The neck should be in proportion with the rest of the body.

✳ It should be muscular with a smooth, defined crest.

✳   A slightly longer neck appears elegant.

✳   A slightly shorter neck denotes strength.

- Too long a neck can influence the horse to work on the forehand.

- Too short a neck and the horse may find working in a rounded outline difficult. He may be a *'puller'*, too strong in front.

- A lack of muscle in the neck could indicate that the horse has been off work or is not being worked properly.

- The neck is too muscular underneath, could indicate the horse is not being worked correctly. He may have difficulty working in a rounded outline.

Shoulder

The area just below the withers and extending to the point of shoulder has an effect on the type of movement the horse will be able to offer. The slope of the shoulder may reflect the pastern angle, giving an indication of the type of action the horse will produce.

✳ The shoulders ideally should slope at a 45 - 50 degrees angle from the vertical. (This angle should be reflected in the slope of the pasterns.)

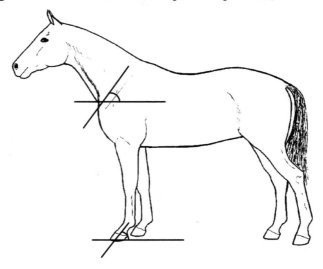

● If the slope of the shoulder is too upright this will restrict movement, creating short, choppy paces, with little extension of stride.

- If the shoulder slopes at a greater angle, although this will give a greater length of stride, the shoulder area could prove 'weak', liable to injury.

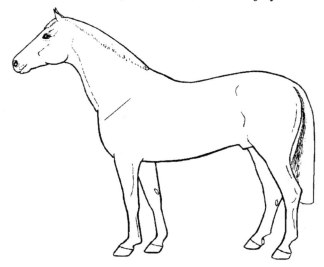

- A small shoulder indicates a restricted movement.

- An overlarge shoulder indicates a lack of agility, particularly when jumping.

Forelegs

When observing the legs, there are certain 'sight lines' which aid in recognising good and bad conformation.

Side view

* The legs should be 'straight' through the centre, from the centre of the shoulder through the forearm and knee to the fetlock.

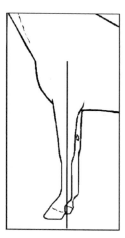

* The legs should fit neatly underneath the body with the knee behind the 'line' dropping from the front of the forearm.

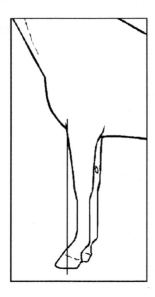

* The forearm should be muscular.

* The length of the forearm should be longer than the cannon bone. Though the cannon bone should in relation to the forearm *appear* short, there is no evidence that short cannons are stronger. It is the bone density that gives strength.

* The knees should be broad and flat. The joints are an important point of conformation, and should be a good size, clear of bumps and lumps.

* The pastern should be a medium length and slope at a 45 to 50 degrees angle, as with the shoulder.

• If the knee is bowed in front, this is *'over at the knee'*. This spoils the appearance and is unacceptable when showing.

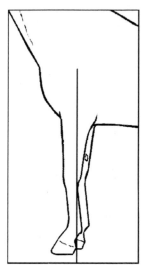

• If the knee is concave, *'back at the knee'*, this is a more serious fault as it will put strain upon the tendons of the lower leg and upon the bones of the knee itself.

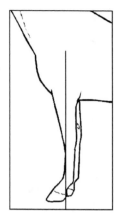

• Leg behind the vertical – the horse is *'under himself in front'*; may cause stumbling, forging, the horse may work on forehand, out of balance.

• Leg in front of vertical – lack of speed, strain put on the tendons and joints. The horse may have suffered from laminitis in the past. Hind limbs may be put under strain and stress.

• Long and sloping pastern gives a springy ride but is also liable to strain.

• Short, upright pasterns are stronger but give a bumpy ride. Causes jarring and concussion of the joints, possibly lameness. (Look at the pasterns in conjunction with slope of shoulder.)

Front view

The chest is the area between the forelegs, often referred to as the *'heart room'*.

✳   From the front the chest should have breadth, sufficient to fit a good hand's width, and be well muscled. Both the forelegs should be straight in line through knee, fetlock, pastern and foot.

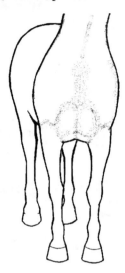 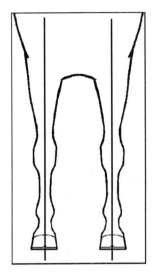

•   A narrow chest will bring the forelegs too close– *'closed in front'* or *'legs out of the same hole'* resulting in poor action, brushing, speedicutting.

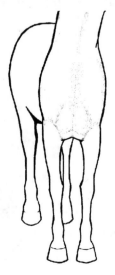 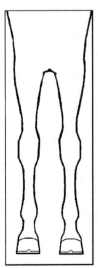

- A wide chest with legs too far apart the horse *is 'too open in front'*. Problems in some gaits, such as galloping or lateral work. This type of horse may also be wide and uncomfortable for the rider.

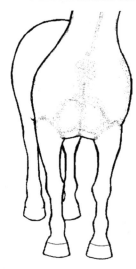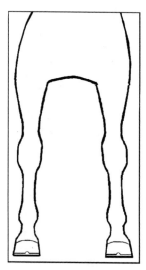

* From the side the chest should be rounded with a smooth continuous line from the base of the neck.

* Prominent chest or breast bone – *'pigeon chested'*, often the horse is a poor mover, lacks balance and has poor paces.

* In young horses or those off work, this area may suffer from a lack of muscle, which will improve with exercise.

✳   The legs should be placed at the 'corners' of the horse with width between them. The forelegs should be in line with the hind legs when the horse is standing square.

●   Legs converge top to bottom so that the hooves are closer together – *'cross-footed in front'*, *'toed-in'* or *'base narrow'* – unequal wear on foot and shoe, muscle and tendon strain on outside of legs, may result in stumbling.

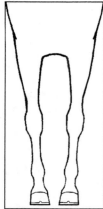

●   Knees come in closer, *'knock-kneed'*.

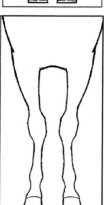

●   Knees widen out *'bench knees'*.

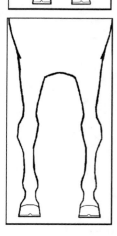

Body

The body stretches from the shoulder, across the ribs and belly to the hip.

* The ribs should be rounded, barrel shaped – *'well sprung'*.

* The horse should look fit and lean, the ribs should be just visible.

• Shallow chest, a lack of depth in trunk and girth, *'showing a lot of daylight'*. Horse will lack stamina.

• If the belly rises abruptly the horse is *'herring-gutted'* and will lack stamina. The saddle may need a breastplate to prevent slipping back.

• If tight around the loins the horse is *'tucked up'*, could indicate illness, colic, digestive problems.

• The belly should not be too large or distended with food, *'pot-bellied'*.

Loins

These are situated behind the saddle and extend to the point of croup.

* The horse needs strength of muscle and breadth here to give a solid base so that the hindquarters can transmit the impulsion to the forehand, essential for balance and performance.

* The last rib should only be a small distance about the width of four fingers (5 cms or 2 inches) from the hipbone *'well ribbed up'*.

• A wide space between the ribs and the hip, thin and poorly muscled, *'slack loins'* indicating a weak back.

Hindquarters

Being the source of power the hindquarters need to be muscular and strong.

Side view

* There should be a good length between hip and point of buttock, and hip and hocks.

* The thigh from the buttock to the stifle should be muscular as should the second thigh or gaskin, from stifle to hock.

* Hips should be broad but not protruding.

• Weak, poorly muscled hindquarters, protruding hips, concave flanks, all denote weakness, lack of stamina and power.

View from behind

∗   Hips should be the same level in height.

∗   Shape across top of the hips should be rounded and equal on both sides.

•   Shape across top of hips is too flat or angled (like the sloping roof of a house).

Hind Legs

Side view with the horse stood straight and four square.

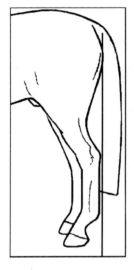

∗   The leg from hock to fetlock should be parallel and almost in line with a vertical 'line' from the point of buttock.

∗   Hocks should be large, outline clean, with a prominent point at the back.

∗   Good length of hip to hock so that the hock to fetlock, the cannon bone, appears short.

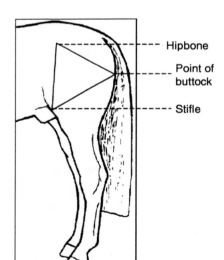

Hipbone

Point of buttock

Stifle

When looking at the hindquarters, take the three points, the hipbone, the point of buttock and the stifle. These should make up an equilateral triangle.

There should be the same amount of distance between these points.

Any deviation shows weakness and will place strain on the stifle and the hock.

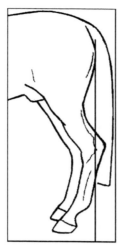 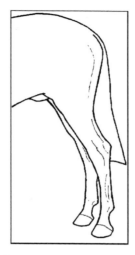 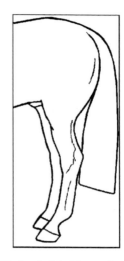

'Sickle hocks' – where the hock is behind the vertical whilst the fetlock is on or before the line. Stress and strain on hock, ligaments and tendons of fetlock and foot.

'Hocks in next county' – both hock and fetlock behind the line. Puts stress on back and loins.

'Under behind' – point of hock touches line but the hindcannon slopes to the front of the line. Causes imbalance in paces, liability of forging.

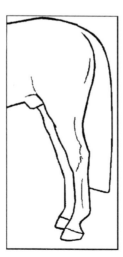 

'Straight hocked' – the upper leg from stifle to hock appears upright. Sign of speed, good for galloping but not jumping.

Poorly developed gaskin (second thigh) is called *'tied or cut in above the hock'*. Lack of stamina and strength.

Viewed from behind.

Line from point of buttock passes through centre of hock, cannon, fetlock and hoof.

'Cow-hocked' – where the hocks turn in. Movement may be awkward with feet splaying outwards. Stress on hock. Foot likely to screw on contact with ground.

'Bowed hocks' – where the hocks turn outwards. Feet normally pigeon-toed, affects movement. Stress and strain on inner leg and ligaments of hock. Uneven wear on outside of foot.

'*Too open behind*', hocks too far apart; places stress on the inside of the lower leg.

'*Closed behind*', legs and hocks inside vertical line, too close together. Brushing, loss of balance and stability, awkward paces.

'*Slit or split up behind*', when the legs are correct but the second thigh muscle is not developed and the horse looks 'wide behind'.

The Feet

The feet are one of the most important points of conformation.

* They should be a round, even shape and a suitable size for the horse.

* Both fore hooves should be equal in size, as should both hinds.

* The wall of the foot should be clean, smooth and shiny.

* The pastern and hoof should be the correct angle to the ground.

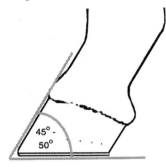

| Angle of front foot | Angle of hind foot |

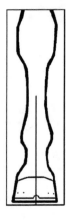

* The feet should point straight forwards.

• Small feet reduce the weight bearing surface and the area that absorbs concussion. This puts more strain on the foot and leg. Possibility of foot problems.

• *'Boxy feet'*, upright feet and pastern. Can give a choppy, short, uncomfortable stride. Also cause concussion of the joints, possible lameness as the frog may not be in contact with the ground during movement.

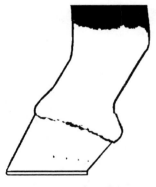

* Long, sloping, large or overgrown feet put strain on the heels, the fetlocks, lower legs, tendons and ligaments. May result in bruising of the soles and tripping.

* Rings on the hoof wall can either show a change of diet or if the rings are deep this can be a sign of laminitis.

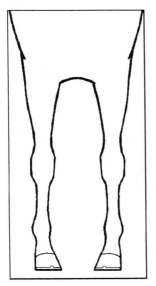 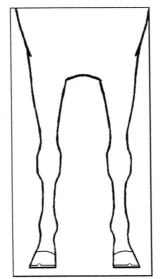 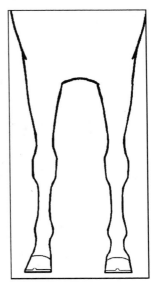

• Feet that turn in facing each other are called *'pigeon toed'*. The horse will be prone to brushing, faulty action and uneven wear of feet.

• When both feet turn outwards, *'splayed footed'*, this puts strain on the tendons and ligaments and causes faulty action such as dishing.

• Occasionally one foot will be correct but the other foot will show a deviation.

Many of the faults with the feet and legs can be improved quite dramatically by a good Farrier and corrective shoeing.

Closer Inspection

Having checked the conformation at a distance and by walking around the horse, now is the time to make a closer inspection by the 'hands on' method. This is a vital part of assessing conformation. Approach the horse as normal, towards his neck on the nearside, pat his neck feeling for the muscular development at the same time. Run a hand over his shoulder and down the foreleg.

✳ Where possible measure the appropriate areas with a hand – two fingers fit in the jowl line, a fist under the jaw between the cheekbones, a spread hand's width for the chest, four fingers' width at the loins between the last rib and hipbone.

✳ Assess the circumference of the cannon just below the knee by hand, a good amount for a horse is 8 to 9 inches of bone (approximately 20 cms). This shows weight carrying qualities – *'a horse with good bone'*. With a small, thin cannon the horse will only be able to carry light riders.

Run the hands down the legs; feel for splints. These cause no particular problems provided they are not so close to the knee or hock joints that they affect its action. Feel the tendons at the back of the legs, should be clean, free from lumps. Feel the joints, knees, fetlocks and hocks, should be large, broad, flat and clean. Feel for windgalls, sign of work and age.

The Foot

Pick up the foot in the normal manner and note how readily the horse complies, another indication as to his temperament. Clean the foot out if necessary.

Check the shoe – observe if the horse has been shod recently. Observe if the shoe is a normal, concave fullered shoe or if the horse is wearing a remedial shoe. If the shoe is worn, note if the wear is more prominent on one side rather than the other, or at the toe. This gives an indication of faulty action. Feel around the shoe for fit, whether or not the shoe is loose.

Check the foot, the sole should be a concave shape. The frog, should feel clean and rubbery, be a good shape, large and in good condition. The heels should be clean and spongy to touch.

The Mouth

The teeth should meet evenly. Where the teeth do not meet evenly, this can affect the horse's feeding and grazing, possibly leading to other digestive problems.

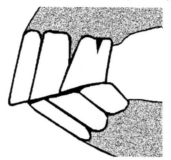 

'Parrot mouth', where the top jaw is long or 'overshoots' the bottom jaw like a parrot's beak.

'Sow mouth', where the top jaw is shorter or undershoots the bottom jaw.

Assessment of Static Conformation

The ability to assess a horse's static conformation comes through observation and experience. Practise assessing horses frequently; observe the relevant points and how these differ between individuals. Then compare these observations with the way in which each horse performs.

Example of Assessment

This is the type of assessment that can be given to each horse in the yard.

In the stable

Name	L.B. (Name often gives hint of gender, but not always!)
Height & build	16.2 hh (measured from own height), medium build.
Colour	Light bay.
Markings	White star on forehead, three white socks.
Injury Markings	White areas behind withers, past saddle sores. May have problem fitting a saddle.
Gender	Gelding.
Breed or Type	Medium Hunter type. Slightly fine in build, but heavier than a pure Thoroughbred, possible part Thoroughbred/Irish Draught.

Condition	Summer coat, fairly good condition, shiny, lying flat over bones. Underweight but not thin, muscle tone is slightly poor.
Proportions	Head looks a little too large but not so much that it detracts from overall picture.
Temperament	Good in box, looking interested, relaxed, kind eye.
Age	Estimate around 12 years (teeth showed Galvayne's groove about one third of way down corner incisor).
Mouth	Has a slightly overshot or parrot mouth. Mouth is large enough to take a double bridle.

Bring the horse out of the box with headcollar and lead rope. Leads well, came out of box quietly. Stands well, head held high for few seconds, having a look around, ears mobile, then relaxed. Quiet to handle.

General impression	The horse seems well proportioned. Head still appears a little large but now can observe that the neck lacks muscle. Would expect a horse of this type to have more muscle.
Stance	**Keeps shifting his weight off the off fore.** Can see that there is no shoe on that foot. (At this point because the foot is suspect possibly have a closer look and pick up the foot.)
Top line	From poll to dock. Good neck, though shows a slight 'ewe-neck' and lacking muscle along crest.
	Prominent withers could make fitting saddle difficult. Good back, right length, loins strong though a little lean. Good quarters, fair length from point of croup to dock. Croup slightly sloping possibly due to lack of muscle. Tail set on in right place, not too high or low.
Head	Big kind eyes, plenty of forehead room, big nostrils. Straight profile. Ears large and mobile, pricked and alert.
Jowl	Good jowl, can fit two fingers in jowl area, plenty of room. Head fits on the neck well. Can fit fist under the head between cheekbones.
Neck	Definitely underdeveloped as far as muscles are concerned. Good sternocephalic muscle but top muscles slack. Length in proportion with body.
Shoulder	A little too upright, reflected in pasterns. Like to see a bit more slope to the shoulder.
Chest	Slightly narrow chest for a horse this size, could be that general lack of muscle. Forelegs inclining slightly inwards 'base narrow' but not 'pigeon-toed'.

Forelegs	Straight legs, conforms to line through shoulders, not over or back at the knees. Holds legs well under body not leaning forwards or backwards. Pasterns slightly upright. Feet large and slightly more sloping than pasterns. Could be flat-footed.
Body	Good breadth of girth from withers to breastbone, plenty of lung room. Space between last rib and hip correct.
Hindquarters	Good length between hipbone and point of buttock and between buttock to hock.
Hind legs	Straight no deviation from line from point of buttock. Good strong, large hocks. Rear view; hips level and wide, hind legs slightly 'cow hocked'.
Off fore	Want to check that leg first. Possibly favouring leg because of cast shoe. Yet general lack of muscle in body leads to hypothesis that there may be a foot injury.
	Horse lifts foot up readily. Immediately see horse very flat footed. Evidence of bruising on sole, discoloration. Horse flinches a little when sole gently tapped with hoof pick.
Other feet	Shoes on three feet show slight but even wear, not yet due for shoeing. Flat feet and soles, frog good shape but flat. This horse would have problems on anything but good going.
Legs	Check legs, run hands down from elbow to foot. Elbow room good, forearm lacking muscle. Knees broad, flat and clean. Measure bone under knee, length from tip of forefinger to tip of thumb is about 7 inches (18 cms) plus about 2 inches more equals 9 inches (23 cms). Good weight carrying.
	Lower leg to fetlock is clean no bumps or scars, tendons quite clearly felt. Windgalls in fetlock area on fore legs, soft so been there for some time. No newly forming windgalls, these would be hard and hot.

General Assessment

The horse's static conformation and underlying bone structure, despite the lack of muscle tone throughout the body, is basically good. His body is well proportioned and, though the head is slightly large, this does not detract from the overall picture.

The horse's head fits well onto his neck. The neck lacks muscle along the crest and this shows in a slight dip (ewe neck) in front of the withers. The withers are prominent and there is evidence of saddle injuries, so care would be needed to obtain a properly fitted saddle.

The legs are straight, the joints large and strong. There are windgalls around the fetlocks but these would cause no problems. The horse has a strong back and hindquarters.

The greatest difficulty with this horse would be his feet. These are extremely flat and prone to bruising, corns and injury. The Farrier may be able to improve them slightly but feel that this is a conformational problem made worse by bad care in the past.

This horse eventually could be worked well on soft ground in an indoor school or well-maintained outdoor sand school. He may jump a little but with great care. If the ground becomes hard, rough, dry or stony the horse cannot be worked on this surface.

Exam Tips

Because the subject has been a matter of debate and argument for centuries, there are many 'horsy' terms for conformation. It is often difficult to remember all the correct terms and, in some cases, these terms denote different meanings in various parts of the country. Memorise those that are the easiest to learn and understand first, for instance 'cow-hocks' and 'ewe-neck'.

In the Stage III when describing the horse's conformation, explain what you see before you and use your own words. *Do not try and use a term that you do not understand.* The Examiners are not testing your memory to learn the conformational terms; they are testing your own personal assessment of the horse.

When bringing the horse from the stable for assessment you may ask for a bridle. You do not know this horse and using a bridle is safer, unless the Examiner states otherwise.

To assess the 'bone' of the horse, discover the length from the top of your index finger to the tip of your thumb with a piece of string then measure this. You will then be able to place your hand around the horse's foreleg just under the knee and estimate the circumference of the cannon bone.

After gaining experience by looking and assessing as many different horses as possible, you begin to develop an 'eye' for conformation. This sometimes becomes almost an instinctive flair. You begin to pick up different aspects. You will also have your own personal likes and dislikes; you are quite entitled to express these feelings. Assess the basic conformation and compare this to the horse's possible action, how certain points may affect his movement and ability.

CHAPTER 11
Dynamic Conformation

Dynamic conformation is the horse in motion, the way he moves. The basis for the horse's action is his skeletal frame and his muscular development. It also, to some degree, is influenced by his training, which should enhance his natural movement.

Action

All horses and ponies have a natural action. There are types of action to observe when assessing the horse. Some of these are good qualities and some are faults, which are preferably avoided.

There are certain terms used to describe action.

Under tracking – when the hind foot fails to reach the fore foot print. Poor pace and movement.

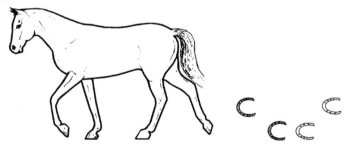

Tracking up – when the hind foot reaches and is placed in approximately the print left by the fore foot. Fair pace and movement.

Over tracking – when the hind foot reaches beyond the fore foot print. Good pace and movement.

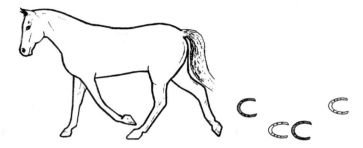

Dishing – the foreleg swings outwards either from the knee or the shoulder. Depending on the degree the limb deviates from normal, dishing can affect movement and pace. Puts strain on leg and shoulder area. Dishing from the shoulder is worse. This action can also be present in the hind legs when the horse dishes from the stifle.

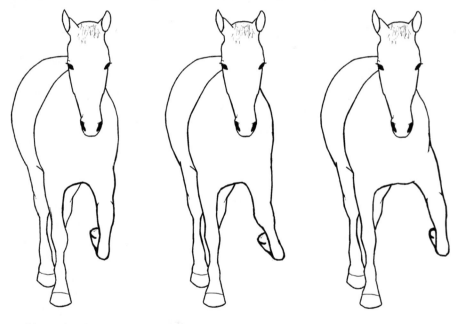

Normal action   Dishing from the knee   Dishing from the shoulder

Over-reaching – when the hind leg steps onto the heel or pastern of the corresponding foreleg. Shows a lack of balance in pace, can cause heel and leg injuries.

Forging – over reaching when the hind foot touches the shoe of the foreleg and makes a noise. Shows a lack of balance or too fast a pace.

Plaiting – when the legs, fore or hind, weave in front of one another.

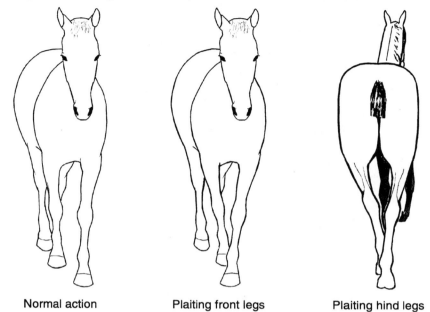

Normal action   Plaiting front legs   Plaiting hind legs

The horse will lack balance in paces, affects quality of pace and can result in injury to the legs, such as brushing or speedicutting.

In Hand Assessment

To check the dynamic conformation, the horse should first be assessed in hand at walk and trot, from the side, the front and from behind. The 'in hand' assessment should be made on level ground and in a straight line, so that any deviation in limb action, such as dishing, can be seen more clearly.

The horse should be encouraged to walk and trot actively. The handler should hold the lead rope or reins a little way from the head allowing the horse a certain amount of freedom. Any nodding of the horse's head, which may indicate unlevelness, can then be observed.

Observations

In both walk and trot the horse's footfalls should have a clear beat. Occasionally a horse will walk with a two-time beat, giving a 'rolling' action.

The limbs should move relatively straight, that is the 'flight of the leg' should be straight. Look for dishing, plaiting, or limbs that move too close to each other, normally associated with a narrow chest or weak hindquarters. Horses who move their limbs close may suffer injuries such as brushing.

Look for a good length of stride. The horse may move with short, stiff, pottery steps. If he is unbalanced in his paces this can cause over-reaching or forging.

Look for action in the hind legs such as 'twisting' the hoof on contact with the ground, usually combined with twisting of the hock. This action puts strain on the joints.

Reason for Assessment

The usual reason for assessing conformation is to purchase a horse. The prospective buyer needs to see the horse in the stable, his reaction when tacked and the type of bit used. Observe also any attachments to bridle or saddle. The horse may be ridden at all paces, if possible.

Walk

Always look for a horse with a good walk, a clear four-time beat, tracking up or if possible over tracking.

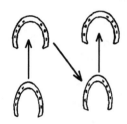

Sequence: near hind, near fore, off hind, off fore.

Think of a capital **N**

Trot

A two-time beat with a clear moment of suspension.

Sequence: near hind and off fore, off hind and near fore.

Think of an **X**

Canter

A three-time beat with a moment of suspension after the leading leg touches the ground.

Sequence: outside hind, inside hind and outside fore together, inside fore (leading leg).

Think of a **%**

Gallop

This is a four-time beat with a moment of suspension after the fourth beat.

Sequence is one hind then the other hind, one foreleg then the other foreleg.

Think of a **Z**

Depending on the type of work for which the horse is being purchased, it may be appropriate to show some fast work, lateral work and jumping. The purchaser may wish to see the horse being lunged and loaded for travel.

Breed and Types

Different breeds and types have specific conformational points that help in establishing their origins. There are often colours and markings prevalent in certain breeds. This section will describe the more popular breeds and types in this country.

Revision

Native Mountain and Moorland breeds of the United Kingdom (Stage II). Hot, cold and warm bloods, Stud books, types – hunter, hack, cob, riding pony (Stage II).

Breed	Height	Conformation	Colours	Characteristics
Arab	14.2 – 15 hands	Dish (concave) face, broad forehead, large dark eyes, tapering face to fine muzzle. Flat knees, short cannons, hard, healthy feet.	Grey, chestnut, bay.	Free floating action. Stamina used for endurance.
Anglo-Arab	Around 16 hands	Straight or dish profile, long head. Sloping shoulders, powerful hindquarters.	Bay, chestnut, liver chestnut, other solid colours.	Stamina and good movement.
Cleveland Bay	Around 16 –16.2	Large convex head. Powerful shoulders, deep girth. Strong back and hindquarters. Good bone.	Bay, brown.	Powerful, used for riding and driving.
Irish Draught	Around 16 hands	Straight face, short powerful neck and shoulders. Longer back with powerful hindquarters. Large feet.	Grey, bay, brown.	Strength and good temperament. Used for jumping ability.
Thoroughbred	Around 16 hands	Smaller finer head, longish neck. Sloping shoulders, longer back. Prominent withers. Thin skinned.	All solid colours, bay, brown, grey.	Speed, jumping ability. Can have difficult temperaments.
Welsh Cob	14 – 15.2 hands	Good head, strong shoulders, powerful back. Good hock action. Compact body, deep girth.	Solid colours.	Hardy and versatile. Good nature. Riding and driving.

The above breeds and their cross-breeds form the majority of the riding horses in the United Kingdom. From these breeds come many of the types used in Riding Establishments and by most of the horse owners in this country.

The term **type** refers to a horse who is not pure bred. These are cross breeds and will vary in build, height, action and performance.

Hunter type – usually based on a cross between a Thoroughbred and an Irish Draught or Cleveland Bay, in height around 16 hands. Varies from a lightweight hunter type showing more Thoroughbred characteristics, a middleweight, or a heavyweight hunter showing more of the Irish Draught or Cleveland Bay tendencies. The horse may be half bred having one Thoroughbred parent and one non-Thoroughbred, or a three-quarter bred having one Thoroughbred parent and one half bred.

Hack – smaller and lighter than the hunter type, in height around 15 hands. Usually bred from a Thoroughbred, Arab or Anglo-Arab stock. A **show hack type** is elegant with extravagant paces.

Cob – stocky, compact, strong type, around 15 hands. Bred from Welsh Cob, native stock crossed with Thoroughbred.

Riding pony –from 12 to 14.2 hands with pony characteristics. Descended from pony breeds, notably Welsh ponies mixed with Arab and Thoroughbred blood.

Polo pony type – in height around 15 hands, a mixture of Thoroughbred blood with native ponies or those from Argentina, the Criollo.

Most horses are described as **types** unless it is obvious that the horse is pure bred or his ancestry is known. This classification includes horses who exhibit the tendencies of a pure bred but whose ancestry is not actually known. For instance, a horse who has the characteristics of a Thoroughbred is classed as a Thoroughbred type. Many breeds are imported such as the Hanoverian and the Trakener from Germany; the Dutch and Danish Warmbloods are becoming popular particularly for dressage.

Teeth

Revision Stage II
Teeth, basic estimate of age, inspecting teeth, dental care and problems.

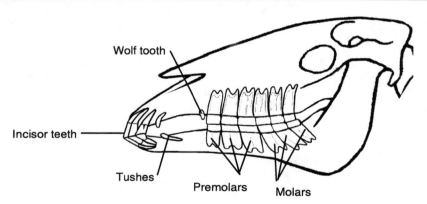

The teeth of the horse are specially designed for a grazing animal. The adult horse will have 12 incisors or cutting teeth, six on the upper jaw and six on the lower jaw. The interdental space divides the incisors from the grinding teeth or molars. There are 24 molars in total, six on each side of each jaw. The first three are termed premolars, the three behind, the molars. In male horses there are also tushes or canine teeth that grow in the interdental space.

Occasionally there are wolf teeth, small molars appearing in the top jaw in front of the premolars. These are normally lost with the temporary or milk teeth, but occasionally they remain and normally cause no problems.

Determining the age of a horse, particularly if his birth date is not known, is usually performed by an inspection of the teeth. There are other signs of ageing, the changes within the body and joints and the depth of the haw above the eye, but these do not give as close an indication as the alterations in the incisor teeth.

For a basic estimation of age, the slant of the teeth and Galvayne's Groove on the corner incisor give a fair indication.

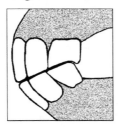

7 years old

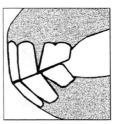

About 10 years old

About 15 years old

About 20 years old

Dental Care

All horses and ponies need dental attention at least every 6 months and at times more frequently. All horses suffer from uneven wear of the molar teeth. The upper jaw is slightly wider than the lower jaw and this, combined with the sideways grinding action, means that sharp edges develop on the outside of the upper molars and the inside of the lower molars. Treatment is given by the Equine Dentist or Vet who will rasp these edges smooth. If not treated, the sharp edges can cause cuts and ulcers inside the cheek or on the tongue.

If a horse develops a problem with his teeth and this is not given attention this will affect his work and health. He may not accept the bit when working or show signs of obvious pain in the mouth. He may start refusing his food, have difficulty swallowing or begin **'quidding'** that is dropping partially eaten food and saliva out of his mouth. All these difficulties will result in an unhealthy horse, lack of condition and loss of performance.

In riding establishments, schools or livery yards, the Equine Dentist or Orthodontist will generally call every few months and attend to several horses. If there is an immediate problem the Vet is also able to give treatment.

Exam Tips

Conformation and action may be included when the candidates trot a horse up for inspection. The Examiners may also ask for an general assessment of the horses after the riding section.

Learning about conformation takes practice. You will need to study the points of conformation in theory and turn this knowledge into practical ability by developing observation, awareness and perception. You should develop your own discriminating judgement, have your own opinions about what you do or do not like.

As part of the Exam preparation, look at different horses and assess them critically with an experienced person. Take a clipboard around the stable and assess each horse, check your answers against their registration papers if possible. Observe pictures from books or magazines and practise assessing the horses, picking out their good points as well as their weaknesses.

Some people prefer to mentally divide the horse into three portions, the forehand including neck and head, the middle portion and the hindquarters. Others will divide the horse into two, forehand and hindquarters. Whilst many horses do seem to have a forehand that does not fit their hindquarters, the horse should ultimately be thought of as a whole.

You will need to develop an 'eye' for conformation, a 'feel' for the reasons behind a horse's strengths and weaknesses. Whilst expressing opinions obviously taken from a book is perfectly correct, it is only so if it fits the horse being assessed. The basic information needs to be sound, but then it needs to be expanded from your own experiences, in your own words. You are quite entitled to have opinions of your own providing you can back them up with facts.

Having some knowledge about breeds and types is essential, their basic characteristics, physiques and abilities. You will need to learn how to distinguish between breeds. The information given here and that in the Stage II book should be reinforced by practical experience.

C H A P T E R   12
Behaviour and Vices

Horses and ponies should be treated with a firm but kind and understanding attitude. Discipline is essential, correction of bad behaviour and rewarding good. By this method the horse learns what behaviour is acceptable and what will not be tolerated.

Problem horses, those with vicious habits, tend to have learnt these habits from a human handler; through fear and pain the horse learns to behave badly. This can influence the way he is treated throughout the rest of his life. It is essential from the start that the young horse is handled in a way that will teach him to act and behave with good manners. Then as the handler becomes accustomed to the horse, and the horse to the handler, so understanding and respect will grow.

Correct Behaviour

Good stable manners can be taught from the beginning almost from birth. Educating the young horse is based on the groom or owner knowing what to teach and how to teach it.

In the Stable

* The horse should be taught to come to the door when his name is called.

* He should learn to stand quietly with his head to the door whilst the groom enters the box.

* The horse should accept having his headcollar and leadrope put on without raising or tossing his head around or moving off.

* He should learn to stand whilst being handled and groomed.

* When restrained in the box he should learn to move over on command.

* He should accept having his bridle put on and open his mouth readily for the bit.

* He should stand quietly whilst having his saddle put on and the girth fastened.

* He needs to be taught to lead in hand in a headcollar and lead rope.

* He should pick his feet up when asked to do so without hesitation or fuss.

In the Field

* Ideally he should come over to the gate or approach the groom when his name is called.

* He should stand quietly whilst having his headcollar and lead rope put on.

* He should lead quietly from the field and stand or move when the groom is unfastening and fastening the gate.

* When being put in the field he should learn to stand quietly whilst his headcollar is removed and the groom has walked away.

In the Yard

* He should accept being tied up and stand quietly in the yard.

* He should not lunge or bite at other horses whilst tied up or being led.

* He should stand quietly for the Vet and the Farrier.

These points are important and every young horse or pony can be taught correct manners. Good manners in a horse and pony make a world of difference to the handler, groom, rider and owner. Dealing with uneducated or vicious horses, those who cannot be trusted in the box or field, makes the groom's job very difficult and dangerous.

Naturally not every owner has the good fortune to start from scratch and most of us come into contact with the horse when his basic training has already been established. We then have to deal with the problems passed on by others.

Also not every owner handles their horse solely, particularly in a commercial Riding Establishment where a number of staff care for the horses. If, though, everyone knew what to expect in a good mannered horse and how to teach, train and re-educate an animal, caring for horses and ponies might be more simple and less hazardous.

The horse is a living creature and will almost always at some time react to external or internal stimuli in a way that is instinctive. The important point is that with good training the horse will learn security, will develop trust for his handler which, in difficult situations, can and does prevent serious accidents.

Training

Most horses, at whatever age, are always willing to learn, willing to please. They are taught, through correction and reward, to associate actions with pleasure or pain. To educate a horse correctly the handler, groom or rider has first to be self-disciplined. Staff at yards should also be taught behaviour to expect and the methods of training the horse.

Education should be:

Consistent – asking for the same action every time. The horse cannot learn if the groom corrects an action one day and allows the horse to be disobedient with no correction the following day.

Correct – knowing the standards to expect. Those who have worked with horses for many years learn how ill mannered horses can make the work harder, even dangerous. The new horse owner or those coming into the industry need to be taught the standards to expect and how to achieve this through correction and reward. This should constitute part of the training for new students and working pupils.

Confident – having the conviction and the firm self-discipline to correct the horse when he is doing wrong. This should not be through bad temper but with a firm, decisive and consistent manner.

Prompt – the horse should be corrected or rewarded the instant he has performed the action. Correcting some time later, even a matter of minutes afterwards, will confuse him. He needs to know exactly which action he should or should not do. The groom should not nag the horse incessantly, a quick correction or reward is sufficient.

Considerate – this is where the self-discipline is important. The rider and groom should never, as far as is humanly possible, unwittingly cause pain. For instance fastening a girth up roughly and pinching the horse's skin; landing on the saddle with a thump when mounting; tying the horse up incorrectly in the headcollar and lead rope so that he pulls back in fear and hurts his poll.

Common sense – will prevent many problems before they happen. Restraining the horse when handling or working around him can prevent bad behaviour in the first place. It is the groom's job to keep the horse out of situations where he will either be frightened, cause pain or become injured.

A good mannered, disciplined horse reflects a good mannered, disciplined groom.

Bad Manners

Bad behaviour is usually learnt from the handler or owner's own negligence, inconsiderate actions or ignorance. Ignorance may be bliss for some, certainly not for the horse. The horse learns to fear pain and will remember situations for years to come. A cold-backed horse has possibly suffered back pain either from an ill fitting saddle or a heavy unbalanced rider. A horse who fidgets or turns round to bite when the girth is fastened has either suffered pain by careless handling or not been corrected.

Constantly feeding titbits will cause the horse to nip or bite. Titbits are a special reward when he has been good. Giving titbits for every good action will make the horse become unruly if he does not receive his treat as usual.

The groom has also to distinguish between plain bad manners and instinctive behaviour. The horse should not be punished for instinctive reactions. He should instead learn to trust the handler in situations, so that his behaviour is modified. For instance travelling to a show or new stable, the handler should confidently and quietly reassure him. The horse is learning trust, obedience, submission and control. The rider and groom are in charge. They, in a way, take over the role of the head of the herd whom the horse follows and obeys without question.

It is important that a quiet, firm discipline is always given for, as well as his physical needs of food, water, exercise and relaxation, the horse needs a mental and emotional security to stay in good health.

Methods of Restraint

There are times when a horse will need restraining. He may be nervous, highly strung, frightened or just being awkward. Restraining him so that he is quiet and compliant is better than having a battle with him, which may lead to a dangerous situation. There are several methods of restraint besides the headcollar and leadrope.

*   Putting his bridle on will offer more control.

*   Patting the horse's neck, scratching his forehead, talking to him, giving him a haynet or feed may distract his attention sufficiently.

*   Holding on to the muzzle and either squeezing it with fingers and thumb or by twisting the lip. This is a mild form of twitch. Avoid interference with the horse's breathing.

*   Pinching some skin on the neck.

*   Holding up a foreleg.

*   Twitching. The top lip is held with either a twitch made of a short wooden pole and a loop of string or the 'nutcracker' type of twitch. It is now thought that the action of the twitch releases endorphins into the blood stream which, acting almost like a sedative, have a calming effect.

*   Gently holding the tongue when the teeth are being inspected. This does need great care to avoid damaging the tongue.

*   Drugging and sedating - the Vet may have to administer drugs.

Any form of restraint should be applied with care. The twitch, for example, should only be left on for five to twenty minutes. Fine-skinned horses will receive a permanent mark if the twitch is left on for longer than five minutes. For thicker-skinned horses, twenty minutes is the maximum, after that the upper lip can become numb. The lip and nostrils should always be massaged after using the twitch to encourage the return of the circulation.

Revision

Stage II types of twitch and methods of twitching.

Stable Vices

Stable vices are behavioural actions caused by physical, psychological or medical problems. Often these are a result of bad handling, fear, stress, boredom, imitation, inherited traits or temperament. Sometimes it is difficult to tell when or why the vice appears.

Stable vices include – weaving, crib-biting, windsucking, eating bedding or droppings, kicking the box, kicking the door, pawing the floor, rug tearing, biting or kicking in the stable, box walking, refusal to lie down, tail rubbing.

Weaving

- A nervous habit when horse sways from side to side. This movement varies from head, neck and body movement to actually picking up and putting down the forelegs alternately.

- The various causes are boredom, lack of activity, imitation of other horses or possibly a medical problem such as painful feet.

- Weaving leads to loss of condition, nervousness and lameness through stress on the front legs.

- Find the cause. If the horse is suffering from sore feet give treatment, call the Vet or Farrier. If boredom or inactivity either exercise more frequently, put the horse out in the field or paddock, feed ad lib hay, or change to a box in a more interesting part of the yard. If caused through imitation, remove the horse to a different part of the yard.

An anti-weave gate successfully stops the horse weaving over the door. Those that are dedicated weavers however, will continue this habit in the box. Some even weave in the field, in which case the horse is probably a confirmed weaver and cannot be cured.

Crib-biting

- The horse grabs hold of projecting wood or metal such as the stable door, manger or fence in the field with his incisor teeth and bites.

- Crib-biting is caused by boredom, inactivity and imitation.

- Crib-biting damages the teeth and, when associated with windsucking, may cause respiratory problems.

- Remove all projecting edges in the box and use Cribox over the remainder. This is a tarry, creosote type paste that is unpleasant to taste. Smear it two or three times for a week over all the areas the horse can bite in the stable.

- Prevent boredom and inactivity if at all possible. Crib-biting often begins when the horse is off work, on box rest. Give hay ad lib and walk in hand if possible.

   When my horse was off work for a few weeks with a leg injury I was horrified to find that he started crib-biting. Whether this began through boredom, lack of activity or because the horse next door had the habit, possibly all three, I could not prove.

   I smeared everything in sight with Cribox, stable door, window ledge, slats of wood on the walls, anything on which he could bite. It caused an awful mess, my hands were sticky for days and the horse finished up looking a tarry mess, but it cured him. He never did it again.

- If this does not stop the habit, a muzzle, a crib strap or a Grinders Bit may be used. These are extreme measures and again personal experience shows that these gadgets will not cure a confirmed crib-biter. However, anything is worth trying to stop the habit, which eventually can also lead to windsucking.

Windsucking

- The horse arches his neck and sucks in air.

- This habit is normally connected with crib-biting and is caused by boredom, lack of activity and imitation.

- This can result in problems with the respiratory system and leads to loss of condition and the possibility of colic. It also develops large muscles under the neck.

- A crib strap may offer a cure. Windsucking and crib-biting are difficult to control once established and must be declared if the horse is being sold, or the contract is null and void.

Eating Bedding

- The horse persistently eats his bed. Though most horses on a straw bed will eat a certain amount, a horse who gorges himself on straw will have problems.

- The causes include lack of roughage in the diet, worm infestation, boredom and inactivity.

- Eating the bedding can lead to loss of condition through a nutritional imbalance. There can also be respiratory problems, when dust, spores or pieces of rough straw become lodged in the throat or cause an allergy in the respiratory tract.

- Bed down on different bedding such as shavings, shredded paper or peat. Check the horse's diet to assess if he needs more roughage. Give him ad lib hay, put him out to pasture more frequently and try worming him with a different Wormer or more frequently for a period.

- If it is necessary to use straw, the bed may be sprinkled with disinfectant to discourage eating. There is also a specially treated straw on the market. However both these methods can cause other problems; the horse may develop an allergic reaction such as conjunctivitis (an eye condition) or dermatitis (a skin condition).

Eating Droppings or Chewing Wood

- The horse consistently eats the droppings or chews wood in the stable or in the field. Eating droppings results in worm infestation and loss of condition through nutritional deficiencies. Chewing wood can result in damage to the teeth or injuries from splinters.

- Both these habits may begin as dietary problems.

- Check the horse's diet for mineral/vitamin or fibre content. Keep the stable skipped out continuously and, if possible the field or paddock clear of droppings. Worm the horse possibly using a different brand of Wormer. Smear Cribox over wood. If the problems persist call the Vet. In extreme circumstances the use of a muzzle, cradle or grass reins may help to prevent the horse eating the droppings or wood.

Kicking Stable Walls

- The horse continuously or periodically kicks the stable walls.

- Causes include irritation from a neighbouring horse, persistent flies and fly bites on the legs or even vermin in the box. It can also be from frustration or boredom in a lonely box. Sometimes a horse in pain will kick the box walls.

- Check the horse's health first to assess if he is in pain and needs medical attention. Check for parasites, insects and vermin. Change the box, put the horse out to pasture more frequently, or exercise more often. Alternatively, as a last resort, the whole box can be padded with straw or straw bales.

Pawing the Ground and Banging the Stable Door

- Normally at feed times, but some horses persist throughout the day.

- Shows impatience when related to feed times. At other times shows stress, boredom and lack of attention. Pawing may also be caused by a lack of bedding. Sometimes the horse just wants to make a noise to attract attention.

- These habits can injure the horse's legs resulting in soreness, bruising and concussion (and a groom's headache).

- Thick matting on the door and floor will prevent the noise. A rubber tyre hung on the inside of the door can discourage kicking. Pawing may be resolved by a deep, clean bed.

Rug Tearing

- The horse constantly turns round to bite the rug, or grabs hold of the front of the rug and tears it.

- This can be caused by irritation, infection, skin problems or parasites. It can also be a result of boredom or frustration.

- Find the cause and treat. Change the rug if the material is irritating the skin. If the habit persists, a strong leather bib under the chin can offer a solution.

Biting or Kicking in Box

- The horse turns vicious in the box.

- These are particularly dangerous habits and can cause severe casualties to handlers.

- These habits usually stem from mismanagement – bad handling, rough grooming and treatment resulting in pain and fear. The horse is relatively trapped in his box and the only way in which he can communicate is by bad behaviour. If the problem is not recognised, understood and dealt with immediately the results are a dangerous, bad tempered horse. There may be a medical cause; the horse could be suffering from pain. It can also be caused by feeding too many titbits. Some horses become 'territorial' when in their box. The box may be too small and the horse feels trapped, claustrophobic, or it could be through boredom causing stress and anxiety.

- Try and discover the cause. Changing boxes, either to a larger box or one in a busier or maybe quieter, part of the yard may help. Assess the horse's health, especially if he is not normally vicious. Stop feeding titbits and prevent other people from doing this by putting a notice outside the horse's box.

- Often the origin of the problem is never known. Experienced staff only should handle the horse in his box. He should be restrained with a headcollar and lead rope whenever he is handled in the box. In bad cases of biting, two lead ropes tied to two rings will prevent him from swinging his head around.

- Firmness in handling is necessary to let the horse know when he is doing wrong. He should be reprimanded every time he tries to bite or kick. A sharp tone of voice or a slap on the muzzle when he tries to bite may discourage him. At the same time he will need kindness and understanding especially if he has been treated badly in the past. Every time he is handled and does not bite, pat him and give him a word of praise. Always reward good behaviour so that the horse learns and understands what is expected of him.

- Groom him with care especially around the sensitive areas of the belly and girth.

Box Walking

- The horse restlessly walks around his box leaving a worn track of bedding.

- This is caused by boredom, claustrophobia, nervousness or illness.

- The horse loses weight, condition and may become 'one-sided'; the muscles on one side of his body develop more than on the other. The shoes become worn more quickly; the leg joints and feet suffer from concussion.

- Check the horse's health. Exercise the horse more frequently or allow him more time in the field or paddock. Feed hay ad lib. A change of boxes could help. In extreme circumstances the horse may have to be tied up for part of the time in the box, though once unrestrained he can tend to walk the box again.

Note: If the horse is overweight, feeding ad lib hay is not ideal. Feed hay in a horseage net (smaller holes) as this will keep his attention longer, or one haynet inside another.

Refusal to Lie Down

- This is sometimes a difficult habit to notice as horses do not lie down specifically to rest. This habit is usually associated with general restlessness and box walking.

- Normally caused by nervousness in the box, illness or insufficient bedding.

- The results will be a stressed and tired horse.

- Check the horse's health. Using more bedding may encourage the horse to rest. Try a different type of bedding. The horse can be given long steady work. If the problem persists and the horse's health is deteriorating, contact the Vet.

Tail Rubbing

- The horse is constantly scratching his tail against the wall of the box, the fence or a tree in the field.

- The cause could be sweet itch or pinworms eggs around the anus.

- Find the cause. If the cause is sweet itch, treat as normal and ask the Vet for assistance. For pinworm eggs use an appropriate Wormer, clean around the anus and shampoo the tail.

- Tail rubbing can be stopped but, as with most habits, the more prolonged the problem the harder it is to eradicate.

Pulling Back in a Headcollar

- The horse pulls back when tied up in a headcollar. Some horses even refuse to be tied up at all.

- This is normally caused by being frightened when restrained. The horse pulled back and subsequently suffered with pain around the poll area, especially if he was tied to a solid object and could not break the lead rope. Sometime a horse pulls so hard, the lead rope or even the headcollar has to be cut to free him.

- Always tie the lead rope to a piece of string, which will break the moment the horse pulls back. Once free the horse no longer pulls. Twine is satisfactory providing it is not too strong. Nylon string is not suitable.

- Alternatively use a lunge line. This is put through the securing ring so that it can slip whenever the horse pulls back. The handler can keep control so that the horse does not go free. The handler should wear gloves when holding the line.

- This can be a difficult habit to break. Kindness or firmness should both be tried. Often just looping the lead rope through the string makes the horse feel less threatened.

Tack Problems

There are various behavioural problems associated with tack. Most of these are caused by bad management, handling, rough treatment, ignorance, lack of understanding and sympathy. Some are caused through lack of discipline.

There is little wrong with having a soft and sympathetic nature, but when the horse is allowed to behave badly without reprimand, or the discipline is inconsistent, this can cause just as much trouble as roughness.

Biting or Kicking when the Girth is Fastened

- This is a common problem especially with older horses and those that are highly-strung, sensitive or thin-skinned.

- Normally caused by the girth being pulled too tightly too fast, pinching the sensitive skin around the girth, painful memories from girth galls, rough handling, ill fitting girth. The memory of such rough handling and pain will last for years, usually a lifetime.

- This bad behaviour should be reprimanded every time the horse tries to bite or kick when the girth is tightened. The girth should be fastened slowly and gently, particularly on sensitive horses. The horse should be allowed to have some time with a loose girth before it is tightened. Always tighten the girth carefully, avoid pain.

- If the horse tries to bite or kick he should be warned with a stern voice. A mild slap on the muzzle if he tries to bite should discourage him. Hold the reins so that the offside rein is shorter to prevent the horse from swinging his head around. Holding the whip near to the horse's head so that he can see it clearly, often discourages him from swinging his head around.

- Always reward the horse with a pat if he behaves well to show that this is the way he should react in future.

- Every new rider or handler should be taught to fasten and tighten the girth with care. They should also be taught to watch for the horse trying to bite or kick.

Problems with the Bridle

- Some horses react when the headpiece is placed near their poll. Others refuse to open their mouth for the bit or raise the head so high it is almost impossible to reach.

- Rough handling, memory of pain around the poll, bad manners, lack of discipline, sore mouth all contribute to these bad habits. Sometimes caused by being led incorrectly in a bridle, when the handler 'pulls' the horse along and hurts the poll or mouth.

- Firmness, patience and kindness must all be tried. The horse has to learn to accept the bridle and the bit. If the horse is sensitive around his poll, keep trying slowly and patiently to stroke him around his ears. This can take years and some horses are so badly frightened that the bridle has to be dismantled before being put on. Keep trying with patience. Be strict every time and again use patience if he is frightened.

Cold-Backed when Mounting

- The horse moves around, pulls back, is fidgety and restless whenever a rider tries to mount. In extreme cases the horse may rear, buck or pull back so fast the rider either cannot mount or is thrown on the floor.

- Normally caused by memory of pain through saddle sores, an ill fitting saddle or a heavy rider thumping down on the saddle and the horse's back. May also be caused by back pain.

- Check the horse's back. Call the Vet if any doubt particularly if the horse has recently started being cold-backed. If the horse is genuinely frightened, patience and careful handling will be required. Experienced riders only should mount and ride the horse. Keep his attention with some titbits whilst the rider mounts.

- It may help, particularly on cold winter days, to walk the horse around in his tack for a few minutes before mounting. This will help him to warm up his muscles, especially around his back.

- Discipline is essential; the rider is more vulnerable when mounting than at any other time. The horse must learn to stand still. It does sometimes help if only one person mounts and rides him for a while, especially for a school horse used by many clients.

Bridle Lameness

- The horse backs off the bridle and will sometimes appear unlevel in action.

- Caused by bad, rough riding, an ill-fitting bridle, sore mouth, memory of pain.

- Check the horse's health with particular attention to the head and mouth areas. Patience, good riding, well fitted tack and time hopefully will erase the bad memories.

Problems when Ridden

- The horse is nappy, that is he refuses to go where the rider wants. He may lean or veer towards the rest of the ride, another horse, the school door or menage gate. He may even spin round, refuse to go forwards, buck, rear, twist and turn to avoid going in a particular direction.

  Horses do perceive the world in different ways and it may be that something is frightening the horse, or he associates a particular place with pain. However he cannot be allowed to persist in being nappy. The horse ultimately has to learn to obey the rider under almost all circumstances. If he is allowed to disobey the rider, this will cause endless trouble. After all in a competition the horse has to go where the rider asks, he has to become accustomed to outside noise and movement without flinching.

The rider can attempt to calm the horse, to build his confidence and in some circumstances this works. At other times, it takes firmness and persistence from the rider to insist the horse goes where the rider wants.

- The horse's behaviour changes, he does not work as well as normal. He may find flatwork difficult or not move as he should. He may start refusing at jumps, jump badly or start to run out at fences.

If the horse is normally keen, there could be a physical problem. He may be feeling pain in which case call the Vet. If the problem is mental, it may be that he has experienced pain through bad riding. This will take time to build up his confidence again. He may be tired of jumping, in which case give him time off. Either work him differently, flatwork, lungeing and hacking, or give him a short holiday. Horses sometimes rush fences because they have experienced pain, probably through the bit if the rider pulled on the reins over the jump.

For riding problems it is always worth considering physical pain or illness first. If there is no apparent physical reason, then the problem could be mental. The rider needs to use his experience and knowledge to discover the reason for riding problems.

Whatever the problems and difficulties, at all times the horse needs a strong, firm, disciplined leader, one in whom he can place his trust. In many circumstances even when the horse is frightened, being firm gives him the confidence to face his fears and overcome them. Always correct bad behaviour, reward good.

Exam Tips

Dealing with stable vices and behavioural problems is closely associated with horse psychology. A study of the horse, his natural lifestyle, his characteristics and instincts will help any owner, handler or groom to understand why the horse behaves in certain ways to various stimuli and environments. Experienced riders and grooms become aware of a possible difficulty before it happens and will either avoid the situation or be prepared to deal with the problem.

In the Stage III Examination you will be asked about stable vices, their possible causes, prevention or cures. Safety should always be the most important aspect. If a horse is behaving in a dangerous manner, never try to handle the situation if this puts you in danger. Keep yourself safe first, then when the horse has quietened down, deal with the problem or ask help from someone more experienced.

C H A P T E R   13
Ride and Lead

This exercise, where the rider rides one horse and leads another, is useful in a variety of circumstances. There are precautions, which are necessary for the safety of the horses and rider.

Reasons for Ride and Lead

1) Variety of work – a different form of exercise.

2) Alternative to lungeing – if the horse cannot be lunged for some reason such as no area to lunge safely.

3) If the led horse cannot be ridden – tack sores, lack of time.

4) The owner's inability to ride – through illness, injury or lack of time.

5) Fittening work – at the start of a fittening programme before the horse has developed sufficient muscle to wear the tack everyday. If the horse is saddled this can harden the saddle and girth areas without the rider.

6) Staff shortages – if the yard does not have sufficient staff to exercise the horses.

7) Leading another horse for a rider – the rider may be injured and the horse has to be led home. The rider may be meeting the ride and the horse is not able to be transported by box. This happens occasionally when hunting.

8) The horse or pony being led is used as a pack carrier or as a substitute when required – often on trekking holidays.

Advantages

* Time saving especially for a yard with few staff, or possibly an owner with two or more horses to exercise everyday.

* Labour-saving, one person can work two horses at the same time.

* Keeping the horse fit if he cannot be ridden, particularly if the alternative is keeping the horse in the box. This applies to horses with illnesses that make riding impossible. Obviously the horse should not have a contagious or infectious disease.

Disadvantages

❖   The rider has to be competent to lead and to deal with situations if they arise.

❖   Possibility of injury to either horse. Even when the rider is competent, the horse being led is not under as much control as when ridden, and accidents can occur.

❖   Demanding on the rider who has to concentrate on two horses instead of one. If both horses misbehave or become frightened, the situation can be more difficult to control.

❖   The horse being led does not work as hard as if ridden. Over a period of time, the horses can be alternated, so that each horse is ridden every other day.

Equipment

The rider and both horses need to wear protective clothing and the correct tack for maximum safety.

The Rider

The rider should wear all the correct clothing, a correctly fitted BSI approved hat with three point harness, gloves and, if necessary, a jacket fastened properly. A body protector will offer further protection. Long boots will be safer than short jodhpur boots, offering more protection if the rider's leg becomes trapped between the two horses. The rider should carry a short whip.

The Horses

The horse being ridden is tacked as normal, bridle, saddle, girth fastened sufficiently tight.   The horse being led should **always wear a bridle**; this offers more control than a headcollar. Though a snaffle bridle is preferable, the horse may be led in a double using the bridoon reins only. The curb reins can be twisted and held safely out of the way by being looped through the throatlash. A running martingale should be removed completely, or have the rings detached from the reins and secured through the neckstrap.

Saddle

If a saddle is used on the horse being led, the girth should be checked before the start. The stirrups should be safely secured as if for lungeing.

If the stirrup leathers are quite loose on the stirrup bars, the catch can be pushed up to the 'closed' position to prevent them from sliding and dropping off. If the leathers are quite tight or secure with the catch in the 'open' position, there is no need to close it. If the leathers do become caught on a bush or tree they will slip off; this is safer than the leathers becoming entangled and the horse panicking.

The saddle may have the extra safety of a breastplate; particularly useful at the start of a fittening programme when the saddle may not fit snugly and slide backwards. A breastplate will also keep the saddle steadier preventing saddle rubs or friction sores.

Leading Rope

The horse can be led either with the bridle reins or a lead rope. The reins are passed over the horse's head and used straight from both bit rings. If using a lead rope, this may be attached to the nearest bit ring or the far bit ring (usually the left ring) and passed under the horse's chin through the nearest bit ring. The rope should have a knot or loop at the end so that it does not slip out of the rider's hand.

If there is a leather coupling joining the two bit rings the rope can be attached to this. Alternatively a lungeing cavesson can be used with the rope fastened to the middle ring at the front. When leading with a lead rope, the bridle reins should be made safe by being twisted and secured through the throatlash.

Saddle Cloths and Exercise Sheets

Numnahs or saddle cloths may be worn by both horses providing they are fitted securely and will not slide and fold up under the saddle.

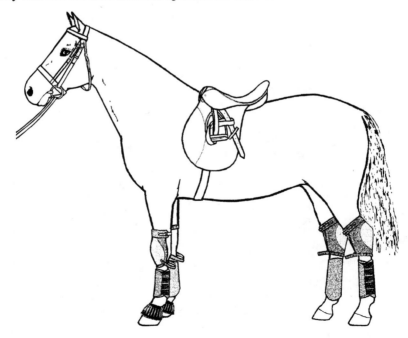

In cold weather the horses may need an exercise sheet each, which can be fitted and attached to the saddle. The exercise sheet must have a fillet string to fit under the tail so that the sheet does not blow up over the horse's back.

Protective Clothing

The horses should wear as much protection for their legs as possible. Brushing boots on all legs. If there is only one set of boots then the horse being led can wear a fore and a hind boot on his offside legs and the ridden horse on his nearside legs. Though this is not ideal, at least the horses will have protection against injuring each other.

Knee caps and hock boots, if available, will give protection to these joints. Overreach or petal boots protect the coronet and heels.

Bandages are not advisable. If these become loose they may wrap around the horse's legs. If boots come off they generally drop away neatly and can be collected later.

Method

Check the tack and boots before taking the horses out of the stables, and certainly prior to mounting, especially if someone else has tacked up the horses.

Preparation

If there is an assistant to help, this will make mounting easier. The assistant can hold the horse to be led until the rider is safely mounted then hand the horse to the rider. Often, though, there is no help and the rider has to organise the two horses alone.

Take one horse from the stable and tie him up safely with a headcollar over the bridle. The tack can be checked again now. Take the other horse from the stable and check the tack. Collect the restrained horse and take both horses to a safe place to mount.

Mounting

With the horse to be led on the left or nearside of the other horse, first position the horses at right angles to each other.

Keep them apart for safety.

Position the horse being led so that his head is adjacent to the ridden horse's shoulder.

Holding the lead rope, reins and the whip in the left hand, mount as normal. Pass the whip into the right hand and walk off slowly. The whip is held in the rider's right hand, except when signalling to the right.

Riding

The reins or lead rope of the horse being led are held in the rider's left hand. The length should be kept fairly short so that the horse's head is level with the ridden horse's shoulder or the rider's knee. The horse being led should never be in front of the ridden horse or allowed too far back behind the rider's knee. In these situations either horse may bite or kick the other.

When riding and leading on the road the horse being led should be on the left of the ridden horse, between the ridden horse and the kerb.

Signalling

During the ride and lead, follow the rules of the road. Always look behind before signalling, observe thoroughly the situation behind and in front before manoeuvring.

When turning left and signalling with the left hand, the reins of both horses and the whip are held in the right hand. When turning right, the reins are held in the rider's left hand. The top of the whip is also held in the left hand. The rider should not signal with the whip in the hand.

Make the hand signal clear, at shoulder level. Continue to look around and observe the traffic conditions.

The Public Highway

If possible it is wiser to avoid ride and lead on roads, especially busy main roads and winding, narrow country lanes. The volume of traffic on main roads make this hazardous, motorists are not always patient or aware of the dangers. On country lanes motorists often drive too fast mistakenly thinking that these roads are quieter and therefore safer.

Unfortunately it is almost impossible to avoid riding on roads or lanes. Wearing bright fluorescent clothing during the day, or reflective clothing in murky conditions will increase the safety of the rider and horses. Any type of fluorescent or reflective clothing and tack will make the rider and horses more visible; tabard, hat cover, arm bands, brushing boots, tail bandage, exercise sheet, even stirrup lights in really dark conditions.

The Highway Code

When riding on the public highway, the rider should know and obey the rules of the Highway Code.

* The rider should never ride on the pavement unless it is absolutely necessary.

* Verges may be ridden on, providing they are not privately owned or are in a district where the bye-laws prohibit this action.

* Avoid riding on verges if these are dangerous, that is with potholes, ditches, rubbish.

* When riding on the public highway always look behind, ahead, around and behind again before signalling or performing any manoeuvre.

* Allow a wide berth to stationary vehicles.

* When turning right, either at a junction or into another road, keep to the left, walk straight across. Do not cut corners or ride in the centre of the road.

The Country Code

When riding in the countryside, riders need to show consideration to pedestrians and be aware of dangers such as yapping dogs.

* Horses should not be ridden over fields especially if the fields are ploughed, or have crops growing.

* Horses should not be ridden through livestock in fields.

* Ride around fields keeping to the track.

* Ride on permitted bridleways only.

* Leave all gates as found.

* Ride past pedestrians and other riders with care, if possible at walk.

Weather Conditions

Horses still have to be exercised in bad weather, but there are some conditions in which it is dangerous to ride out especially on the public highway.

* Avoid riding at dusk, night times or in murky conditions.

* Avoid frosty, icy or slippery conditions, heavy snowstorms, thunder and lightening, heavy gales.

Dismounting

Bring both horses to a halt.

* Ask the ridden horse for a quarter turn on the forehand to the left so that his hindquarters move to the right.

* At the same time allow the lead rope out slightly.

* This will give ample room to dismount.

The offside stirrup can be laid over in front of the saddle before the rider dismounts.

The near side stirrup can either be laid over the saddle or secured as normal.

Tie the led horse up, then put the ridden horse into the stable and remove the tack. Put away the other horse and untack him.

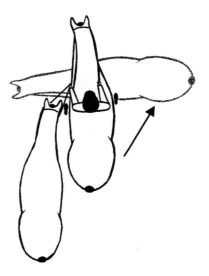

Safety

Before taking two horses on a ride and lead, the rider should first check if the horses are accustomed to this type of exercise. Practise in a safe area, an indoor school or outside menage before taking the horses out of the yard.

This is also a good time to check if the horses are compatible. Occasionally horses react when another horse is brought near; some mares, especially in season, can behave badly.

Keep to a safe route. Avoid any hazards if possible, such as road works, busy main roads.

Unless absolutely necessary the rider should avoid dismounting whilst out on the ride. Trying to mount again with two horses out on the road or in the countryside can be very difficult and dangerous.

Avoid halting and standing still for any length of time, in case the horses become restless.

The safety precautions for ride and lead are extremely important. Riding one horse in the countryside or on the road may be hazardous enough; taking two horses out doubles the risk.

It is frightening how many people who do ride and lead have little idea of safety. All too often motorists are faced with the lead horse in a headcollar and lead rope on the right hand side, next to the traffic, with the rider apparently having little or no control. The British Horse Society is concerned with the safety of both riders and horses. If more riders were aware of the dangers and of the simple safety precautions there would be fewer accidents.

Problems

If at any time problems do occur the rider will need to react quickly, quietly and efficiently.

- If the led horse suddenly pulls back, slow the ridden horse down or halt. Encourage the led horse to return to his position and walk on quietly. Talk to the horses to reassure them.

- If the led horse continues to pull back and resist, rather than lose the horse or be pulled off the saddle, it may be necessary to dismount and lead both horses home.

- If either horse becomes nervous and naps, speak quietly but firmly and try to encourage forward movement.

- If a situation arises which is dangerous, for example if one of the horses continues to nap and becomes disobedient, rather than have a battle, dismount and lead both horses. Alternatively the rider can dismount, mount the led horse and lead the other horse. This is one reason why it is better for the horse being led to wear a saddle.

- Always inform someone responsible at the yard of the planned route and the approximate time it will take.

- Take a portable phone or some money for a public telephone in case of emergencies.

- If the worst happens and the led horse escapes, either follow him home quietly or dismount and catch him if he is stood grazing nearby. Ask for help, if possible, from a passer-by. At all costs keep safe; do not rush off after the horse.

The ride and lead exercise can be useful in the work schedule for keeping horses fit whilst saving time. The type of exercise can last up to one hour as a normal work period. If the horse is being exercised as part of a fittening programme the time can be reduced accordingly.

Exam Tips

Preparation for this part of the Stage III will need practice at least three or four times before the Examination. As part of the study preparation for the ride and lead revising the rules for the Riding and Road Safety Test before the Stage III may help.

Revision

Riding and Road Safety Test – Stage II book.

During the Examination, always check the tack of both horses before mounting, even if the horses have been used before. The Examiner may ask if you are satisfied with the horses' protective clothing. If not, then express your opinions and reasons.

To prepare the ridden horse check the nearside stirrup first then, keeping the horses apart, lean over the saddle and push the offside stirrup down. If this is not possible, you may mount then push the stirrup down. The offside stirrup can be changed when mounted; remember to keep both feet in the stirrups if altering the length.

You will have to mount the horse yourself, so keep the led horse at right angles and away from the ridden horse giving yourself plenty of room to mount. *Once mounted remember to change the whip to the right hand.*

You will be asked to make the appropriate hand signals for turning. Even if riding in a car park or field, the Examiners will need to see the correct sequence of look, signal and manoeuvre as if you were on the Public Highway.

You will be asked to trot for a short distance. Warn the horse being led before you start off by saying 'trot on' whilst giving the leg aids to your own horse. Remember to look behind over your right shoulder first, to check for 'traffic' both prior to trotting and before returning to walk.

C H A P T E R   14
Travelling

Transporting horses or ponies requires careful preparation and planning, particularly if the horse (or owner) is not accustomed to loading, unloading and travelling to different places. Forward planning is vital, especially when travelling to an important show or event.

Revision Stage II

Travel clothing – poll guard, rugs, tail and leg protection. Putting on and fitting the travel clothing. Planning and preparation. Restraint in the box. How to load and unload. Loading problems. Animal Transport Certificate and new legislation for travelling.

Preparation for Travelling

Horses and ponies are transported for various reasons, to a new home, to an event or competition, for a hack, a sponsored ride, to have a lesson or training session. Even sometimes to the Vet's to be given medical attention. Whatever the reason the aim is to load, transport and unload the horse with as little stress as possible and with safety.

Preparation can begin days ahead.

❖ Entry forms for a show generally need to be completed and returned a few weeks or days in advance.

❖ Plan the route, especially if travelling to a new location. There is nothing worse than losing the way to an important show, arriving late and stressed. Consideration should also be given when planning the route. Driving along winding, narrow country lanes is not advisable with a large vehicle.

❖ Timing – calculate the time required to prepare the horse and box for loading, travelling to the venue, unloading and working the horse in, then, in addition, include extra time in case of loading or traffic problems.

❖ The travel equipment and tack will need checking before the day of travel. Any cleaning, repair or replacement can then be done in plenty of time.

Travel Equipment

Making a list of all the items required helps to ensure that vital equipment is not forgotten.

∗ A map or route to the destination.

∗ Money for the phone or a portable phone (in case of emergencies).

∗ Telephone numbers of the AA or RAC, insurance, the Vet, the Farrier.

∗ Dressage sheets, entry forms, horse's registration card, horse's inoculation card (this is compulsory at some shows), any other documentation necessary.

∗ Medical kit.

∗ Grooming kit including a hoof pick and plenty of elastic bands or thread for plaiting.

∗ Tack - bridle, saddle, numnah or saddle cloth, martingale or breastplate, spare girth if possible and any surcingle girths necessary. Boots; brushing, overreach.

∗ A can of oil is useful in case the fastenings or catches on the trailer or box become stuck.

∗ Water and water bucket. There is usually a water supply on the show ground but not always and for long journeys water may not be available. It is also more hygienic to take water particularly if large numbers of horses are drinking from the same trough.

∗ Feed and feed bucket - if out all day or for several hours.

∗ Hay - two haynets – one for the outward journey in the trailer and one for return. For long journeys it is wise to take extra.

∗ Skip and small shovel. If the horse messes the trailer on the way out this will need clearing for the homeward journey.

＊ Rider's clothes – hat, gloves, whip, body protector, showing jacket, jodhpurs if changing. Tie and shirt can be worn under a sweatshirt and even jodhpurs can be kept clean under a pair of strong, jogging trousers. Waterproof jacket, short and long whips, riding boots.

＊ Travel clothes, boots or bandages and fibregee, overreach boots, kneecaps, hock boots, tail bandage, tail guard, poll guard, headcollar and lead rope. Rugs, sweat sheet, summer sheet, New Zealand. A piece of string is useful if the horse needs to be tied up at the venue.

Each type of equipment can be put in a separate box; this makes it easier to find when needed. For example a medical box, a tack box, a grooming kit box, a travel boot or bandage box, a rider's box for clothes and a documents box. The stacking boxes are very useful and take up less space.

The Horse

A few days before, the horse's general health will need monitoring whilst being exercised. His shoes will need checking and if he is due for shoeing, it may be possible to have him shod a couple of days early before the event. If he is due to be wormed or vaccinated these should be done 3 to 5 days before travelling.

If the horse has never been boxed before, has not travelled for some time or it is not known how he will react, he should be introduced to the box or trailer before the day. Taking him on a couple of small journeys first will help him to be calm and confident. Waiting until the day of the show to discover that the horse is nervous, difficult or will not go in the box will not do anyone's nerves any good.

The Trailer or Box

The trailer or horsebox should be checked a few days before: tyre pressure, fuel, lights, brakes, and towing bar. The inside may need brushing or cleaning out if it has become dusty. Check the towing vehicle: brakes, lights, tyre pressure, water, oil.

The Day Before

Preparing as much as possible the day before travel will save time and energy. Clean the tack and check the travel clothes. Travel boots or bandages, tail bandage or tail guard should have been washed and dried after their previous use. Check the medical box and grooming kit. Then collect everything together and load as much as possible into the towing vehicle or horsebox.

If starting off early the next day it saves time to loose plait the horse's mane, that is plait but leave the plaits hanging down. The horse may rub one or two plaits during the night but these can easily be plaited again in the morning. The horse's tail should not be plaited overnight as he will probably rub the tail and then the hair becomes very knotted. If the horse or pony is out at night and he has had a bath, putting a light New Zealand rug on him overnight will keep him relatively clean, providing the weather is not too hot.

Prepare the trailer or horsebox and fill up with fuel. It is easier to sort out any problems and to fill the tank the day before, than at 6 a.m., on a cold and frosty morning.

Preparing to Travel

The trailer or horsebox is prepared first. If the horse is dressed in his travel clothes first and he is highly strung, nervous or just excited about going out, he will be as high as a kite by the time the transport is ready.

Lights and brakes are checked again, and the tyres on both towing vehicle and trailer, better safe than sorry.

✷   To check the headlights, indicator and brake lights, ask someone to go behind the trailer or box and to call out when they see the lights.

✷   For trailers, check that the trailer is firmly attached to the towing vehicle, that the safety line is secured correctly. There have been occasions when the towing vehicle has been driven off leaving the trailer and horses behind.

✷   Check that the brake is off on the trailer.

It is advisable when travelling with a trailer to take the wheel clamp on the journey. If the trailer has to be left unattended, for instance if travelling alone, the wheel clamp should be attached to the trailer in case of theft. Trailer theft is on the increase and it only takes a few minutes to fix the wheel clamp for security.

Some bedding can be laid down on the floor of the trailer or box if necessary. Trailers with rubber matting may not need bedding. Put the rest of the equipment into the towing vehicle.

Check the string inside on the securing rings and tie up the haynet, or nets, if more than one horse is travelling.

Park the trailer parallel to a fence, if possible, so as to block one line of escape. Position the trailer with the interior facing towards the light so that horse is not walking into a black hole.

Take the ramp down and make sure it is steady on firm ground.

Close the groom's door or the front ramp, if open, so that the horse does not attempt to go out the front. Double trailers sometimes have a central partition that moves to offer more room. It is better if the horse will load without moving the partition as this means fiddling around when the horse is loaded.

Once everything is ready with the trailer or box, prepare the horse: groom, plait if necessary and put on the travelling clothes.

The handler should now put on a riding hat, gloves and be wearing boots. These may seem irrelevant with a quiet well-behaved horse, but every horse has his moment and the handler needs protection against any possible injury.

Loading

It is always safer and easier to have assistance. A horse may be loaded by a single person, but it is risky and more awkward.

Ask one assistant to stand by the open side of the ramp, that is, the ramp away from the fence. If the other side is open, ask another assistant to stand at that side. The assistants need to stand about a foot away from the side of the ramps. If they are too close they may intimidate the horse or become trampled if the horse suddenly steps sideways.

Designate one assistant to fasten the breech bar or strap (the bar or strap behind the horse's hindquarters) once the horse is loaded. If the assistant is unsure how to do this, demonstrate beforehand so that everything is slick and efficient when the loading begins.

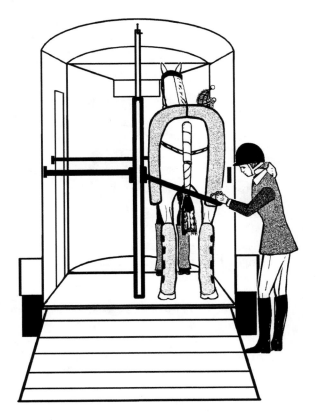

The assistant fastening the breech bar should stand to one side as much as possible in case the horse kicks. Never allow anyone to stand directly behind the horse when he is in the trailer.

Bring the horse to the trailer leading him quietly on the nearside, not pulling him, but walking beside him. **Never wrap the rope around the hand.**

With an unfamiliar horse, or one that may prove difficult, a bridle can be put on over the headcollar for further safety and control. The bridle can then be removed once the horse is safely in the trailer.

Lead the horse straight to the ramp and, without looking back at him, walk up the ramp and into the trailer; the horse should follow quietly.

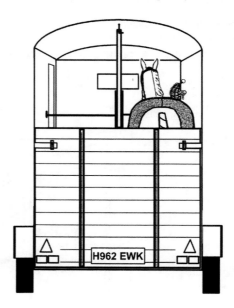

When one horse travels, and there is a partition, the horse should travel in the right hand side of the trailer. Travelling on the crown of the road is smoother and keeps the trailer balanced.

If one horse only is travelling and there is no partition, use two leadropes tied to two rings, one on each side of the trailer.

If there is room, stand beside the horse whilst the breech bar is secured. If not, slip underneath the front bar and hold the horse. Do not tie the horse up until the breech bar is up and fastened. Then restrain the horse on a fairly short length of rope, long enough so that he can eat his hay but not move his head too much.

Once ready tell the assistants to raise the ramp. It often helps if the assistants call out that the ramp is being raised, the person inside is then warned, can talk to and calm the horse.

The ramp should be raised slowly and as quietly as possible. With one horse travelling fasten the side that is empty first and then the side on which the horse is loaded. Again stand to the side whilst fastening the ramp. There have been cases where people have been crushed beneath the ramp when the horse kicked out before the fastenings were secure.

Make sure all doors and partitions are properly secured. Exit through the groom's door and lock it.

Single Person Loading

In circumstances where one person is loading, the horse does need to be accustomed to travelling and good to load. A lunge line can be attached to the headcollar and the horse taken into the trailer or box as normal. The line is passed through the string of the securing ring and the handler, holding onto the line, can secure the breech strap or partition. If the horse does start to move or back out the line can be held firmly to prevent him. Once the breech strap is in place, the lunge line can be unattached and horse tied up with the lead rope.

Alternatively the lead rope can be passed through the securing ring and left untied whilst the breech strap is fastened. Some horses will go into the trailer or box on their own; if they are trained and accustomed to doing this it is normally quite safe.

Loading Problems

When loading any problems should be dealt with firmly, promptly and quietly.

If the horse hangs back, walk by his shoulder and encourage him to walk on. Pulling the horse from the front with the lead rope often has the opposite effect. The horse can back up, holding his head high and resisting. An assistant stood at a safe distance behind the horse may also encourage him to move forward.

If he refuses to load, discover the cause if possible. The horse may be frightened or nervous. Entice him with food, a carrot or some food in a bucket.

In a trailer removing the partition or opening the front ramp may encourage the horse, as the trailer looks lighter and more spacious. If the front ramp is down, remember to keep the front bar up to prevent the horse walking straight through.

If the horse persists in being difficult, a couple of assistants standing a little distance away from the hindquarters may prevent the horse from stepping back. The assistants must stand to one side out of kicking range. One assistant carrying a whip may give the horse a slight tap on the hindquarters.

Speak to the horse firmly at the same time. If he is just being stubborn knowing that his handler is quite determined can sometimes work wonders.

Often a travelling companion already loaded will encourage the horse to enter the trailer or box.

Two people with a lunge line held between them can slowly walk towards the horse's hindquarters. Keeping the line taut, hold it against the horse just above the hocks and encourage him forwards. Alternatively one end of the lunge line can be tied to one side of the box. The other end of the line is held by an assistant and used against the horse's hindquarters in the same way.

In almost all cases the horse will load but dealing with difficulties needs lots of patience balanced with firmness. The horse should not win otherwise he will be impossible to load next time. The handlers or assistants should never lose their tempers or hurt the horse, this will give him a bad memory, and horses have an excellent memory for pain. With plenty of bribery, deviousness and persistence the horse will go into the trailer or horsebox.

Travelling

On the road the trailer should be driven carefully especially around bends, corners and roundabouts.

The maximum speed for a vehicle towing a trailer is 50 mph but this is really only possible on motorways or dual carriageways. Avoid potholes, ramps or other uneven surfaces as much as possible or at least drive over them slowly. Drive at a regular, steady speed so that the horse does not constantly lose his balance.

Think ahead, stopping takes more time with a trailer or horsebox. Anticipate traffic lights, junctions or other hazards so that braking is gradual. Avoid slamming on the brakes and coming to abrupt halts, except in an emergency.

Long Journeys

If the journey takes more than four hours, the horses should be checked and allowed a break. If they are too hot, sweating, breathing rapidly, replace the rug with a lighter cooler rug or blanket. If too cold, shivering, cold at the base of the ears, add another rug or blanket. Offer water and more hay.

If the journey is to last over six hours the horses will need a feed. It would also help, if at all possible, to take them out of the box or trailer and allow them to stretch their legs.

Clothing

In really cold weather a horse should certainly wear a stable rug. He may have a jute rug and blanket. When transporting more than a single horse the atmosphere is usually quite warm. A single horse in a large box may become quite chilled.

In hot weather the horse may not require a rug or blanket. A light, cotton summer sheet is quite useful to keep draughts off his back, to keep him clean and as a protection against flies.

Tack

For short journeys the horse can travel wearing his tack. A bridle can be put on underneath a headcollar. The reins should be made safe by being twisted up and held under the neck with the throatlash. In a large box, the saddle can also be put on but only if really necessary and there is no risk of the saddle being caught up on the partitions. A rug or blanket can be put on top of the saddle if travelling tacked up, providing this is properly secured.

In a trailer it is wiser to leave the saddle off especially if the trailer is narrow, has a partition and the horse is to be unloaded from a front ramp.

Brushing boots can also be put on for travelling but should have a travelling boot over the top for protection in the trailer or box.

When the horse is travelling for a long time, over four hours, a tail guard should be used instead of a tail bandage. The bandage may restrict circulation after a period and cause damage to the tail or dock.

Unloading

Park in area where the horse can unload in safety away from other parked vehicles or moving traffic. A flat piece of ground so that the ramp is steady and where the horse will have plenty of room to unload. If the trailer is front unload, remember which side the ramp will be lowered. Parking next to a tree and being unable to lower the ramp will mean moving the vehicle and trailer.

Enter the trailer by the groom's door and then close it. Untie the horse. Leave the front bar up, especially with front unloading so that the horse does not rush out before the ramp is down. Stand by him and quietly talk to him until everyone is ready.

With front unload, once the ramp is down, undo the front bar, move the partition and slowly lead the horse out. If he does try to barge, speak to him firmly telling him to be steady. Placing an elbow into the horse's chest area can encourage him to move more slowly. Then lead at a steady pace. Assistants stood to either side of the ramp at a safe distance can prevent him from jumping off the ramp.

If unloading two horses, each horse should have a handler. The horse nearest to the ramp should be unloaded first. The partition can then be moved for the other horse to prevent him squeezing past, injuring himself and squashing the handler.

For a rear unload, the ramp is lowered and an assistant then unfastens the breech strap, again standing to one side in case the horse rushes backwards or kicks. Gently, slowly back the horse down the ramp. Allow him time to stop and look around if he wants. Then encourage him to walk straight back so that he does not slip over the ramp and scratch his foot. One assistant standing to one side of the ramp can help to guide the horse down. Keep talking to the horse so that he is calm.

For a horsebox the horse must be made to wait until all the partitions are secured, then led quietly down the centre of the ramp.

Single Person Unload

For a front unload trailer and a horsebox, lower the ramp and enter. Untie the horse and leave the rope hanging through the ring. Undo the front bar and move the partitions. Lead the horse out.

For a rear unload trailer enter by the groom's door and then close it. Untie the horse and leave the rope through the ring. Lower ramp and undo breech strap. The horse may back out quietly on his own in which case catch the lead rope as he is coming down the ramp. Alternatively return to the horse and, holding the lead rope, persuade him to back out down the ramp.

Care on Arrival

After arriving and unloading the horse, check that he has not suffered any injury during the journey. Remove the travelling boots or bandages, any protective boots and the tail bandage. If it is a cold day, the horse can keep his rug on. Alternatively the horse can be tacked up and his rug put on over his saddle.

The horse may be quite nervous or excited; there will be a charged atmosphere. Other horses may be calling or being ridden close by. The horse should not be left on his own. If it is necessary to go somewhere, for example the show secretary for entry details, ask someone to watch the horse.

The horse should be given at least ten to twenty minutes to settle down before the start of the show. He will probably need exercising or lungeing to relieve stiffness, especially after a long journey.

If the trailer and towing vehicle or horsebox is to be left unattended whilst the horse is competing, these should be fully locked and secured.

Care at Home

Before loading to return home, any droppings should be cleaned out of the trailer or horsebox.

On arrival at the yard, the horse should again be checked for injury and then put away in his box to relax. If he is a seasoned campaigner he will probably slip back into his routine quite happily. If he is unused to travelling it may take him a while to settle down and during this period he should be given regular checks for sweating.

The trailer or horsebox will need cleaning out thoroughly. Any droppings left will rot the box floor and eventually turn mouldy or hard. The vehicle should be checked for any damage.

Care after the Competition

After the competition keep the horse warm and see to his needs immediately. If necessary walk him round to cool him off. The horse should not be boxed and taken home if sweating and hot, he needs to cool off properly first. If riding home, keep him moving steadily.

On arrival at home, put the horse into his stable and untack him. Do not let him stand about in the cold. Observe him in case he breaks out in a sweat, in which case he will need walking around to cool.

Check the horse for cuts, bruises or thorns. Check his feet, shoes and legs for injuries or swellings. Rug up or thatch a sweat rug, bandage his legs if necessary and undo the plaits. Give him hay and a little drink when ready.

Feed the horse when he is cool, usually with his normal feed. If he is tired dampen his feed to make it more digestible. Alternatively, if bran is available in the yard, adding some wet bran to his feed or giving him a bran mash will help to keep his digestive system working. Leave the horse to unwind and settle.

When he is relaxed brush off quickly. Do not strap, as he needs the rest. Check his rugs and if wet change them. Keep checking the horse to see if he is warm, not chilled or hot. (Feeling the base of his ears is a good indication of body warmth. These will be icy if he is chilled, or hot and sweaty if he has not cooled down sufficiently.) If there is time, check and clean all the tack especially if this has been wet. Set fair the box and put all items away.

Fix the wheel clamp on the trailer. When trailers are parked in their static position it is best to leave the brake off. If the brake is left on and the trailer is not moved for weeks or months the brake can lock the wheels.

All tack, feed or water buckets should be cleaned as soon as possible. Travel clothes should be thoroughly cleaned and dried ready for use next time.

Forms of Transport

There are regulations covering the transportation of animals that the horsebox and trailer owner/driver should know and observe. These can be found in the current edition of the 'Transit of Animals' from HMSO.

The type of transport used is normally a trailer, a horsebox or some type of lorry specially adapted to carry horses. Any vehicle transporting horses should be strong. Horses are large, heavy animals and having metal shod hooves can cause extensive damage.

All vehicles have a plating certificate, which describes the weight that each axle can carry. To exceed these limits is not only dangerous but is also an offence.

Before buying a horsebox or trailer, check its measurements and its weight carrying capacity to conform to EC regulations. All vehicles with an unladen weight of 30 cwt and over must have an annual test at the HGV Ministry of Transport.

❖ If the vehicle is over 7.5 metric tonnes gross weight the driver must hold a HGV licence and be insured to drive the vehicle.

❖ The box and trailer must display a registration number, (for trailers this should be the same as the towing vehicle, so be aware of this when changing vehicles).

❖ All indicator, brake and headlights must work properly.

❖ A trailer must display a red triangle on the back.

❖ Tyres must conform to the legal limit.

❖ There must be internal lighting in the box or trailer.

❖ All vehicles and trailers must display clear warning notices at the front and back that horses are being carried.

❖ Any vehicle transporting horses should be strong. The bodywork is usually steel framed and may be constructed of aluminium, fibreglass, glassonite, steel, hardwood or wood. The floors must be safe, sound, non-slip and easy to clean and can be made out of wood, rubber composition on wood or rubber grannalistic. Wood floors should have treads, as they become slippery.

❖ Ramps should be wide enough for the horse. They can be made out of wood or metal and covered with a non-slip surface or heavy-duty matting, wooden treads can be used.

❖ The groom's door is a small door at the side. This gives an attendant access to reach the horses without opening the ramp. Some boxes have an entrance from the cab.

❖ For a horsebox there should be adequate ventilation by means of sliding windows (protected by bars and made of toughened glass).

❖ Lighting from windows and internal lighting are legal requirements.

❖ All vehicles and trailers should be given regular servicing and safety checks both from the maintenance aspect and for safety of the animals.

Trailers

Trailers are available in different sizes, designed to carry one to four horses. They are usually built on a double axle having four wheels, which allows better stability and allocation of weight. Trailers with one axle or two wheels may be lighter and more manoeuvrable but are far less stable and only suitable for ponies.

Trailers are built with differing heights. If transporting larger horses it is better to look for a trailer with a higher headroom.

Some trailers have a front ramp that lowers on the right hand side. For a situation where the horses have to be unloaded by the side of the road, this means they will be exiting onto the road possibly into a stream of traffic. Some trailers feature a left-hand ramp where the horses can be unloaded onto the verge.

Advantages

The advantages of a trailer are:

* Low-loading with a shallow ramp.

* Relatively inexpensive to buy compared with boxes.

* Inexpensive to use.

* They do not need testing for a plating certificate every year.

* Easy to maintain.

Disadvantages

• Trailers can be narrow, lightweight and not as sturdy as boxes.

• Little space to store equipment, so tack and kit have to be carried in the towing vehicle.

• Smaller, more confined space and lower head room. This can put off a tall or larger horse for loading and travelling.

• Most trailers can only transport two horses at a time.

• Towing vehicle needs to have sufficient engine capacity to tow. Towing with a light vehicle with a small engine can be very dangerous. New regulations regarding towing capacity are being introduced.

• Trailers can be unsteady in certain conditions for instance a high wind.

Horseboxes

These vary in design from the modified small box to the luxurious box with living quarters.

Advantages

* Far more sturdy than trailers.

* Some horses prefer loading and travelling in a box where there is more space.

* Can transport more horses at one time.

* Safer to drive, less likely to be unstable in weather conditions.

* Better suspension than a trailer giving the horse a smoother ride.

* Except for small boxes, there is space for storing tack and equipment.

* Some boxes have living quarters, kitchen and facilities.

* Easier to unload than a rear ramp load/unload trailer.

Disadvantages

- Expensive to buy.

- Expensive to maintain.

- Needs to be tested for plating certificate every year.

- Can be more difficult than a small trailer to park and store.

- Can be more expensive to run, fuel costs, insurance and road tax.

Insurance

All trailers, horseboxes, towing vehicles should be insured. Some companies will only insure for third party, fire and theft. Trailers are usually insured only for one particular towing vehicle. It is best to investigate several insurance companies because rates do differ and sometimes different companies offer incentives.

Some equestrian insurance companies will offer a trailer or box insurance together with the horse insurance.

New Regulations

There are new regulations relating to drivers when they tow trailers and drive lorries. These only apply to drivers who passed their driving test after January 1997. Anyone who has passed their driving test after that time can only drive a lorry or a towing vehicle and trailer, the combination of which does not exceed a maximum laden weight of 3.5 tonnes. Any new drivers are advised to check with the Driver and Vehicle Licensing Authority.

Regulations are also being introduced in respect of the towing vehicle for trailers. Towing vehicles will need to be of a certain size; this is to prevent trailers and horses being towed by light vehicles such as family cars.

Those persons who transport horses for business or trade will have to complete an Animal Transport Certificate.

Exam tips

At Stage II candidates covered loading and unloading in theory. At Stage III you will be requested to give a practical demonstration by loading and unloading a horse into a horsebox or trailer.

The horse is normally prepared in his clothes for travelling. You will be asked about the clothing, whether you consider it offers sufficient protection, what you may use as an alternative or whether you prefer travel boots to bandages and your reasons.

Your group, normally consisting of three candidates, may be asked to check the trailer or box to assess if it is ready for loading. You will be questioned about safety checks, brake, indicator and headlights, towing bar, fuel in the tank and tyres. You should not be expected to check these in practice but you will need to know how this is done.

The group will then be expected to load the horse into the trailer or box. If the group has not inspected the trailer or box you may ask the Examiner if you can do this before the horse is brought out. You will need to check how the partitions fasten and unfasten, if there is string on the securing ring and if the ramp is steady ready for loading. In practice the trailer or box is certainly prepared fully first and checked before the horse is brought from his box. No use having the horse hanging around on the yard becoming impatient and restless because the trailer is not ready.

First ask if there is a bridle to lead the horse. This is an unfamiliar horse, which you have never loaded previously, to be safe he should be led in a bridle. There may be a bridle available or the Examiner may say that this horse is quite safe for loading in which case you can proceed.

In a group situation where three or four have been asked to load the horse it is better if the group decide who is going to do what job. Organise yourselves quickly so that one person leads the horse, whilst the others stand by the ramp.

Once the horse is safely loaded, the candidate holding onto the horse can quietly say, when ready, that the breech strap or partition can be moved into place. The person inside can then remove the bridle and ask for the ramp to be raised. Occasionally, in a box, the candidate inside may have to tie the horse up and then leave before the ramp is raised because there is no other exit. However, in most cases the person should stay with the horse until everything is secure.

The group will then be requested to unload the horse. For this you should not need the bridle as the horse has probably loaded well. One candidate enters by the groom's door and closes it behind them, in case the horse tries to exit that way. The other two lower the ramp and stand quietly either side. The horse is untied and led out, down the centre of the ramp or backed out if the trailer has a rear ramp only.

Preparation for the travelling section of the Stage III means practice. Load horses into different trailers and boxes if possible. Observe the different designs of boxes and trailers. Visit shows and competitions and observe how others load and unload. At any event you will be able to watch and see how it should, and should not, be done.

C H A P T E R   15
Nutrition

This subject of nutrition is concerned with the buying, storing, monitoring, weighing and preparation of the feeds as well as the nutritional value of each food. One of the most important parts of the yard, therefore, is the feed room. This is the central control where the feed charts are planned and the food prepared; it may also act as the storeroom for the feed and feeding utensils.

The Feed Room

The three main points about the feed room are:

1.   hygiene and cleanliness
2.   efficiency
3.   security

Hygiene and Cleanliness

Though this may seem irrelevant, as the horse eats grass out in the field and sometimes food and hay from the floor of the stable, it is of vital importance. The problems of dust, dirt, stale food, vermin and parasites pose a real threat to the horse's health.

All utensils should be cleaned thoroughly and regularly. Access to water is therefore essential.

*   An outside tap or hose pipe for cleaning feed buckets and skips.

*   A sink and clean towels for washing hands, knives, spoons, scoops.

Feed bins and hoppers should be cleaned out regularly so that no stale food remains. The floor should be swept twice a day to clear stale food in corners or under bins, then washed and disinfected once a week to discourage vermin.

Especial care should be taken when using drugs or medicines. Some equine drugs are in constant use and staff can become immune to the dangers. As well as keeping drugs under lock and key, the staff must always wash their hands after administering medicines.

All food should be kept in strong containers. Galvanised bins with lids are excellent, as vermin cannot chew through the metal. Plastic bins are useful providing the plastic is strong. The lids must always be replaced firmly; vermin can squeeze through any little gap. Paper bags of food should be stored in bins, never left on the floor. Mice will chew through paper and thin plastic. Food bins can be placed on pallets as added protection against damp.

The room itself should be large enough for all necessary items. It should also be light, airy with good ventilation to minimise dust.

Efficiency

To be efficient, feeding should be quick, relatively easy and error free.

* All food should be clearly labelled. It could be fatal if the wrong type of food was given; for instance sugar beet cubes instead of pony cubes.

* Each horse should have a feed chart, either in the feed room or outside his stable. Any alterations or supplements should be clearly marked on the chart.

* Ideally each horse should have his own bucket, clearly named. This is impractical though for a large riding school and not so essential if the buckets are thoroughly cleaned regularly.

* An efficient stocking system should be used so that no food runs out or is kept too long. Feed does have a 'use by' date and stale food should never be fed to horses. This can cause colic.

To be economical there should be as little waste as possible. The stocking system should be calculated on how much feed is used per week, how long it takes to order and deliver more feed.

Fresh supplies should be placed behind old sacks so that the older food is used first.

* Steamers or boilers for linseed or barley should be positioned by a window allowing the steam to escape. This will prevent other foods becoming damp, musty and mouldy.

Security

* Each feed bin should be capable of being locked or padlocked.

* The room should be secured at night or when the yard is unattended. This is particularly important on competition or racing yards.

* The room needs securing against horses breaking in and gorging themselves on the food.

* All rubbish should be removed; paper bags, feed sacks, packing. This will reduce fire hazards.

✷ NEVER leave a feed made up overnight if possible and certainly not if it is unprotected or uncovered. Rat's urine in a feed can kill a horse.

✷ All medicines should be clearly labelled and kept in a locked medicine cabinet.

Utensils and Storage

The feed room may include:

✷ Food storage - metal or plastic bins. Food hoppers. Plastic bins for soaking sugar beet. Scoops or measures. Airtight containers for salt. Salt should not be left in metal containers as it is corrosive. Use a plastic jar and plastic spoons.

✷ Slow cookers for boiled oats, barley and linseed.

✷ Pair of weighing scales, hanging scales for hay.

✷ Washing facilities – sinks with hot and cold water, clean towels, antiseptic.

✷ Labels and pens, feed charts, (a blackboard or whiteboard is useful).

✷ Electric kettle, power points.

✷ Good, bright lighting.

✷ Scissors, knife, clean bowls, buckets.

✷ Broom, dustpans and dustbin.

✷ Lockable cabinets for medicines and clearly labelled shelves for supplements.

Food should be stored in low, even temperatures, low humidity, no direct sunlight, good ventilation, with adequate protection from vermin, insects, birds and mites.

Vacuum-packed food bags must be carefully stored as the food will deteriorate quite quickly if the bag is ruptured or torn.

Buckets should be heavy duty and strong. They should also be easily cleaned, portable yet safe for the horse. Rubber skips are ideal for feeding. They are sturdy, almost indestructible, easily cleaned, easy to carry and safe. They can be left in the stable overnight without any harm to the horse.

The essential aspects of the feed room, as with any organised system, are simplicity and efficiency. The more complicated a system the more chance there is of it going wrong. If everything is kept in place, clearly labelled and a control book or file used for stock taking then the feed room will work. Feed charts should be clearly written or typed and easily visible for all the staff. Any alterations or supplements should be clearly marked on the charts and all staff taught the organisation of the feed system.

Nutritional Value of Food

To be of any value, food has to contain the nutrients necessary to sustain life. It has to provide the energy for the functioning of bodily systems, for growth, repair and replacement of tissues, to maintain body warmth and for work.

In his diet the horse needs carbohydrates, proteins, fats and oils, vitamins, minerals, fibre and water. Some of these are organic compounds. (Organic compounds are derived from living plants or animals and contain carbon.) Some, such as minerals, are inorganic. (Inorganic compounds are not produced by growth; they do not have the characteristics of a living organism.)

Carbohydrates

This is a group of organic compounds essential for:

* **energy** for vital bodily systems such as breathing and the muscle contractions of the heart and for muscle performance during work.

* **growth,** body warmth and weight.

* **resistance** to disease.

Carbohydrates should make up two-thirds of the horse's feed.

Carbohydrates are present in plants. They are produced by the action of photosynthesis converting the simple compounds of water and carbon dioxide into the more complex compounds; carbohydrates.

Carbohydrates are divided into three main types: **sugars, starch and fibre.**

Sugars – simple sugars contained in foods such as oats, barley, molasses, sugar beet and grass.

Starch – made up of different types of sugars contained particularly in seeds and grains: oats, barley, maize, beans and peas, and grass.

The sugars and starches are digested in the small intestine. A certain amount is used for energy; the excess is stored as glycogen in the liver and muscles. When necessary, glycogen is reconverted into sugars.

Fibre – contained in the structural part of plants, seeds and grains. It contains cellulose which, being an insoluble carbohydrate, resists enzyme action in the digestive tract. **Fibre is converted into energy only by the bacteria living in the large colon and caecum.**

Fibre also contains lignin, which horses cannot digest. As plants grow older the amount of lignin increases making the plants nutritionally less valuable.

Fibre is absolutely essential for the horse's digestion. At least 30 % of the horse's diet should consist of fibre. It stimulates the action of the gut, encourages the passage of food and slows down the digestion rate allowing a greater absorption of nutrients. The main sources of fibre are grass and hay. Other sources are oats, barley, bran, sugar beet and carrots.

A deficiency of carbohydrate will result in a thin, emaciated horse, lacking energy. It will stunt his growth and make him prone to diseases and parasitic invasion.

If fed in excess, carbohydrates are stored as fat eventually resulting in an obese horse. This in turn puts stress on the body, the heart, the muscles, the limbs and the feet. It can result in illnesses such as laminitis and colic.

Proteins

Proteins are made up from approximately 20 different amino acids in varying combinations. About half of these amino acids can be made (synthesised) within the horse's body but the remainder need to be provided in the diet. These are called essential amino acids; the most important of which is lysine.

Proteins are essential for:

✳ **growth** particularly necessary for young stock.

✳ **repair** of cells and tissues particularly in older and invalid horses.

✳ **development** and maintenance of muscle tissues.

Plants extract nitrogen from the soil and combine it with carbon, hydrogen and oxygen from the air. Through photosynthesis these are made into proteins. Grass has a higher content of nitrogen in spring in the young shoots. This decreases as the summer progresses when more nitrogen is contained in the flower heads and seeds.

Foods high in protein include beans, peas, soya bean meal. Other foods containing proteins include oats, barley, bran, clover, lucerne, linseed meal and grass.

A deficiency of protein in the diet results in poor condition, dull coat, stunted growth, poor muscle development. Foals will be small for their age and brood mares will have a reduced milk production.

Excess proteins in the body are stored as fat and excreted through urine.

Fats and Oils

With traditional horse foods the fat and oil content is quite low, but horses can digest fat efficiently.

Fats and oil are important for:

* **heat** – used as energy to maintain body temperature and as an insulating layer under the skin.

* **growth** – hair, skin, cells and membranes.

* **lubrication** in joints, tissues and membranes.

* **metabolism** – chemical reactions in the body; the conversion of one substance to another.

* **energy** and stamina – particularly useful for endurance horses.

* **providing certain vitamins**.

Some oils and fats, such as corn oil, are very digestible providing more energy than the equivalent starch in the diet. For endurance horses and three-day eventers this is an excellent alternative for providing energy and stamina; starch can be fed in smaller quantities.

Fats and oils are present in linseed, corn and vegetable oil, oats, barley, maize and grass.

Vitamins

Though a number of vitamins are essential to the horse, the main nutritionally important ones are vitamins A, B complex, (B1, B2, B3, B5, B6, B12), C, D, E and K. The actual amounts and proportions required vary with each individual horse.

Vitamins can be split up into two groups – the fat-soluble vitamins and the water-soluble vitamins. The fat-soluble vitamins can be stored within the body so that vitamins contained in the summer grass can be utilised throughout the winter. Fat-soluble vitamins, because they can be stored in the body, can be toxic if fed in excessive amounts.

Water-soluble vitamins cannot be stored in the body. Some are obtained from food, but most are synthesised by the bacteria in the horse's gut.

* Vitamin deficiency will result in loss of condition, deterioration of general health, poor metabolism and possibly disease.

* An excess of vitamins, in particular the fat-soluble vitamins, can be toxic causing a metabolic imbalance and illness.

Feeds will vary in the amount of vitamins they offer depending on the where they are grown, soil types, weather conditions, the methods of harvesting and storage.

Fat soluble vitamins A, D, E, K, (All Donkeys Eat Kebabs)

Vitamin A *(retinol)*

✳ Sources include grass, leafy plants, carrots, apples and cod liver oil. Vitamin A, obtained from spring and summer grass, is stored in the liver and used through the winter.

✳ Essential for vision, reproduction, growth, resistance to disease.

• Deficiency results in poor vision, night blindness (difficulty seeing in dim light), infertility, abortion, poor and slow growth, susceptibility to disease.

EXCESS IS TOXIC – any supplementary feeding of Vitamin A should be carefully monitored.

Vitamin D *(calciferol)*

✳ Vitamin D is produced by the action of sunlight on the skin. Other sources are milk from lactating mares, cod liver oil.

✳ Horses living out in summer, providing there is sufficient sunlight, may obtain and store enough Vitamin D to last the winter. Horses whose pasture time is limited, who are fully stabled or who go out in rugs may require a supplement.

• Deficiency causes bone abnormalities, skeletal deformities, joint problems and poor growth in young stock.

EXCESS IS TOXIC – any supplementary feeding of Vitamin D should be carefully controlled.

Vitamin E *(tocopherol)*

✳ Sources include cereal grains, seeds and grass. Levels reduce in food the longer it is stored.

✳ Essential for vascular system, red blood cells, muscle tissues, the reproductive system, for stamina and high performance, and may help to reduce nervousness in some horses.

• Deficiency results in muscular problems including dystrophy (muscle wastage), increased red blood cell fragility and infertility.

Vitamin K

* Vitamin K is synthesised within the horse's gut. Sources also include green leafy plants such as lucerne.

* This vitamin is necessary in the process of blood clotting.

• Deficiency leads to poor blood clotting and possibly haemorrhaging. Deficiency is rare though because this vitamin is synthesised and stored in the body. In some diseases, for example navicular syndrome, the clotting time needs to be prolonged to aid the flow of the blood. The use of anti-coagulant drugs reduces the action of vitamin K so that the blood does not clot so quickly.

Water Soluble Vitamins

These include the B complex of vitamins, vitamin C, Folic acid, Biotin and Choline.

Vitamin B1 (*thiamin*), **Vitamin B2** (*riboflavin),* **Vitamin B3** (*niacin),* **Vitamin B5** (*pantothenic acid),* **Vitamin B6** (*pyridoxine),***Vitamin B12** (*cyanocobalamin).*

* Some B vitamins are synthesised in the body, others are obtained from grass, green plants, oils, grains and seeds.

* Essential for enzyme action in the body.

• Deficiencies cause loss of condition, poor appetite, lack of stamina, eye and skin problems, nervousness.

Note: Antibiotics can affect synthesis of B vitamins in the horse's gut.

Vitamin C (ascorbic acid)

* Essential in the formation, maintenance and repair of tissues and skin.

* Synthesised in the horse's body. Other sources include grass and green fodder.

• Deficiency causes skin problems, weight loss, swellings from fluid in the body (oedema).

Biotin

* Used in conversion of carbohydrates, proteins and fats in the body.

* Often fed as a supplement for horses with poor hoof growth or damaged horn.

• Deficiency causes poor hoof growth, skin problems.

Folic acid

* Essential for formation of red blood cells.

* Sources include grass, good quality hay, grains and seeds, oils.

• Deficiency causes anaemia, lack of growth.

Choline (pronounced koline)

* Essential for the formation and maintenance of cells, for utilising fats and for the nervous system.

* Sources in practically all foodstuffs, grass and cereals.

Note: Heavy infestations of parasites in the gut can affect the production of many vitamins and reduce their function.

Minerals

These are inorganic compounds essential for the proper functioning of the horse's body and his good health. They are divided into two main groups, major minerals and trace minerals, depending on the amount in the body.

The Major Minerals

These are calcium (Ca), phosphorus (P), potassium (K), magnesium (Mg), sodium (Na), chloride or chlorine (Cl).

Calcium and phosphorus are essential for bone formation and growth. An imbalance in this ratio causes poor and abnormal bone growth. Calcium is present in grass, green fodder and limestone. Phosphorus is present in grass and grains.

Magnesium, present in grass, clover and linseed oil, is needed to covert the calcium and phosphorus in the body. Deficiency causes muscle spasms and nervousness.

Sodium, potassium and chloride (electrolytes) regulate fluid in the body. Sources include salt, grass and hay. Deficiencies cause dehydration, lack of growth and energy.

Trace Minerals

The trace minerals act in various ways with enzymes to produce chemical changes within the body. Sources of these minerals are grass and normal feed. Deficiencies cause poor growth, bone abnormalities, skin and hair problems. Iron is involved in the formation of red blood cells so a deficiency causes anaemia.

The trace minerals are; cobalt (Co), copper (Cu), fluorine (F), iodine (I), iron (Fe), manganese (Mn), selenium (Se), sulphur (S) and zinc (Zn).

Roughage/Fibre

Revision

Stage I Types of hay and assessing quality. Types of forage, methods of feeding hay in the stable and the field. Stage II Types of hay and vacuum-packed forage. Methods of feeding hay. Haylage and silage.

Fibre is essential in the horse's diet; his whole lifestyle and digestive system has evolved as a herbivore. Without fibre the horse's digestive tract would cease to work.

Some fibre is available in traditional foods, compound foods and some 'openers' such as sugar beet and chaff, but the majority of fibre in the diet comes from grass and hay.

There are basically two types of hay, seed and meadow, and both these can vary in quality. Seed hay is prepared from specially prepared pasture; the grasses being selected and sown. Meadow hay is made traditionally from naturally grown pasture but many farmers now do sow specially selected seeds as well.

The quality of hay depends on various factors.

∗   The types of grasses that make up the hay.

The percentage of rye grass in the pasture determines the grade. Good grade hay consists of around 30% rye; a level of 5% rye is poor. Other top quality grasses include timothy, cocksfoot, meadow fescue, clover and purple moor grass.

Second quality grasses are foxtails, crested dogstail, rough stalked meadow grass. Inferior grasses are slender foxtail, barren fescue, sheep's fescue.

There should be no weeds or poisonous plants.

Occasionally horses dislike hay made from pasture grazed only by horses.

Hay may include some herbs; sheep's parsley, chicory, yarrow, burnet, comfrey, dandelion.

∗   The type of land on which it is grown.

∗   The nutrients in the soil; the position: south-facing land will receive more sunshine.

∗   Land management, how efficient the farming methods.

∗   Time of year the hay is harvested.

Ideally the hay should be cut just as flowering finishes but before seeding begins. If the seeds are scattered the nutrient levels drop. Normally a cut is taken in June.

∗   Drying and storage.

Hay when cut needs to be dried. Either it is left in the field and turned frequently or it is placed in a barn. Rain, soaking through the cut hay, can wash away nutrients and cause mould.

Hay can be made from fields that have an overabundance of grass. The cutting of hay will benefit the field by encouraging the growth of new, young grasses. If neglected and the grass grows long, the field may deteriorate in quality. Fields cut for hay should be ready for grazing in 4 to 6 weeks.

The quality of hay, even from the same farm, can vary from year to year depending on weather conditions. In years when the weather is not conducive to hay making, the quality decreases, as does the availability of good hay. This results in price rises and an increase in the purchase of alternatives such as oat straw or vacuum-packed forage.

Over the past few years the market for vacuum-packed forage has expanded. To meet this demand more companies are producing an increasing variety; where there were two types, high and low protein forage, there are now several types including the high fibre Fibreage. Some of this forage can be too rich for some ponies and horses and it should always be fed in smaller quantities than hay.

Vacuum-packed forage is extremely useful in a variety of circumstances; for horses with respiratory problems who cannot eat hay; when good quality hay is scarce and expensive and for competition horses who need higher amounts of energy foods.

Water

Revision

Stage I Rules and considerations of watering, methods of watering in the stable and the field.

Stage II Importance of water to the horse. Dehydration test. Watering systems.

Water plays a vital role in the horse's body being present in the bodily systems and essential to their functioning. Around 70% of the horse's bodyweight is made up of water. The horse needs around 8 to 15 gallons of water per day, depending on temperature, health, work, milk production, diet and loss of fluids through urine, droppings and sweating.

∗ Water is present in the plasma of the blood.

∗ In the digestive tract water helps to transport food along the gut.

∗ Water is contained in glands where it aids secretions throughout the body.

∗ Water is present in the synovial fluid of the joints and aids lubrication.

∗ Water aids the respiratory system being present in the mucus in the air tubes.

∗ Many chemical changes in the body take place in water based solutions.

∗ Water transfers electrolytes through the digestive tract to parts of the body.

∗ Transportation of waste products from the body is dependent on the lubricating mucus in the digestive tract, which contains water.

∗ Water aids the excretion of waste from sweat glands, also regulating body heat.

∗ Water aids excretion of waste matter in the urine.

Water is so vital that if the horse is deprived of water for a few days the bodily systems begin to deteriorate, the horse becomes dehydrated and will eventually die.

A supply of clean water should always be available to horses whether in the stable or field, at any time of the year. A check should also be made to assess that each horse is drinking and receiving the amount he needs.

The Importance of Grass

In his natural habitat the horse wanders over the plains or mountains of his native home, feeding from grasses, plants and herbs grown on different soils. These offer him a comprehensive range of nutrients including different vitamins and minerals. Rivers or streams, containing soluble nutrients from the rocks and soils through which they flow, offer him water and minerals. Though the domesticated horse is kept in an artificial way, grass is still important.

It provides most of the nutrients he needs and, in particular, fibre. Grass also provides food as hay, vital for the stabled horse and those living out during the winter months.

For a horse who is ill, on box rest or has lost his appetite, taking him out for a quiet walk and offering him grass often works wonders. A period of 'Dr Green' helps the horse to recuperate.

Every horse should spend some time out at grass to meet his nutritional needs from the forage, to obtain sunlight and consequently Vitamin D. He also needs the mental and physical relaxation of being in his 'natural' habitat away from the box and work.

Exam Tips

At Stage I we learnt about the basic rules and considerations of feeding. At Stage II we learnt to differentiate between different horses and ponies; their needs at certain times. By Stage III we need to know more about the nutritional values of each food.

It is important to understand about feeding in this depth because the horse depends on us entirely for his sustenance. What he eats, how much he is given, what type of hay he has, even how many hours he spends at grass, these decisions are all made by us. The horse cannot raid the pantry if he feels like eating something else. We need to understand the values of food and nutrition so that we can give the horse what he needs, when he needs it, and alter the diet at different times of his life.

During the Exam, the section dealing with the feed room will be conducted as a general discussion. As part of the preparation, visit different feed rooms at different stables and look at the advertisements in magazines. Be observant and critical, think of the type of feed room you would like if you were building a new one. What are your likes and dislikes about the feed room at your stable or yard? Make notes on how you could change or improve the feed room.

For the section dealing with nutrition, the Examiners will ask individuals within the group about the nutritional requirements of the horse, the values of different foods, the importance of carbohydrates, proteins, fats and oils, water, fibre and grass in the diet. You will need to know about the different nutrients, their sources, their importance for the horse, the effects of excess and deficiencies.

C H A P T E R   16
Feed and Feed Charts

The horse's daily diet needs to be constant, balanced and any alterations made slowly. To fulfil these requirements there needs to be a system whereby the feeding is supervised. For this reason, especially in large yards, feed charts are essential.

The Feed Chart

Feed charts are an important part of the organisation in any establishment. They are there to cater for the many ponies and horses living under different circumstances. These vary from riding school horses, children's ponies, competition horses, youngstock, aged animals, 'hot' and sluggish horses, livery horses and ponies out at grass. Each of these will have a different nutritional need and for each there will be a feed chart made up to suit his requirements.

Feed charts are important to:

* maintain a balanced, constant diet.

* give information to other staff.

* calculate the nutrients each horse needs.

* make any alteration accurate.

* keep a constant record; in large yards each feed cannot be memorised.

* ensure each horse and pony is fed the right quantity.

To achieve their aim the charts need to be clearly visible, legible, easy to understand and simple to alter when required. Some establishments have a blackboard or whiteboard in the feed room whilst other yards have individual feed charts pinned to the stable door.

Planning the Feed Chart

The first consideration is the amount to feed each day. This is based on the weight of the horse or pony.

Recommended daily allowance estimated from heights–

Height	Daily amount of food
17-18 hands	15.5 kilos (34 lbs)
16 hands	13.5 kilos (30 lbs)
15 hands	12 kilos (26 lbs)
14 hands	10 kilos (22 lbs)
13 hands	8 kilos (18 lbs)
12 hands	6.5 kilos (14 lbs)

The above weights are approximations and should be modified by taking into consideration other factors; whether the horse is **fine or heavily built**, **under or over weight**, his **age** and **environment**. The type of food is also a factor. The traditional amount is based approximately on 2.5% of bodyweight, some Compound feed can be fed at a recommended ratio of 2% of bodyweight.

The next consideration is the percentage of concentrates to roughage based on the amount and type of work the horse is expected to perform.

These percentages provide a basis but **all horses should be monitored constantly** and the feed altered when necessary. Reductions or increases in concentrates can be given when required and a corresponding increase or reduction in roughage.

Percentages of concentrates to roughage estimated from workload

Workload	Description of work	Percentages of food
Maintenance	No work or very light; walking, some trot work up to 4 hours a week	0-10% concentrates to 90-100% bulk
Light work	4 - 6 hours a week - light hacking or schooling	25% concentrates to 75% bulk
Light medium work	6 - 12 hours a week hacking, schooling with a little jumping	30% concentrates to 70% bulk
Medium work	6 - 12 hours a week includes hacking, schooling, dressage, show jumping	40% concentrates to 60% bulk
Hard medium work	12 - 14 hours a week schooling, show jumping, dressage, hunting once every one or two weeks	50% concentrates to 50% bulk
Hard work	12 hours and over, schooling, show jumping, eventing, hunting twice a week, point to point, racing, endurance riding. Concentrated work	60% concentrates to 40% bulk

The next decision is to the type of food to give. Feeding traditional foods such as oats and barley, or manufactured Compound food, depends on various factors; suitability, economy, convenience and preference.

Each type of traditional food has its own particular nutritional content and quality. The horse will need a mixture to receive a nutritionally balanced diet. Oats, for instance, whilst offering the best balance of nutrients for the horse of any grain, do lack certain minerals and vitamins.

Compound feeds have been researched and developed by nutritionists to create a complete food. There are also different types of Compound feeds consisting of additional nutrients to suit various horses in different circumstances.

Traditional Food

Revision

Stage II detailed descriptions of types of foods, values, deficiencies, qualities, appearance and uses. Cooked foods, supplements, openers or mixers.

Oats – contain carbohydrates, proteins, fats and oils, high fibre content from husk, vitamin B1. Deficient in certain minerals particularly calcium. Provides energy without weight gain. Tends to make some horses and ponies temperamental 'hot and fizzy'.

Barley – contains carbohydrates (higher level than oats), proteins, fats and oils, fibre (lower than oats). Deficient in certain minerals such as calcium. Provides energy without the 'heating' effect of oats, causes weight gain, can be fattening. Fed as an alternative to oats for some horses and ponies and to put weight on a thin horse.

Maize – high level of carbohydrates, slightly lower in protein than oats and barley, contains fats and oils. Lower fibre content. Provides energy and weight gain. Can have a 'heating' effect as with oats and is fattening. Feed sparingly, no more than 25% or quarter of total grain food.

Bran – contains carbohydrates, high in fibre (levels lower than oats: some of this fibre contains lignin). High in protein (some is indigestible protein). Contains fats and oils. Bran absorbs water easily so has a laxative effect. Useful as a mash for ill horses, those off work or before the horse's day off to clear out digestive system.

Incorrect calcium/phosphorus ratio: nutritional experiments have shown that bran is high in phosphorus and low in calcium. If fed in large amounts, especially to young horses, without the addition of extra calcium, this may cause **nutritional secondary hyperparathyroidism (NSH)** or Bran disease. The calcium deficiency in the blood triggers the release of a hormone by the parathyroid gland, which removes calcium from the bones to make up the deficiency. The bones grow weak, brittle and develop abnormally.

*Bran is coming back into popularity especially as part of a feed or as a mash in combination with limestone flour or sugar beet to make up the calcium imbalance. Dried bran added to a feed can help in cases of diarrhoea (scouring).

Sugar beet pulp – this feed, under estimated in the past, now becoming recognised as a **valuable feed for horses**. Contains carbohydrates, proteins, high in fibre and calcium. Suits all types of horses in various disciplines. Whilst being palatable as an 'opener or mixer' it also has value nutritionally. Provides energy in two forms, quick release energy from easily digested sugars: slow release energy from the fibre. Good for endurance horses, riding school horses, hunters. Can be bulky in gut feed sparingly to horses in fast work. Acts as a laxative on some horses.

Linseed – high in oil and proteins, good source of vitamin B. Improves condition of hooves and shine on coat. Linseed must be cooked or it is poisonous. As the seeds absorb water can act as a laxative.

Peas and beans – contain carbohydrates and some fibre. Good source of proteins particularly lysine, required for growth and performance. Gives energy, particularly good for youngstock, performance horses and horses in hard work. Feed sparingly as can be heating and fattening.

Soyabean meal – good source of protein for horses becoming fit and in fit condition. Feed sparingly. Low in fibre, fats and oils.

Corn and soyabean oil – high protein, good source of energy for endurance horses and horses in hard work. Feed sparingly; the horse's concentrate feed may be reduced, for example feeding up to 1 pint of oil a day, reduce oat ration by 1½ kilos or 3 lbs. This is particularly useful for horses who should not be fed so many oats but need the energy.

Approximate nutritional values of foods

Food	Carbohydrates	Proteins	Fats and Oils	Fibre	Notes
Oats	59%	12%	5%	12%	Provides B1 Deficient in calcium
Barley	64%	12%	2%	7%	Deficient in calcium
Maize	70%	9%	3%	8%	Higher in carbohydrates Lower in protein
Bran	52%	16%	4%	10%	Calcium/phosphorus ratio imbalance
Linseed	22%	24%	36%		High oil content High in protein
Sugar Beet	58%	9%	-	19%	High in calcium, salt and potassium. Provides fibre
Molasses	63%	3%	-	-	Provides sugars
Peas & Beans	57%	23%	1%	4%	High in protein and lysine
Soyabean Meal	30%	51%	-	3%	High protein. Low in fats and fibre

Carbohydrates provide short term energy through the starch and sugar and long term energy (stamina) through the fibre (cellulose). Proteins develop and maintain muscle tone, required for a horse in training, fittening and to sustain fitness in constant work. Fats and oils provide stamina and improve condition.

Compound Food

There are many varieties of Compound feed and similar grades have different names depending on the manufacturer. Here is a brief list of the main grades.

Horse and Pony cubes and mixes – designed for horses and ponies at rest, in light or medium work. Several types some for weight gain, some high fibre, non-heating.

Pasture cubes and mixes – designed for horses and ponies in light or medium work. Includes grass pellets and herbs.

High Performance, Racehorse cubes, Competition mix – horses and ponies in hard work, fit horses competing.

Convalescence, Cool mix, Cereal meals – for ill, invalid horses at rest, recuperating from illnesses.

Oat balancer – designed to be fed in combination with oats or other grains. For horses in hard work, younger horses in training to add extra vitamins and minerals to an oat diet.

There are many varieties of Compound feed currently on the market, to suit every horse and pony, under all circumstances and every owner too. Some horses will prefer one type or brand to another, some prefer cubes, some the mixes.

The practical method of choosing which compound to feed is to decide which energy level would suit the horse best, that is a pasture mix, a competition or high performance mix, and then experiment by giving this to the horse and monitoring him over the next few weeks or months.

It is possible to combine two types of Compound feed. For instance, for the horse who is a little sluggish on Pasture Mix, but not doing enough work to be fed Competition or Performance Mix, these two types can be added together in varying amounts. A horse could be fed two or three scoops of Pasture Mix and one or two scoops of Competition Mix if required. When changing the balance of the food this should be done gradually over a couple of weeks.

The next step is to assess the horse or pony, calculate his needs and requirements so that a suitable feed chart can be compiled.

Assessing the Horse

Deciding on the horse's daily diet the main considerations are:

❖ **type of horse**

Some horses are naturally 'good doers', others become easily excited and temperamental when fed on high-energy foods. Some horses will put weight on easily whereas others remain underweight.

❖ **type of work**

Riding school horses, children's ponies or small horses, beginners and novice horses all need a diet which will keep them quiet and steady. School horses who work almost everyday need stamina, some work at higher levels and will also need more energy. Horses competing at events, show jumping or dressage will need energy to sustain performance. Short distance sprinters need quick bursts of energy, whilst long distance endurance horses need stamina.

❖ **health and condition**

If the horse is ill and convalescing he will need a different diet to encourage healing. There are also foods that the horse may need to avoid at certain times of his life. For instance if he is not working, an excess of carbohydrates may result in azoturia, an excess of rich grass can cause laminitis. It can be just as vital to the horse's health to know what not to feed and the nutrients to avoid when necessary.

❖ **rider's ability**

This is closely associated with the work the horse is to perform. For children, novices or nervous adults the horse needs to be quiet and reliable. For those who wish to compete the horse will need a different type of food to sustain that type of energy.

❖ **economy, time and labour**

Traditional foods are less expensive than Compound foods and in a large yard with a number of horses and ponies this is an economic consideration. Alternatively it can be less time and labour consuming to feed one type of Compound food than to weigh and mix two or three traditional types. The decision depends on the judgement of the owner and those feeding the horses concerned.

❖ **present diet**

When a new horse or pony is purchased the type of food to give him will first depend on what he has been fed previously. There should be no drastic change of diet straight away. The pony or horse can then be monitored for a few months and his feed altered gradually if necessary.

In the examples that follow there are suggestions for traditional foods and compound foods. *Not all the traditional foods mentioned need be used; normally a mixture of two or three is given.* It depends on the individual horse and his circumstances but these are possibilities for each category.

* A young horse (3-5years) needs more protein for growth; vitamins such as calcium and phosphorus in the right ratio to build up his bones. **Traditional feed**: barley, small amount of soyabean meal, corn oil, sugar beet, chaff. **Compound feed**: Horse and Pony Cubes or Pasture Mix

* An older horse needs proteins to replace body tissues lost through degeneration. **Traditional feed**: boiled barley, oats or maize, corn oil, soyabean meal, sugar beet, molasses. **Compound feed**: Cereal Meal or Pasture Mix.

* Ill or recuperating horses need proteins to rebuild their tissues and fight disease. **Traditional feed**: boiled barley, bran, sugar beet, chaff, plenty of roughage. **Compound feed**: Convalescence Mix, Cooked Cereal Meals.

* A horse in hard work needs carbohydrates for energy, starch for stamina and sugars for quick bursts of fast work. **Traditional feed**: oats or barley and/or maize, sugar beet, corn oil, chaff. **Compound feed**: Performance Cubes or Mix.

* A horse in a fittening programme needs carbohydrates for energy and protein to develop muscle fibre. **Traditional feed**: oats or barley and/or maize, soyabean meal, corn oil, sugar beet. **Compound feed**: Horse and Pony Cubes or Mix, Performance Mix possibly a combination of both.

* Riding school horses will need stamina. **Traditional feed**: oats for cob types and sluggish horses, barley, sugar beet, chaff. **Compound feed**: Horse and Pony Cubes/Mix.

* 'Hot' horses, those with fiery temperaments need lower carbohydrates and more fibre (unless competing). Feeding horses like this a large amount of oats is asking for trouble. **Traditional feed**: barley, sugar beet, chaff. **Compound feed**: Horse and Pony Cubes or Mix.

* Sluggish horses need their energy levels raising. They can be fed higher proportions of carbohydrates, monitor their weight. **Traditional feed**: oats, maize, barley, sugar beet. **Compound feed**: Performance Mix.

* Hunters need energy giving foods, carbohydrates and protein to build the muscle tissue. **Traditional feed**: oats and barley, soyabean meal, corn oil, sugar beet. **Compound feed**: Performance Mix.

* Endurance, long distance riding horses travelling at speed over distances need short and long term energy. They need to develop muscle power without excess weight. Carbohydrates are essential but not too much bulk food. Corn oil added in small amounts offer an easily digestible energy food without making the horse too excited. Oil can replace grain in the food. **Traditional feed**: oats, barley, corn oil, soyabean meal, sugar beet. **Compound feed**: Performance Mix.

✳ Horses in strenuous work; racehorses and eventers, need extra protein such as small amounts of soya bean meal added to their feed. This should not be fed in excess. **Traditional feed**: oats, barley or maize, soya bean meal, corn oil, sugar beet. **Compound feed**: Performance mix or Racing Cubes, (Racehorse Mix).

✳ Dressage horses need long term energy to maintain the more concentrated level of work. The dressage season continues for long periods and the horse will need to maintain fitness without the fast burst of energy. **Traditional feed**: oats, barley or maize, sugar beet, corn oil, chaff. **Compound feed**: Performance Cubes or Mix.

✳ Show jumpers need bursts of energy; carbohydrates are vital. The jumping season lasts over long periods. The show jumper needs to be kept fit over a long period of time. **Traditional feed**: oats, barley or maize, sugar beet. **Compound feed**: Performance Cubes or Mix.

✳ Show horses need condition, in weight and appearance. They need foods that give condition without the 'heating' effect as their manners need to be exemplary in the show ring. **Traditional feed**: barley, sugar beet, small amounts of linseed oil, chaff. **Compound feed**: Horse and Pony Cubes, Pasture Mix.

The types and amounts of feed can vary throughout different times of the year. During the summer if the horses and ponies are feeding on more grass, the barley ration can be reduced to prevent excess weight gain. Sugar beet can also be added to the Compound feed.

Salts as electrolytes and minerals will be needed to supplement those horses in fast, strenuous work that makes them sweat. Add electrolytes to food or water and keep a salt and mineral block in the stable.

Succulents such as carrots, apples, turnips, swedes will always be appreciated by the horse and can be added to the feed.

Ponies

Most people when thinking of feeding consider horses, but ponies are just as important, perhaps more so as their riders are usually children. Most native ponies are also good doers and thrive on little food. Some may even need their food restricting especially at certain times of the year.

A good diet will create a quiet sensible pony.

Ponies can be divided into four groups.

1. The small, woolly native pony – Shetland, Exmoor or Dartmoor.

2. The larger native pony – Highland, Dales, Fells, Welsh cobs, New Forest.

3. The more finely bred pony – Connemara or Arab cross, Welsh riding pony.

4. The part Thoroughbred pony.

Groups 1 and 2 are good doers and thrive on very little. Many ponies, especially out at grass, do extremely well during spring, summer and early autumn whereas during the winter, particularly through January and February, they can lose weight. Weight loss at this time of year is not always noticeable because of the thick coat.

Groups 3 and 4 are not such 'good doers' and they are usually worked harder, possibly stabled for longer periods.

Beginners ponies. Group 1

Need to be quiet and calm. Small amounts of concentrates particularly if out at grass most of the time during the spring and summer months when a handful of Pony Cubes after a ride is sufficient. During the winter, small feeds, barley and sugar beet, or Horse and Pony Cubes/Pasture Mix particularly if the pony loses weight at any time.

Family Ponies. Groups 1 and 2

Need to be quiet and calm though probably doing more work. Feed small amounts of oats or barley, sugar beet or Pony Cubes/Pasture Mix calculated on their workload and time at grass.

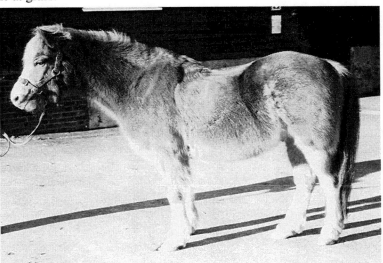

Riding School ponies. Groups 1, 2 and 3

Need concentrates to maintain energy and condition. Feed as per workload, Horse and Pony Cubes or Pasture Mix with sugar beet or chaff.

Hunting Ponies. Groups 3 and 4

Living in during the night and out during the day, exercising in the week and hunting every Saturday need concentrates as per workload. Some oats, barley, sugar beet, chaff, linseed oil or a mixture of Horse and Pony Cubes/Pasture Mix with Competition Mix.

Show ponies. All groups

Need special care as the pony should be in good condition but be well mannered. Should look well covered and have elegant movement, great presence and impeccable manners. Food could include barley, or Horse and Pony Cubes with sugar beet.

In all cases, with both ponies and horses, there is one important point that should be remembered; it is better to slightly underfeed than overfeed. Overfeeding causes far more problems, physical and mental. Obesity puts strain on the limbs, the lungs and the heart.

Once the relevant calculations are known, daily amount, percentage and type of food to give, a feed chart can be designed to suit each pony and horse. It is advisable to have one standard weighing system for the whole yard, either by weight or by scoops. Giving the amounts in scoops is more usual and simpler.

Example 1

Name: Rufus   Age 5

	Oats	Barley	Sugar beet	Hay
Breakfast	1	1	1	Ad lib Dry hay
Lunch	½	1	1	Ad lib
Tea	½	1	1	Ad lib

Example 2

Horse	Oats	Barley	S. beet	Nuts	Mix	Chaff	Additives	Hay
Bella	1		1				Biotin	2-1-2
Ace	2		1				Red Cell	2-2-3
Harry	½	1	1					2-2-3
Sue			1	1				1-1-2

Please note these are examples. If feeds are measured by weight then the food weight of each scoop should definitely be noted. For instance a scoop of oats has a different weight from a scoop of pony cubes. Each scoop of food needs to be weighed to obtain an accurate amount. Also it should be mentioned whether the scoops are level or heaped amounts.

Feeding horses and ponies is an art developed from the knowledge passed on by those with experience. Every horse and pony is different and will vary at certain times in their lives. The rule is to know your horse, monitor constantly and adapt the feed gradually to suit his requirements.

Exam Tips

You should now be able to speak through experience about the different foods, traditional, compound and roughage and give advice on what foods to feed to different ponies and horses in different circumstances. Always with the proviso that each horse and pony will be monitored constantly.

When discussing feeds and feeding in the Stage III, base your answers on experience if possible and practical knowledge. For instance if a friend were to ask you about the 15 hand hunter she has just purchased, what amount and type of food to give him; you would first discover more information.

What food was the horse being given previously? Even if changes are to be made, it is essential that this is done gradually. What type or build is he? What work is he expected to do? Is he allergic to any food? Is he a good doer? What type of hay is he having? Does he have it dampened or dry? Is he going out to grass? Find out as much information as possible. On this basis you can make an assessment of how much and what type of food he will need in the future.

It may help to take a note of the horses and ponies on the yard and make up feed charts to suit them. This will give you some experience of assessing the horse and pony, their workload and in deciding what type of feed they would require.

C H A P T E R   17
Fittening

A fittening programme is a schedule of exercise and stable management designed to bring the horse from an unfit or 'soft' condition to a sufficiently fit state for the work he is to perform.

Horses are given time off for a holiday, as a break from work to prevent staleness or as a recuperation time after an illness or injury. Hunters are turned out to pasture during the summer months, event horses take a break during the winter, dressage and show jumpers have time off at different periods during the year. The more high powered the work the horse is performing the more vital it is to give him a holiday for relaxation. Riding school horses are often given a break to prevent staleness and deterioration in their 'way of going'.

Fittening Programme

Revision Stage II

Fittening timetable and considerations. Variations for fittening programmes, methods of fittening. Hazards of the fittening process, injuries through concussion.

The fittening programme is designed to suit the type of horse and his work.

Type of Horse	Work	Length of Programme
Riding Club	Small cross-country events, Prelim/Novice dressage competitions, hacking	6 weeks
Hunter	Cub hunting in September - full hunting in November 1 – 2 days a week	6 weeks cub hunting 8 to 10 weeks full hunting
Dressage	Dressage competitions	8 to 10 weeks
Show Jumper	Show jumping	8 to 10 weeks
Long Distance	Endurance riding, long distance hacking. Needs to build up stamina	10 to 12 weeks
Novice Eventer	Novice dressage, show jumping and cross-country	10 to 12 weeks
Three day Eventer	Dressage, show jumping, steeple chasing and cross-country	12 to18 weeks
Golden Horse Shoe	Endurance riding over greater distances	12 to 18 weeks

The more advanced the horse and work the greater the amount of time and the variation in time. To build up fitness the horse has to also build up muscle fibre. When muscles grow 'soft' their fibres diminish and reduce in size. The fibres must then be built up gradually to create thicker and stronger fibres. Tendons and ligaments too need to become more supple, more strong to cope with exercise.

Method of Fittening

The three aspects of the fittening programme, stable management, exercise and feeding, should all be related to each other. Preparations can be made prior to the horse being brought up from grass.

* The stable is thoroughly cleaned and disinfected a few days to a week before the horse is brought in. Bringing him into a stable immediately after using strong disinfectant may give the horse skin problems or weepy eyes.

* Bedding can be placed in the box the day before. This should be as dust free as possible. May use shavings at first and change to straw later if required.

* Check that the ventilation in the stable is airy but not draughty.

* All tack and clothing, such as blankets, should have been cleaned and stored, they may now need airing and checking.

* New food can be ordered. Old, stale food should have been thrown away; the horse should never be fed on stale food.

A few days to a week before the fittening programme starts the horse may be brought into the stable for short periods. He can be given a small feed, a handful of pony cubes or pasture mix and some hay. This will help to condition his digestive system to the 'new' food and his body to the change in temperature and atmosphere in the stable.

Grooming can begin with a quick brush down. Gradually the grooming can be increased to quartering.

He can be wormed, inoculated if necessary, have his teeth seen to by the Vet or dentist and have his shoes put on. Remember **W.I.T.S.** worming, inoculations, teeth and shoes.

Check the horse's tack; his shape will have changed and he may need a different saddle to start with or numnahs underneath his normal saddle to prevent sores and galls. Surgical spirits can be rubbed gently into the saddle and girth area to harden the skin.

He may have his tack put on for short periods, possibly be led in hand for 15 minutes or so, to help him become accustomed to wearing this again and to prepare his skin and back.

Exercise and feeding are closely related, but exercise should come first. The longer and harder the exercise, the more 'hard' food is then fed. If too little or too much exercise is done in relation to feed then problems can arise.

The exercise is balanced to build up the horse's physical fitness gradually, to 'harden' his legs slowly to the effect of exercise and to prepare him mentally for work. At first the majority of the horse's feed is roughage. This should be meadow hay to begin with changing later in the programme, if required, to seed hay or vacuum-packed forage.

Planning the Programme

Depending on the type of work for which the horse is being prepared, many owners plan the timing of their fittening programme based on the date of the horse's first competition or event.

Most owners will have a date for their first competition and, working back, count the number of weeks to the start of the programme. They may then add a couple of weeks to allow for any problems.

Ideally the horse should peak at the competition date. If he should peak a week before though, this is no problem as he can be kept 'ticking over' for a week with a more relaxed work schedule. It is better that a horse is a little too fit for the competition rather than unfit.

Most importantly the programme needs to be adjustable and adaptable to allow for any situation that may arise. If the horse becomes injured in the middle of the timetable, the programme should not be adhered to rigidly as this would be risking increased injury.

* The programme needs to be adjusted even to the point where the first competition is postponed until the horse is ready. The golden rule is to monitor the horse closely throughout the programme.

* The fittening programme given as an example is suitable for most hunters, more advanced horses will be need extra time.

* Higher performance horses will need longer periods for walking and slow trot work. The longer the fittening process takes the longer the horse will stay fit.

* Riding club and school horses are normally fit for full work within six weeks. It does though depend on the horse. These types of horses will generally not have any specific date to work towards.

* Horses coming back into work after recuperation from an illness or injury may need longer to become fully fit.

Example of fittening timetable for a Hunter over eight weeks

Week	Exercise	Feed Hay	Concentrates	Comments
1	**15 minutes** increasing **to 45 minutes. Walk** on flat ground.	90%	10% Low energy compound or barley, sugar beet and chaff.	Continue some hours daily at grass. Check tack areas. Quartering - pull mane and tail. Protect with boots for exercise.
2	**45 minutes** increasing **to 1 hour. Walk** on **flat**, including some **roadwork**.	85%	15%	Reducing time at grass. Protect with boots, for roadwork. Check tack areas. Watch condition for excess sweating.
3	**1 hour per day Walk** up and down **hills. Trot** -short periods **up to 1 minute** increase to two or three times in 1 hour.	80%	20%	Check tack areas. Grooming now upgraded to strapping.
4	Increase work to **1½ hours per day Trot** work increase. **May introduce schooling sessions** for 10 to 15 minutes **couple of times a week.** Short **canter** by end of the week.	70%	30%	
5	**Trot** up and down hills. Slowly increase **trotting** and **cantering** time each day. **Increase schooling on flat to 30 minutes on some days.** May introduce **jumping** over small fences.	60%	40%	Keep monitoring horse in stable and at exercise. Check tack areas and shoes.
6	Increase work **so that on some days the horse is doing up to 2 hours**; long hack or two single hours in one day (one hour hack and one hour flatwork and jumping.) **Horse could be lunged.** Introduce **short canter up hills.** Include fast canter by end of week.	60%	40% Oats may be introduced or Competition Mix.	Horse needs shoeing. Worm before day off. Horse may go cub hunting, a shorter, quieter hunt.
7	**One good gallop** (pipe opener) during week. Horse is now in full work.	60%	40% Energy food increased.	
8	**Increase canter work** up and (carefully) down hills.	60%	40%	Keep checking tack areas.

General Points

There are various points that will improve the effectiveness of the fittening programme.

∗   Introduce variety in the work. Change the course on hacks, school in different schools or paddocks if possible, loose school or jump in an indoor menage. Keeping the work varied will prevent the horse becoming stale.

* Modify the work according to the horse. If he becomes too excited and sweaty, keep the any canter work to short bursts. Alternatively if he is fit a long canter may calm him down rather than quick short canters.

* Modify the exercise according to weather conditions. Particular care should be taken in hot, humid weather, when the horse may sweat excessively, and in dry, dusty conditions.

* Watch the ground. Keep to good going if possible. Work slowly on hard or very muddy ground. On the roads trot only on straight areas.

* Change the rein frequently when schooling and lungeing to avoid one-sidedness. Change the trot diagonal and alternate the canter lead when hacking for the same reason.

* From the start insist that the horse works correctly. Use the fittening programme as a training programme as well. Encourage a good walk with the horse seeking the contact. Trot work should be an active, balanced trot. Even with a steady, slow trot at the beginning of the programme, insist the horse trots correctly. Do not allow the horse to jog trot, this is an evasion. Insist on smooth obedient transitions.

Problems

There is always the risk of injury, a kick in the field, a cut or scratch, but a carefully designed fitness plan will prevent most problems, injuries and accidents from occurring.

* Tack sores, girth galls, open wounds around the tack areas, can be caused by the tack rubbing on a soft skin.

* Dietary problems are numerous if the horse's diet is not changed gradually, colic, azoturia, filled legs and even mental problems.

* The horse may suffer from respiratory problems coming in from a pasture to the dry, dustier atmosphere of the stable: coughs, colds and chills.

* Boredom through long hours in the stable can lead to bad habits, weaving, crib biting. The horse needs to be worked steadily and allowed frequent pasture time.

* The horse may even suffer from exhaustion if pushed too hard and this in turn can lead to accidents and injuries. Weariness will also lead to mental stress and loss of condition. A tired horse will be much more susceptible to other diseases and illnesses.

Concussive Damage

Injury to joints, tendons, ligaments and muscles can be a potential hazard of the fittening timetable. Working on hard ground particularly early in the programme, working the horse too much too quickly, fast work before his musculature is prepared can all lead to injuries.

The results of concussive damage are windgalls, formation of splints, navicular syndrome, ringbone, bruised muscles and tendons, sidebone and arthritis.

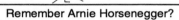
Remember Arnie Horsenegger?

Concussive damage can cause real problems.

It is necessary to judge the horse's capabilities. Work on the road at walk and slow trot is valuable for hardening the legs, but an excess of work on hard ground and fast work over stony areas and brick hard mud can lead to weeks off work and a serious setback in the programme.

Judging Fitness

Each horse is different and the cliché 'know your horse' plays an important role in judging fitness.

Body   his body will begin to muscle up. He will look leaner and stronger in his frame. His muscles will begin to show under the skin particularly around the neck, crest, shoulder, back and hindquarters. His skin may look shinier.

Respiration   his respiration rate will alter through exercise. At first only small amounts of exercise will make him breathe faster, as the programme progresses this increase in the respiration rate will occur later through his work.

Sweating   though no horse should sweat excessively, an unfit or overweight horse will sweat quite easily at first. Later in the programme he will perform work without too much sweating and, when fit, he will sweat hardly at all, except in hot weather.

Exercise   he will progressively find the exercise easier. He may even start to become a little springier perhaps even a little full of himself at times. Whilst no horse should be pushed to continue working when he is tired, it will become apparent that the horse can progressively do more work with ease.

For higher performance horses the fitness can be more precisely judged in a type of fittening plan called 'interval training'.

Interval Training

This is a specific type of fittening process normally used for horses performing harder, faster work such as eventers and long distance endurance horses. It involves timed periods of cantering and walking, building up the muscles and improving the heart and respiration rates to a higher degree. The heart and respiration rates can be closely monitored to keep a record of progress.

Interval training can *begin around week 6 of the normal fittening programme*. Some horses, younger, older or less fit, may need to wait *until the 7th or 8th week*. The horse can begin interval training after he has had two or three canters within the normal programme.

The interval training schedule may be as follows

The horse is warmed up first with an initial period of walk and trot.

1st and 2nd weeks   3 minutes canter followed by 3 minutes walk repeated three times. This is done **every fourth day** and will take 18 minutes in total.

3rd and 4th weeks   5 minutes canter followed by 3 minutes walk repeated three times, **every fourth day**. This will take 24 minutes in total.

5th and 6th weeks   7 minutes canter followed by 3 minutes walk repeated three times, **every fourth day**. This will take 30 minutes in total.

The canter should ideally be done on flat ground. If cantering on hilly ground the time of each canter should be reduced as this is more strenuous. During the non-interval training days the normal work continues: schooling, hacking, jumping and the horse's day of rest.

The heart and respiration rates are monitored between each canter, each interval training day. The respiration rate can be monitored by counting the breaths per minute during the walk period. The heartbeat is monitored by a stethoscope or a special heart monitor attached to the horse.

The horse's heart and respiratory rates should improve during the training period. Both rates should increasingly return to normal in a shorter time. Once the rates stabilise, that is return to normal at a similar time after each session, the horse has achieved fitness.

To be precise the horse should be worked over the same ground in the same weather conditions, but this is not always practical and any slight deviation should be taken into consideration.

The horse should never be pushed beyond his capabilities and if he breathes heavily and does not recover within the three-minute walk period, the training should be reduced and limited until he is sufficiently fit to cope.

Note: whilst some riders find interval training extremely beneficial to their horses, others do not endorse this type of training. It depends on personal preference, experience and the individual horse. The point about interval training is that it gives a structured approach for training a horse to further fitness and a basis on which to monitor the horse systematically over a period of time.

Maintaining Fitness

Once the horse has achieved fitness, the next point is to maintain this fitness throughout his work. This is a balance between exercise, feeding and relaxation.

The type of exercise and food depends on the horse and his work. Most horse will keep fit on a work schedule of one hour a day; some need a little more to keep to the level of fitness they need for competition. Variety in the exercise schedule is important for horses in any discipline. All horses will need a mixture of schooling on the flat, hacking out, lungeing, jumping and some time spent at pasture to relax.

Preparation of Horses for Events and Competitions

Preparing a horse for competition or showing involves day to day care. His food, exercise and relaxation will be carefully designed to keep him in the condition he needs to compete. Any competition is the result or culmination of months of hard work from both rider and horse.

Ultimately the horse needs to be trained for his specific discipline and the rider or owner will need to be consistent, constant and firm if the horse is to be successful.

Whatever the standard of horse, whether he is a school horse, a riding club horse or a high performance horse, his training should be as correct as possible from the start. If a horse is taught the correct basics he will find his work so much easier (as will the rider). Even with an older horse the fitness programme can be taken as an opportunity to teach discipline.

* The horse should stand still and quiet when having his tack put on and when the rider is mounting. He should stand still until the rider is ready to move and has given the signal.

* He should walk with active forward steps seeking the bit. For a young horse or one just coming back into work, the walk should not be 'on the bit' to start with as this can destroy a good walk. The horse should stretch forward into the rider's yielding hand.

* He should never be allowed to jog. On hard surfaces such as roads the horse should trot slowly. This will harden the hooves and strengthen the bones without the risk of slipping and concussion. Though in some countries the jog is a recognised pace, and very pleasant to sit to, the horse unless taught to jog uses this as an evasion. He is either refusing to walk or trot correctly. On good surfaces the horse should walk actively or trot actively.

* When coming to halt he should be persuaded by the rider's back, seat, legs and hands to halt squarely with his hocks underneath him. If he does have one leg out of line the rider should quietly correct this or walk on and halt again.

* He should be taught responsiveness to the rider's aids particularly the leg aids. If he is disobedient, he should be reminded by a tap with the whip.

* He should be discouraged from napping either on a hack or in the school. The rider needs to be firm about his veering towards or slowing down by the door, gate or other horses.

* The rider should keep the horse balanced in all paces, avoiding any sudden stops or sharp turns. These may also cause tendon or ligament injuries.

Care of all horses through the fittening programme is important if they are to remain in good health, condition and continue to compete successfully.

Exam Tips

At Stage II the fittening programme was covered basically, at Stage III the Examiners will be looking for more practical experience. You should know the relevant fittening times for each type of horse and the timetable of exercise, feeding and stable management throughout this programme. You should also know the hazards of the fittening process particularly the dangers of concussion if the horse is worked too hard too quickly.

For owners, working pupils and competitors who have had to take a horse through a fittening programme, the knowledge and experience will be evident. Not everyone though will have this type of experience. Reading articles in magazines about the fittening process, or books written by actual competitors who bring their own horses on, will certainly help widen your knowledge.

C H A P T E R   18
Saddlery

The cleaning, maintenance and storage of saddlery are important aspects of stable management. Tack that is allowed to become dirty, worn, cracked and generally dilapidated will cause problems, accidents and injuries, for both horse and rider. The tack room needs to be organised so that all saddlery is kept in clean, dry and secure conditions.

The Tack Room

Ideally the tack room needs to be situated centrally and conveniently near to the yard and stables. Having to carry heavy tack some distance, especially in the pouring rain, would certainly not be convenient or efficient.

Some larger yards have two or even three tack rooms. These may each serve a stable block, or be divided into school tack, livery tack and competition tack.

Space

The room should be spacious to accommodate all the tack and any clothing, such as rugs, with ease. It may include cleaning facilities and if so, there should be sufficient room for cleaning without staff having to clamber over each other or bump into bridle hooks hanging from the ceiling.

Temperature

* The temperature should, if possible, be kept fairly constant, cool rather than cold or hot. Electric fan heaters can be placed high on the wall *away from the tack* to warm the room in winter. Direct heat onto tack is a fire hazard and will also crack the leather.

* Electric fans could also be used to cool the temperature in summer.

* The room should be well ventilated to allow a free flow of air, but not draughty.

* The room should definitely be dry. The roof, walls, windows and guttering should be well situated and maintained to prevent rain from leaking into the room and onto the tack.

* Leather deteriorates in constantly changing temperatures and wet or damp conditions.

Construction

∗   Ideally the room should be brick built with a slate roof. The floor, usually of concrete, should allow good drainage.

∗   Wooden buildings are prone to quick temperature changes and are a fire hazard.

Lighting

∗   Lighting needs to be good; electric strip lighting is best.

∗   Sunlight should be restricted; the heat will crack the leather and the sun fades the colour.

Fittings

∗   There should be a fire extinguisher.

∗   Each saddle should have its own named rack and each bridle a named semicircular holder. The bridles and saddles should be positioned on the opposite walls so that they do not become crowded and entangled together. The saddle racks and bridle holders should be high enough to keep the tack from trailing on the floor but not too high to make it difficult to put the bridle and saddle away.

∗   There should be plenty of room between each saddle rack and bridle holder so that the tack does not become crushed and damaged. Cramped space makes it difficult to put tack away and there is then a tendency to just dump it on top of other tack, or on the floor.

∗   Any other equipment such as lungeing cavessons, lungeing reins or side reins should have their own area.

∗   There may also be places for spare girths, bits, stirrup irons and leathers, breastplates and martingales.

∗   Numnahs, saddle cloths and seat savers could be kept in marked lockers.

∗   There may be wooden saddle racks as extra places to put saddles and numnahs.

∗   A notice board or blackboard is useful for noting the position for each horse's tack and for tacking up lists and worksheets.

Other items that may be kept in the tack room if there is space are grooming kits, a clock, cupboards for bandages, brushing boots, knee and hock boots, overreach boots.

Security

All tack rooms need complete security. Tack thefts are common and even if left during the day, the door should be locked.

The door should be strong and have a lock and padlock. The windows should have bars. There should be a burglar alarm and a security light within the yard. Any connecting doors should be bolted from the inside.

Tack can be numbered and registered. There should also be a list of all the tack and other equipment kept in the room. If the tack is insured, the insurance company may wish to check the security arrangements.

Cleaning facilities

The tack cleaning area may be situated within the tack room or be in a separate room.

* The floor needs good drainage to prevent damp and condensation. An extractor fan to extract damp air would help to keep the atmosphere dry.

* Saddle racks and bridle hooks will be needed. The bridle hooks should be situated out of the way or, ideally, on telescopic cords so that they can be raised and lowered when required.

* There should be a sink with hot and cold water. Alternatively a boiler or geyser could supply hot water. The sink will need a draining board.

* There should be plenty of work surface and cupboards for sponges, cloths, soap, saddle soap, oil or leather dressing. Shelving would also provide space for various items.

Other items that may prove useful are: an electric kettle, a dustbin, a clock, a radio, plenty of clean towels. There should be space for dirty equipment ready to be cleaned and perhaps a locker or cupboard for tack that needs repairing.

Organising the Tack Room

No matter how splendid the tack room, organisation is essential for its efficient use and the care of tack.

1. All tack should be put away correctly after use. Saddles on their racks, bridles hung correctly with the reins secured by the throatlash.

2. All tack and equipment should be clearly named. The name of the horse can be displayed above the bridle holder and saddle rack.

3. The floor should be swept clean daily.

4. The working surfaces should be cleaned after use.

5. All litter and rubbish should be thrown away as this poses a fire risk.

6. The stock can be checked regularly and inspected for repair or replacement.

7. Electric lighting, fans, heaters, kettles should be checked regularly and mended or replaced if faulty.

8. The alarm system, padlocks, door locks, window bars and other security measures should be checked and maintained.

9. Any leaks from windows, doors, walls or ceiling should be repaired immediately.

10. It may be difficult to monitor people going in and out, but everyone on the yard should be aware of strangers and challenge them or inform a senior member of staff if someone unfamiliar is around. In yards where the tack is valuable or there is a large amount of tack it may be worth installing video surveillance.

Rugs may be kept in the tack room if this is large enough, but ideally there should be a rug room. Wet rugs should be kept away from the tack. If the tack room is efficient this will be evident throughout the yard. Staff will be able to prepare the horses and ponies quickly and extra tack will be easy to find when needed. Most importantly the tack will be in good condition, clean and safe to use.

Saddlery

There are many designs of bridles and saddles plus accessories, which have been developed over the centuries to help riders and horses.

Bridles and Bits

There are seven main types of bridles and bits.

1. The snaffle
2. The gag (gag snaffle)
3. The pelham
4. The kimblewick (often classed with the Pelham)
5. The bitless bridle
6. The curb (normally associated with the double)
7. The double

The bridle is designed to indicate to the horse, through various contact points around his head, the rider's intentions. Most bridles, apart from the bitless bridles, are centred around the type of bit used in the horse's mouth.

Revision

Stage I The snaffle bridle, points of. Snaffle bits, points of, materials, types, double jointed, single jointed, straight bar and mullen mouth. Bitrings, loose ring, eggbutt, D ring, full-cheeked snaffle, loose ringed fulmer. Nosebands, types of, cavesson, flash, drop, grakle. Putting on and fitting a snaffle bridle. Removing the bridle. Cleaning the bridle.

Stage II Snaffle bridle, points of. Fitting the bridle. Kineton noseband. Types of bit. Principles of bitting. Action of bits, single jointed, straight bar, mullen mouth. Size of bit, measuring, checking. Overbitting. Accessories, bit guards, brush pricker, Australian cheeker, grass reins. Poor fitting and dirty tack. Martingales and breastplates.

In this section the other bit types are covered, with descriptions of their action and uses.

The Gag

This bridle usually has a single jointed or straight bar bit. The rings of the bit are adapted with extra holes to allow a rein to pass through and be attached to the headpiece.

∗ The extra leverage of the gag exerts **pressure on the poll as well as on the mouth**.

∗ Though the bit is often used with one rein only, the gag should have two reins, the gag rein and an ordinary rein.

The English Gag with two reins   The English Gag with one rein

∗ As the gag snaffle has the effect of raising the horse's head it is effective on horses who stick their heads down to their chests and pull.

∗ This is designed for horses that are strong or for riders who are not yet strong enough to keep the horse at the required pace.

∗ Fitted as a normal snaffle bit, high enough to wrinkle the horse's lips at the corners of his mouth.

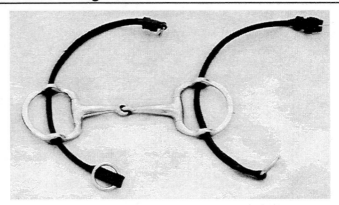

*   There are different designs and variations of the gag snaffle. Some gag bits have multiple rings; the American gag features a long shank with a ring at the top and lower ends.

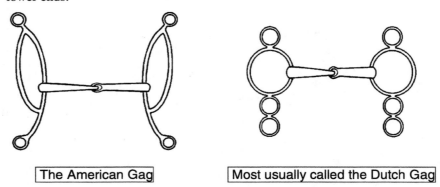

The American Gag   Most usually called the Dutch Gag

The Pelham

Originally the Pelham was designed to combine the action of the two bits of the double bridle. The Pelham can have a straight bar mouthpiece, sometimes with a port, or a single jointed mouthpiece. The mouthpiece can be made of vulcanite. The reins are attached via two rings, one where the mouthpiece connects and the other to a small ring at the lower end of the shank. There is also a small ring at the top for the curb hook and a connection for the lipstrap between the mouthpiece ring and the lower ring.

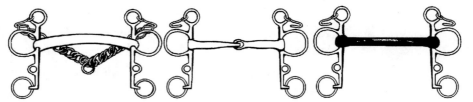

*   Pressure is applied to the **bars of the mouth, lips, chin groove** via the chain and the **poll**.

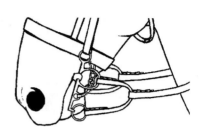

* Can be used with two reins or with one rein attached to leather loops called roundings, though the use of roundings lessens the effect of the Pelham.

* Usually used on **stronger horses** or for children on strong ponies.

* Strong **cobby** types go well in a pelham as their short, wide jaws suit this kind of bit.

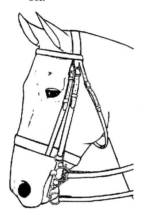

* Used in the show ring if the double bridle is unsuitable for some reason.

* Fitted a little lower than the snaffle close to the corners of the mouth, without wrinkling the lips.

* The curb chain is normally fitted inside the bitring next to the horse's face. (It may be fastened through the bitring so that the hook does not chafe.)

The curb chain is fitted onto the offside hook and then twisted in a clockwise direction until straight. The lipstrap hook should lie to the bottom of the chain. The chain is fastened to the nearside hook so that it lies flat against the horse's chin.

Another variation is the Army Reversible Pelham. This features cheeks with slots at different heights. The leverage is altered by fastening the lower rein to the higher or lower slot.

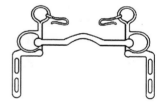

The Pelham helps certain horses, making an improvement in their work. Some horses, though, do not suit the Pelham at all. It makes them heavy in the hand, encouraging them to lean on the bit. It also can make them strong in their way of going.

The Kimblewick

This is a straight bar bit with an arched mouthpiece (a port or tongue groove), a fixed 'D' ring and a curb chain. The bitring can either be solid or contain slots.

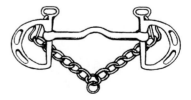

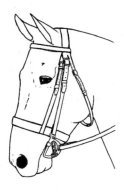

- This bit is especially suitable for children on strong ponies as the action is stronger than a snaffle.

- It acts on the **bars of the mouth, the chin groove and the poll**.

- Fitted as the Pelham close to the corners of the horse's mouth without wrinkling the lips.

Similar to the Pelham, this bit can be useful on some horses and ponies. On others it makes them stronger, lean on the bit or in some cases, back off the bit refusing to go forward.

The Bitless Bridle (often termed the Hackamore)

The bitless bridle as the name implies has no bit or mouthpiece. There are a variety of designs available.

∗   Puts pressure on the **poll and the nose**.

∗   Used on horses who have an **injured or sore mouth, poor mouth conformation**, or who **object strongly to a bit**.

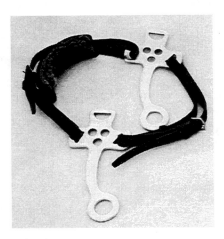
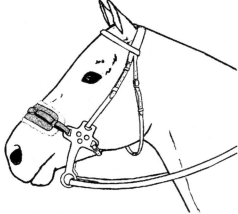

The Blair's pattern bitless bridle

Excellent for use on horses who need a rest from wearing a bit; many horses do thrive on this type of bridle. Some horses though do not like the effect, which can be quite strong. Some cobby types or stronger horses often ignore it completely and riding these types in a bitless bridle can be a nightmare.

The Curb

The curb is a bit in its own right but, rarely used on its own, it is more commonly combined with the bridoon to make up a double bridle.

The Double Bridle

Consisting of two bits, the bridoon and the curb, each has a set of reins. The double bridle, providing a refined feel, is used primarily for flat work and is compulsory in advanced Dressage Events. The right hand ring of the bridoon is attached to a cheekpiece. The left hand ring to a sliphead (a headpiece and cheekpiece combined). The cheekpiece and sliphead fasten on the right side of the horse's face. The cavesson is the only noseband that should be used with a double bridle.

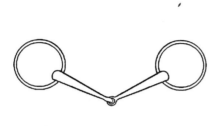

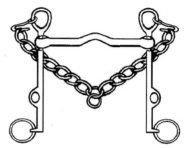

The bridoon bit

A sliding cheek Weymouth bit with mouth port and long cheeks.

The curb bit is attached to cheekpieces connected to a headpiece. The curb chain can be single or double ringed and is attached to the hooks on the top rings of the curb bit. The chain should have a single 'fly link' in the centre which, when the chain is fitted, should lie to the lower end of the chain. This enables the lipstrap to pass through the link and hold the chain in place. Sometimes curb chains are covered with leather.

The lipstrap has a longer and shorter part. The shorter portion is fastened to the lipstrap ring on the horse's left hand side. The longer portion is connected to the right hand ring. The lipstrap passes through the fly link in the curb chain and fastens on the left under the horse's chin.

The functions of the lipstrap are:

* It helps to keep the chain in place, preventing it from rising too high and catching the sensitive bones under the jaw.

* It holds the chain in place should the chain come unfastened.

* Modifies the action of the cheeks of the bit preventing them from swinging from side to side.

* It prevents the horse from grabbing hold of the cheeks of the bit.

There are two reins, one attached to the bridoon bit and one to the curb. The curb reins attached to the lower ring on the cheeks, should be narrower in width than the bridoon reins.

Points of the Double Bridle

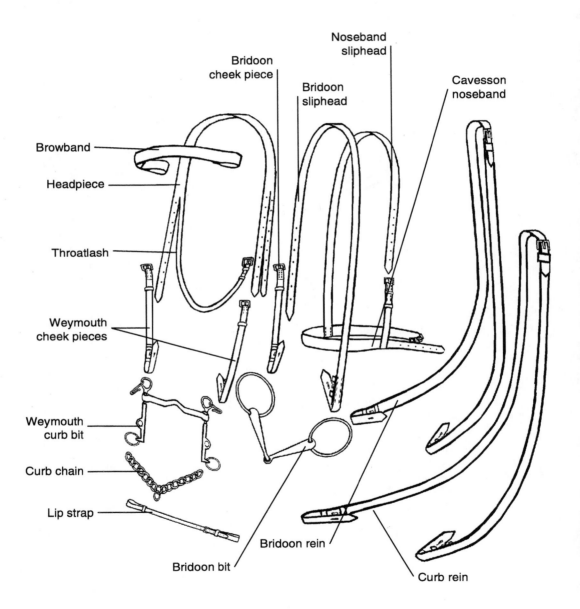

Browband

Headpiece

Throatlash

Bridoon cheek piece

Noseband sliphead

Bridoon sliphead

Cavesson noseband

Weymouth cheek pieces

Weymouth curb bit

Curb chain

Lip strap

Bridoon bit

Bridoon rein

Curb rein

Action of the Bridoon

As in the normal single jointed snaffle, this bit encourages the horse to raise his head, if this is held too low. When the horse holds his head low the joint of the mouthpiece comes into contact with the roof of his mouth.

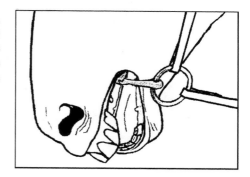

Action of the Curb Bit

The more complicated curb bit is based on a lever action. The reins bring the lower end of the cheeks backwards putting pressure on the curb chain under the chin, and onto the poll through the cheekpieces and headpiece of the bridle. The longer the cheeks, the more leverage can be exerted and the more severe the bit.

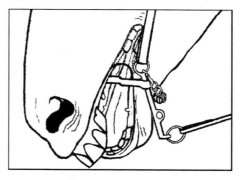

The aim is to use the refined aid of the curb to encourage the horse to flex through a supple poll and relax his mouth, head, neck and back. This is achieved by applying a very delicate, light pressure with the curb bit. The horse should be encouraged to use himself with a better balance and self-carriage.

* Allows a lighter, finer feel on the horse's mouth.

* Helps to balance and control the horse.

* Puts **pressure on the bars of the mouth, lips, chin groove and poll**. Lower cheekpiece puts leverage on the curb chain. Upper cheekpiece puts leverage on the poll.

The whole feeling of using the bridoon and curb should be one of a light, quiet contact with the horse coming forwards into inviting hands.

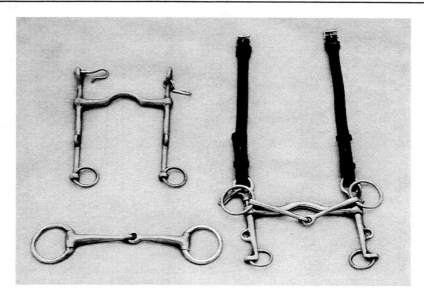

1. Top left a weymouth bit
2. Lower left an eggbut bridoon
3. Right a bridoon and weymouth together

Putting on the Double Bridle

Make an approximate measurement of the bridle as normal by holding it by the horse's head with the headpiece and the mouthpiece in their relevant positions. Any alterations can then be made prior to fitting. Once the bridle looks correct, undo the headcollar, refasten it around the horse's neck as normal, remembering to slip the leadrope so that it is hanging loose through the string of the securing ring.

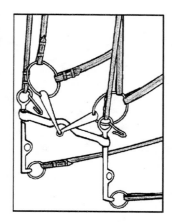

The two bits are held in the left hand with the bridoon bitrings inside, and behind the curb. The bridoon mouthpiece lies in front of the curb mouthpiece; the joint in front of the port on the curb bit. The top of the bridle is held in the right hand as normal and the bits are slipped gently into the horse's mouth.

Fitting

Both bits should be sufficiently wide, approximately 5 mm or ¼ inch wider **on each side of the horse's mouth**. Too narrow and they will pinch perhaps causing sores. Too wide and there will be excessive movement in the horse's mouth, which could be uncomfortable.

The bridoon should just wrinkle the corner of the mouth. The curb bit should be slightly below the bridoon. There should be room for the tip of the thumb to fit between the bridoon and the curb. Too close and the bits will interfere with each other. Too far apart and the bits will either be too high or low in the mouth, or have a totally incorrect action.

The curb chain has to rest flat against the horse's chin in the chin groove. Place one of the end links on the offside hook. Twist the chain around clockwise until all the rings are flat against each other. The fly link should be at the lower edge of the chain. If not adjust the chain on the hook again.

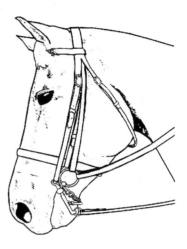

Once the chain is flat turn the chain again halfway and place the link onto the nearside hook. The chain should now be flat against the horse's chin.

To check that the curb chain is the correct length, take the curb rein and gently bring the curb cheek backwards. The chain should touch the horse when the curb cheek is approximately at a 45° angle to the horse's mouth. At times the chain may be slightly tighter but this requires a knowledgeable rider. Any looser and the chain will be ineffective.

Thread the lipstrap through the fly link and fasten on the nearside.

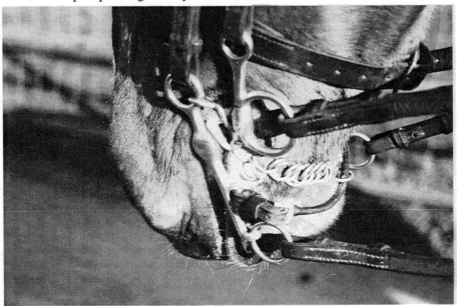

Leading with a double bridle

The horse should be led with the bridoon reins only. The curb reins should stay on the horse's neck. The bridoon reins should be arranged so that they are **inside** the curb reins. If the horse is led with the bridoon reins outside this will interfere with the curb bit and the horse may object.

1. To arrange the bridoon reins, first make sure that the reins are not tangled. Lie them on the horse's neck just above the withers with the bridoon reins in front of the curb reins.

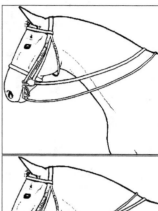

2. Now pass the curb reins over the top of the bridoon reins and place them in front.

3. Take the bridoon reins and pass them over the top of the curb reins and over the horse's head.

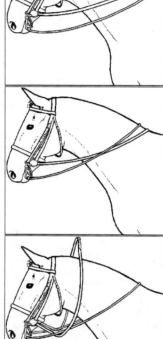

4. The bridoon reins will now be inside the curb reins and the horse can be led as normal.

This method ensures that the horse is led from the bridoon bit, not the curb and that the bridoon reins do not interfere with the curb.

The Principles of Bitting

With many different types of bit and a seemingly endless variation within each group it can be quite difficult to make the right decision as to which bit to use. Mostly it is the preference of the rider. Many will swear by one bit whilst others utterly deplore the use of the same. There are those who believe that only a snaffle should be used in a horse's mouth.

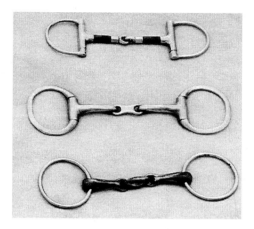

1. Copper roller D ring snaffle

2. French link eggbut snaffle

3. German KK training bit with link

The best method of choosing a bit is to begin with the mildest one possible and to experiment until one is found which suits the horse and rider. After all the aim is to keep the horse's mouth soft and relaxed with him working forwards in a rounder shape into the bit. If a horse is wearing a bit that causes him pain, he naturally will either run away from it or refuse to work into it.

Each horse and rider is different and what suits one combination will not necessarily suit another. Some horses will relax more in a straight bar bit or even a Pelham than a single or double jointed snaffle. Some riders prefer the feel of a double jointed snaffle than a straight bar or a bit with a single joint. Some horses and riders prefer a loose ring rather than an eggbut. Whatever suits the horse and his rider, making them relax with each other, is the right bit for them.

Some tack shops hire out bits, or it may be possible to borrow from friends. Eventually with experimentation and experience the right bit will be discovered for the benefit of rider and horse.

Young horses

Young horses should ideally be started on the mildest bit possible. This does depend on the horse, his mouth conformation and the rider. The snaffle is best, particularly the loose ring German training bit, double jointed with egg shaped link. This is a mild bit and having seen many young horses trained in this, particularly for dressage, it does seem to work very well. Other snaffles are the D ring which will help with steering or an eggbut which prevents the ring pinching the horse's lips.

For young horses learning to accept a double bridle the Tom Thumb can be used. This is often beneficial for young show horses. The Tom Thumb has short cheeks and, having less leverage, is milder.

Difficult horses

As with all horses the bit is just one part of the whole system, which includes the rider's balance, riding skill, use of leg and body aids and then the hands. So many times riders try to find a bit suitable for their horse when really the horse and the rider just need to improve their training and skill.

We cannot all be excellent riders overnight (I wish!) so we have to keep learning, improving and expanding our understanding and skill. It is surely better to find a bit that suits both horse and rider and which makes both happy, than to try and muddle along with a 'correct' or 'prescribed' bit which suits neither.

With difficult horses the approach should be to first discover the problem. Riding a horse in a stronger, more severe bit does not always solve the difficulties. Sometimes the situation is made worse, especially if the horse is suffering from a sore mouth or simply with troublesome wolf teeth.

For a horse with a sore mouth the obvious alternative is the bitless bridle or hackamore. For a horse with a dry, fixed mouth a copper roller or a synthetic apple scented bit. The Nathe bit or nylon covered bits are generally very mild and will help a horse whose mouth is tender.

For stronger horses the Pelham can be very effective and some horses do work better in this type of bit. For strong ponies the Kimblewick can be tried. Sometimes though horses can learn to 'lean' or back off these types of bits in which case reverting to a milder snaffle can have a good effect.

Bit Attachments

Sometimes bit attachments are as good at mending problems as changing the bit. For the horse who has tender lips because the bitring chafes, rubber bit guards are used to protect the mouth. A brush pricker, a rubber bitguard with bristles, can be used to discourage a horse from leaning to that side. A tongue grid is often used to stop a horse putting his tongue over the bit.

Different nosebands, the flash, drop and grakle, are used with certain bits to prevent the horse evading by opening his mouth or crossing the jaw. Martingales are used to prevent the horse tossing his head upwards, sometimes dangerously, or from weaving the head from side to side.

It does depend on the horse and his problem and often it is through trial, error and experience that the right type of bit or attachment is found. Hopefully the problem is a temporary one and the horse can return to his normal bit when this is solved.

Saddles

Revision

Stage I and II, types of saddles, points of the saddle, materials, functions. Putting on and checking the fit of a saddle. Attachments, martingales, breastplates, cruppers, functions and fitting. Types of girth, numnahs and saddle cloths.

Saddles are available in different designs to suit the various disciplines, but no matter which type of saddle is used, the essential element is that it fits the horse correctly and is also the right size for the rider.

Whilst the saddle should not be blamed for poor riding, the frequent statement of 'the saddle does not make a difference' is totally untrue. Anyone who has sat on a uncomfortable, painful saddle will testify that the saddle can make a world of difference to the riding.

Riders do come in all shapes and sizes and it is important that the rider can sit comfortably and be able to use the leg aids effectively. A saddle can be a very personal possession, but in riding schools where a number of riders sit on the same saddle and horse, a good GP saddle that accommodates a range of riders is worth its weight in gold.

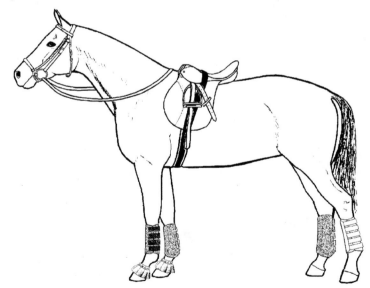

Surcingle girth

This is used primarily for extra safety on a cross-country course, in case the normal girth comes undone or breaks for some reason. It fits over the top of the saddle and around the horse's body on top of the normal girth. It is fitted firmly with the fastening positioned under the horse's belly in the centre of the normal girth.

In Competition

In competitions there are rules governing the types of tack and attachments that may be permitted.

Type of tack permitted for the three disciplines

Tack/discipline	Dressage	Show Jumping	Eventing
Bridle	*Prelim/Novice*: snaffle *Elementary/Advanced medium:* snaffle or double bridle *Above:* double bridle	Gag, pelham, bitless bridle, snaffle	*Dressage:* snaffle or double bridle *Show jumping*: gag, Pelham, snaffle, bitless bridle *X-country*: gag, pelham, snaffle
Saddle	Dressage or GP	Jumping	Dressage/jumping/X-country
Permitted bridle attachments	None	Bitguards, martingales	Bitguards, martingales
Nosebands	Cavesson, flash, drop	Any	Cavesson, flash, drop, grakle in all three phases
Permitted saddle attachments	Breastplate	Breastplate	Breastplate, surcingle girth in X-country
Boots/bandages	None	Brushing, tendon, overreach	Brushing boots or bandages, overreach boots

Exam Tips

The section dealing with the tack room and its organisation will normally be in the form of a general discussion. Observe various tack rooms, noting their good and bad points. Design your own tack room using your preferences and experiences so that you can understand why this room needs to be organised in an efficient way. Be critical, consider your likes and dislikes about the tack room in the yard where you work or usually ride.

Candidates need to know the different groups of bits, the actions of each bit and why one bit would be used as opposed to another. It is possible there will be various bits available for you to name and describe. Sometimes this section may take the form of a general discussion or the Examiner could ask about bits whilst you are tacking up a horse for a competition during the Practical section. Each group of candidates will be asked to put on and fit a double bridle. Take your time to check the tack, feel the bits, measure them for width and correct distance from each other.

You will be requested to tack a horse up for a competition, dressage, show jumping or eventing. A variety of tack will be available and you will need to chose the right type of bridle and bit, saddle, attachments, boots, girths. The Examiner may then ask you about the fitting of the tack, bridle, saddle and any attachments; if this tack is suitable for the horse and discipline and if you could suggest any further tack required.

C H A P T E R   19
Rugs and Bandages

Rugs are primarily used during the winter, to keep the horse warm in the stable and dry when out at pasture. These rugs include a stable rug or Jute rug, Witney blanket and the New Zealand rug. There are other rugs designed for specific purposes; the summer sheet, exercise sheet, woollen day rug, the sweat rug and the cooler sheet.

Sweat Rug and Cooler Sheet

These types of rugs are primarily used during the summer months when the horse becomes wet either after a bath, in the rain or through hard work and sweat. If he is allowed to stand around and dry too quickly, especially in a nippy wind, he could become chilled. This could lead to illnesses such as pneumonia.

To prevent his body temperature from dropping too rapidly and the possibility of illness, the sweat rug or a cooler sheet can be put on the horse to regulate the drying and cooling effects.

Sweat rugs have the appearance of large string vests. Cooler rugs are similar except their mesh is tighter preventing the loss of body heat more effectively.

The mesh traps air between the body and the rug, keeping the horse warm. At the same time the holes allow a certain amount of body heat and dampness out so that the horse cools and dries. If an ordinary rug, such as a stable rug, is used on a wet horse the damp becomes trapped next to the skin possibly causing skin problems.

In cold conditions, if the horse becomes wet or damp, the sweat rug or cooler sheet can be used under another rug. This will still allow a passage of air to dry the horse but the other rug will prevent too rapid a loss of body heat.

The rug can also be thatched, that is have a layer of straw placed underneath. Again this will prevent loss of body heat but allow drying. The cooler rug with its closer mesh is similar to a thatched sweat rug.

Both the sweat rug and cooler sheet can be used when the horse is dry, particularly when travelling. In hot weather when even the use of a summer sheet could make the horse sweat, the sweat rug or cooler sheet will keep him relatively cool. Again this type of rug can be used under a summer sheet as an extra layer to keep the horse warm but prevent him from becoming too hot.

The sweat rug and cooler sheet normally have a front fastening. A fillet string at the back fits under the tail to prevent the rug from blowing in the wind, flying back over the horse and frightening him. In windy weather a light elasticated surcingle can be put on to prevent the rug flapping.

This type of rug or sheet is a good investment for the horse owner. The sweat rugs are relatively inexpensive for a standard mesh, with a slight increase in price for a fine mesh. Cooler sheets can be a little more expensive.

Both rugs are made from 100% cotton with nylon fastenings and are available in a variety of colours, some even two tone. Sizes range from small, medium, large and extra large or from 63 inches to around 84 inches rising in 3 inch lengths.

Some 'cooler sheets', with very fine mesh, are more like summer sheets and are used to keep the horse warm. Made from cotton, some feature a thermal material specially designed to remove the damp from the horse whilst allowing moisture to evaporate.

Care of Rugs

During the spring and summer the rugs used on the horse over the winter need repairing, cleaning and storing so that they continue to give good use for years to come. Stable rugs made of cotton or synthetic materials can be cleaned in the washing machine. Alternatively many launderettes will take in rugs, wash and dry them. Use non-biological washing powder; strong detergents can affect the horse's skin.

Providing they do not shrink, (read the manufacturer's instructions if in any doubt) under-blankets may also be washed by machine. Alternatively they may need to be dry-cleaned at the local launderette.

Jute rugs are more difficult as the fibres can shrink when washed. Some tack shops will not clean Jutes for this reason. The best way to clean a Jute is in cool or cold water. Spread the rug out on the ground and spray it with the hose pipe, or pour a bucket of cold water over it if there is a hose pipe ban. Then scrub with a brush. Hang the rug out on the line to dry in hot weather or put in a warm, dry place in the house.

New Zealand rugs need specialist cleaning because of their waterproofing. Most tack shops will take New Zealands and clean them. They will also make any repairs that are necessary. It is best to take the New Zealand to be cleaned in late spring or early summer. By late summer and early autumn everyone has remembered that their New Zealand needs repairing and cleaning, and usually at this time it may take weeks before the rug is returned.

New Zealand rugs may also need waterproofing, especially if there is damage to the rug, holes, tears or loose seams. The repairs and waterproofing can be done at a tack shop. If the rug needs waterproofing only, a can of waterproofing may be purchased from a tack shop and this job done at home. The rug is laid out flat and the waterproofing substance sprayed on to it.

All leather straps or fittings will need to be cleaned with saddle soap and oiled. Before washing a rug with leather straps, grease the straps well with Vaseline to prevent the water from cracking them. Any metal fittings will need cleaning with metal polish and given a covering of Vaseline to prevent rust.

Storage

When rugs are put away and stored, it is essential to fold them neatly. Rugs flung on the floor will inevitably become damaged, torn and dirty, which is a waste of the time and money spent in cleaning and repair. Some greaseproof paper can be inserted between the folds to keep the rug completely dry.

The rugs should then be put away in a large, strong box or plastic container to prevent vermin making nests or eating the rugs. Do not use plastic bags or sheets to cover or store the rugs. Plastic makes the rug 'sweat' causing condensation, dampness and mould. If there are a number of rugs to be stored, each rug should have the horse's name clearly marked or attached to it.

All rugs will need to be stored in a dry, airy place. An attic or upper storey of a barn is ideal providing the rain does not leak in. If rugs become damp, they will deteriorate, mould will form on them. This can be very difficult to remove. Leather will become cracked and unsafe; metal fittings may rust.

Moths cause holes in rugs. Placing mothballs or anti-moth substances around the rugs will deter them.

Rugs used during the summer months, cotton sheets, woollen day rugs, anti-sweat and cooler sheets can all be washed, dried and stored in a similar way during the winter.

For the horse's safety and good health as well as for economy, rugs do need to be looked after carefully. If they are repaired, cleaned, stored and used correctly they will last for years. Good rugs can be an expensive item, but the better quality rugs will offer more warmth and protection against the elements, and last longer than cheap rugs that may need replacing after a year or two.

Bandages

Bandages are used in a variety of situations: when travelling to protect the legs; in the stable for warmth; for support; to keep the legs clean; medical reasons and also when exercising.

Protection during Exercise

Every horse when exercising or hacking should wear leg protection either as boots or exercise bandages. Most horses are sufficiently balanced to avoid injuring themselves, but there is always the situation where they may stumble, be caught by another horse or knock against some object. Boots or bandages can prevent injuries and wounds that may result in weeks, maybe months, off work.

❖ Young horses are particularly vulnerable, because they usually lack balance and rhythm tending to trip, stumble or catch themselves when exercising.

❖ Horses and ponies being lunged should wear protection. Working on a circle increases the possibility of leg injuries.

❖ During the ride and lead exercise, both the led and the ridden horses will need leg protection.

❖ For show jumping and cross-country, the legs need protection against knocking the jumps.

❖ When hacking, protection is needed against overreach and brushing injuries, and from wounds caused by thorns.

Exercise Bandages

Some riders and horse owners prefer to use exercise bandages (leg wraps) in place of boots. There are times when bandages are more useful than boots and conversely when boots are more suitable.

Advantages

Bandages do have their advantages.

∗ Offer more support for the tendons during exercise, than boots do.

The support effect of bandages is now a debatable point, as some believe that the actual supportive effect is minimal. Bandages do offer a degree of support to the tendons, more so than boots. Research suggests that bandages cause the legs to sweat and because the heat cannot be dispersed sufficiently quickly the tendons weaken. Breathable boots or Porter boots are now being recommended.

∗ The 'stretch quality' of bandages allows slightly more freedom of movement in legs and tendons.

∗ Bandages are more useful for a horse with a rub on the leg.

∗ Boots can have a tendency to cause friction injury especially if used in a sand school when the sand works up and under the boot. Bandages lying closer to the leg minimise this risk. They also do not 'move' as much on the leg so that any rubs will not be made worse.

✳   Bandages, when properly fitted, tend to stay on. Boots, especially older ones with worn fastenings, can drop off and be lost when hacking or competing on a cross-country event or ride.

Disadvantages

•   More time and labour consuming to put on and remove.

Bandages are more awkward to put on. They should ideally have padding underneath, Gamgee or Fibregee, to protect the bone and tendon from the edges of the bandage. (Many riders, particularly on the continent, do not use any padding underneath. They mainly use bandages made from a soft material such as a woollen mixture.)

•   Unless well fastened bandages can come loose when the horse is working. This can be dangerous if the loose bandage becomes wrapped around the horse's legs.

•   Unless well fitted bandages can cause injuries to the leg. A bandage that is too tight can bruise the cannon bone or the tendon. The blood circulation can also be restricted to the tendon and cause lumps or sores. Padding underneath does partially relieve this effect.

•   Bandages can tighten, particularly if they become wet; they may shrink slightly when drying.

•   Should not be used for long rides, hunting or endurance. They have a 'tighter' effect than boots and can injure the legs.

Materials

Most exercise bandages are made from stretch materials, crepe, stockinette or elasticated webbing and are available in a variety of colours. The fastenings are either tapes or Velcro.

Bandage straps can be used for extra security. These are placed around the bandage, pass through a metal loop and doubled back to fasten. PVC tapes can also be purchased and again used as extra security to hold the bandage in place.

Types of padding include Gamgee, Fibregee and high impact pads such as Prolite or Porter boots.

Fitting the Exercise Bandage

Padding should be used underneath the exercise bandage. This gives more protection, makes the bandage more comfortable and cushions the leg from the edges of the bandage.

The bandage is put on below the knee or hock and extends just to the top of the fetlock joint.

There is a current trend for horses doing flatwork schooling or dressage training to have the bandage extending over the fetlock. This protects him against bruising of the sesamoids and brushing the inside of the fetlock. Others feel that this would cause the bandage to interfere with the joint movement. In most cases the fetlock is left free so that the action of the fetlock is not impeded.

Method

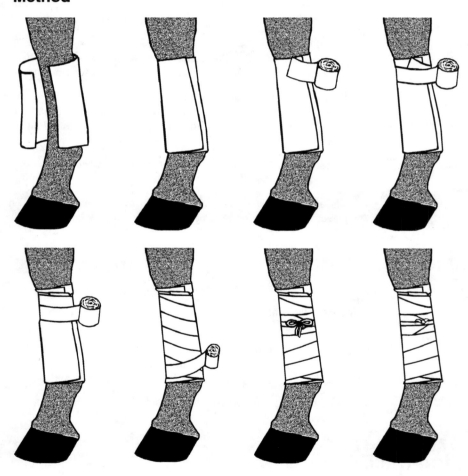

a)   Wrap the padding around the leg so that the outer edge faces backwards on the outside of the leg, ideally in the gap between the bone and the tendon.

b)   Hold the padding in place; start the bandage on the outside of the leg.

c)   Roll from the front to the back of the leg, in the same direction as the padding. Leaving a flap at the top, roll the bandage around the leg neatly.

d)   After one or two turns, fold the flap down and bandage over it.

e)   Repeat the bandaging down the leg, until the top of the fetlock is reached.

f)   Start to bandage up the leg again. To tighten the tension, pull the bandage *against the cannon bone at the front* of the leg, not the back tendon. *Keep the same tension all the way* so that no part of the bandage is looser or tighter than the rest.

g)   When the end is reached fasten the tapes or Velcro on the outer side of the leg. Tapes should be tied firmly but not too tight, and the tape ends tucked away neatly to keep them safe. With Velcro, check that it is sufficiently cohesive to stay firmly in place.

As an extra protection, particularly for cross-country courses where a loose or flapping bandage could be extremely hazardous, the bandage is stitched with needle and thread to make absolutely sure it is secure. Another method is to use insulating tape or a bandage strap wrapped around the bandage.

 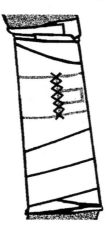 

Test the tightness by inserting a finger in the top of the bandage. There should just, and only just, be room to fit the index finger. Check that the bandage is neat and the same tension all the way down the leg.

To remove the bandage, undo the fastenings or cut the thread. Unroll quickly passing the bandage from one hand to another. Rub the leg to restore the circulation.

The bandages should then be washed, dried, rolled and stored for future use. Padding should be thoroughly cleaned as this lies next to the horse's skin.

To roll the bandage, take the tape or Velcro end and wrap the fastening into neat loops or folds. Roll with the fastening side **inwards** so that this side is the last to be unfolded and will be on the outside when next bandaging the horse's leg.

Boots

There are so many new designs of boots and protective leg wear to suit almost every occasion. Schooling boots are now available that fit over the pastern, some competition boots fit over the fetlock joint giving protection to this area whilst allowing movement. There are brushing boots with larger portions at the front fitting over the knee. Almost any area on the horse's leg, from the knee down, can be protected by one boot or another.

Boots are definitely easier and quicker to put on and remove. The tough plastic or leather covering of boots does offer more protection against brushing especially when the horse's shoe comes into contact. This is often evident as small scratch marks on the inside of the boot. With a bandage this could cause bruising as the material is not tough enough to withstand the impact. This is more important with a young horse who is just becoming accustomed to wearing shoes.

The use of boots or bandages does depend on personal preference, the horse, the type of work and the environment. It is better though for horses to have some protection as even the slightest knock or cut can lead to lameness, infection and pain.

Exam tips

During the Exam, the subject of rugs may be in the form of a general discussion. Any practical experience of buying, maintaining, cleaning and storing rugs will be useful. Visit the local tack shop or look around the stalls at a show and find out the prices of rugs, the varieties on offer, the different sizes. Read the manufacturer's instructions as to care and cleaning. Ask at the tack shop if they take in and clean rugs and how much they charge.

In the Stage III each candidate will be asked to put on an exercise bandage. This does need practice, as much as possible, to give you the efficiency you need. You will then be asked to comment on your bandage and about the advantages or disadvantages of using bandages whilst exercising or competing. It is not usual during the Stage III to have to stitch a bandage, but if you can do practise stitching a bandage for the experience. You may have to tape a bandage in which case the length of tape is cut first then wrapped around the bandage. If the roll is wrapped around, this can make the tape too tight.

CHAPTER 20
Shoeing

The horse's feet need constant, regular care if he is to perform his work and stay in good health so shoeing is a vital part of the horse's welfare. Whereas humans can perform many actions and fulfil job roles with a damaged or injured leg, the horse cannot work if one leg is lame. The role of a good Farrier to the horse and his owner is of fundamental importance.

Revision

Stage I – foot structure and points. Indications that shoeing is necessary.

Stage II reasons for shoeing, hot and cold shoeing, the Farrier's tools. Shoeing procedures, inspecting the newly shod foot. Daily care of the horse's feet. Parts of a shoe, concave fullered, plain stamped, Hunter shoe, grass tips.

The Newly Shod Foot

Once the horse has been shod there are signs that will show he has been shod correctly.

✻ The horse is sound. This can be checked when the horse is led away from the Farrier to his box or to the field.

✻ The shoe fits the foot. The shoe should always be made to fit the foot and not the foot the shoe.

✻ The balance of the foot is correct. There are two points to look for here.

    1. Side view – the slope of the hoof both in front and at the heels should continue the angle of the pastern; the Foot Pastern Angle (FPA).

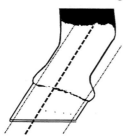 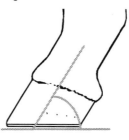 

Angle through pastern and foot   Front foot, FPA 45°-50°   Hind foot, FPA 50°-55°

2. Front view – the hoof walls of the foot, the medial (inside) and lateral (outside) walls, are equal in length.

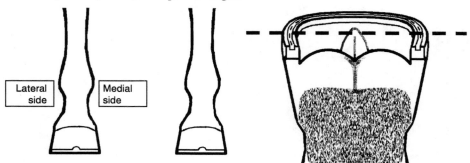

Check also by picking the foot up, viewed from the heel the sides of the foot should be level.

*   The clips on the front feet are in the centre of the toe, directly in a straight line from the middle of the pastern.

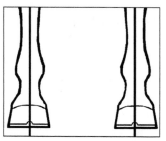

*   The hoof and shoe are flush. There should be no spaces between the hoof and the shoe.

*   The clenches are ideally about a third of the way up the hoof and in a straight line. They are flush with the hoof wall.

*   The horse has the correct shoe, a lighter shoe for a lighter horse doing work on good ground, a heavier shoe for a heavier horse doing work on very soft or hard ground. The Farrier may fit remedial shoes when he is correcting some foot defect.

*   Toe clips on the front feet and quarter clips on the hind are flush with the hoof wall.

*   The shape of the foot is correct. The front feet are rounder whilst the hind feet are more oval in shape.

*   The frog comes into contact with the ground. This will be evident by picking up the foot. The frog should be at the same level or slightly less than the sides of the foot.

Variations

There are times when the Farrier has to vary the method of shoeing.

* Balance of foot FPA may not quite be correct.

  If the horse's foot has been allowed to grow too long, through incorrect or infrequent shoeing over a period of time. It may take the Farrier six to nine months to correct this defect. If the foot is very long the Farrier cannot pare the foot back all at once he can only reduce the length over a period of time.

* If the horse has a natural upright or sloping foot the FPA may not be correct.

  The Farrier will still need to maintain the straight line through the pastern to the base of the foot even though the angles may not conform to the ideal.

* The toe clip on the front foot may not be in a direct line through the centre of the leg and foot.

  If the horse has a natural defect in the foot, so that his foot is slightly off line, the farrier may need to place the toe clip a little to one side.

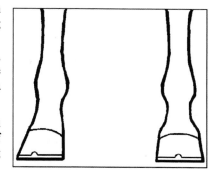

* The shoe may not be flush with the foot on the hind feet. To minimise the effect of overreaching, the hind toe may overhang the shoe slightly.

* The clenches may not be the correct height on the foot or in a straight line. Occasionally if the hoof is weak or suffers from cracking, the Farrier may place the nail in a different area from the original hole. In this case one or more nails may be in a slightly higher or lower position.

It is therefore possible for slight deviations if the Farrier has to make adjustments in the shoeing.

Faulty Shoeing

There are signs that indicate faulty shoeing. The horse can be checked for any evident problems so that the Farrier, if possible, may correct these whilst he is still in the yard.

* The **horse is lame**.

  If he limps immediately after being shod the Farrier should be told. It is possible for the horse to become lame a few days after being shod, in which case the Farrier should be contacted as soon as possible.

  The lameness could be the result of nail prick or nail bind.

Nail prick – When the nail is driven in too deep and penetrates the sensitive laminae in the foot. This causes a puncture wound, pain and possible infection.

Nail bind – when the nail is driven in close to the sensitive laminae. This causes pain and soreness.

- **Incorrect shoeing**.

If the shoe is too small it may press against the seat of corn causing bruising and soreness. *Bruised sole and corns.*

- The **clenches are incorrect**.

The clenches may protrude from the hoof wall. These may catch the horse in action and cause injury. *Brushing or speedicutting.*

Coarse nailing – the clenches may emerge too high up the hoof wall. This could possibly cause *nail bind.*

Fine nailing – the clenches emerge too low down the hoof wall making the shoe insecure and more likely to come off (be cast). The hoof will also be more prone to splitting and cracking. *Grasscrack.*

- The **foot** has been **made to fit the shoe**.

The foot may have been 'dumped' that is the toe has been cut back or rasped excessively to fit a smaller shoe. This can cause damage to the toe area, cracking or splitting of the hoof. *Grasscrack.*

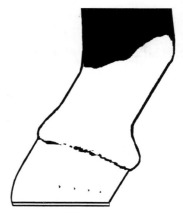

- The foot may not have been trimmed correctly, leaving the toe long. This could cause contracted heels, tendon strain, navicular syndrome, sesamoiditis.

- The heels of the shoe are too long at the back. If the horse, or another, treads on the heels the shoe could be wrenched off, causing damage to the hoof.

- The heels of the shoe are not long enough. The foot will be lower at the back causing *contracted heels or tendon strain.*

- The balance of the foot is incorrect. If the foot has been left over long or dumped the FPA line will not be straight.

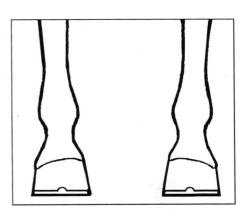

The horse may have a longer medial or lateral side. This will cause problems both in the foot and in the leg. The joints, tendons, ligaments and muscles on both sides will suffer from abnormal and inconsistent stress. This could cause *strains, sprains and joint injuries, ringbone and sidebone.*

- The frog has been overpared.

The frog will not come into contact with the ground. The circulatory system will not work efficiently in the foot. The foot grows smaller and the heels contract. Possible tendon strain, navicular syndrome.

The effects of faulty shoeing are varied and can be serious.

- ❖ **Long toes and collapsed heels**
- ❖ **Grasscrack, brittle horn**
- ❖ **Ringbone and sidebone**
- ❖ **Navicular syndrome**
- ❖ **Strained tendons**
- ❖ **Sesamoiditis**
- ❖ **Faulty action, brushing, overreaching, speedicutting**
- ❖ **Withered frog**
- ❖ **Puncture wounds, injured laminae**

Hot and Cold Shoeing

There are two methods by which the Farrier shoes the horse – hot and cold shoeing.

❖ With hot shoeing the Farrier will first find a shoe that is approximately the right size. Then the shoe is heated in a forge and hammered into shape. Many Farriers have a portable forge.

❖ With cold shoeing the horse's foot is measured and the Farrier will bring a shoe approximately the correct size. A cold shoe can be hammered to some extent but not as effectively as in hot shoeing.

The advantage of hot shoeing is that the shoe can be more precisely fitted and shaped to the horse's foot. The shoe is pressed to the foot whilst hot and gives an indication where the shoe has to be altered. The shoe should not be held against the foot for too long as this will burn the horn excessively causing it to become brittle and disintegrate.

Dressing the Foot

This simply means preparing the foot prior to fitting the shoe. It includes trimming the hoof, paring away any excess horn and frog, rasping to make a level surface and, with hot shoeing, placing the heated shoe against the foot to assess the fit.

Poor foot Care

There are other reasons, besides faulty shoeing, that cause the horse's foot to deteriorate.

Poor daily foot care can result in diseases such as thrush. If the feet are not cleaned out daily, or the bed is allowed to become dirty and wet, the infection that causes thrush will enter around the frog.

Irregular shoeing; various problems stem from this type of negligence. The toe of the foot will grow too long. The horse will be prone to stumbling and consequent injuries; he will suffer from brittle feet and possibly grasscrack. The heels will contract, which will put strain on the back tendons and may lead to navicular syndrome. The feet will grow flat causing bruises to the sole. The horse will eventually suffer lameness that could be permanent.

Poor diet and condition will lead to poor horn formation and weak feet. This again can lead to permanent lameness.

Too rich a diet may lead to laminitis, a condition that varies in intensity. The hoof conformation may be affected.

All horses should have their feet attended to by the Farrier at least every six weeks and sometimes as often as four weeks. The resulting problems caused by leaving it for any longer will only escalate in seriousness if the frequency of visits is delayed over a period of time.

Types of Shoes

Different designs of shoe have been used with variations to deal with different situations.

Plain stamped – is a shoe used for heavy horses in slow work. It is flat and even on both ground and bearing surface. This makes the shoe heavier but more resistant to wear.

Concave fullered – is the most popular type in use. The inside edge is concave continuing the shape of the hoof wall and sole. A groove is cut in the ground surface (it is fullered) providing extra grip and making the shoe lighter in weight. This shoe does wear out more quickly as the ground surface area is reduced.

There are normally seven nail holes, four on the outside and three on the inside, but this number can vary. The heels of the front shoes may be pencilled, that is they taper towards the end. This helps to prevent the heels being caught by the hind shoe and ripped off.

Hunter shoes – are similar in design to the concave fullered except that the hind shoe is provided with a *calkin* and *wedge*. The *calkin* is a square raised portion on the outside heel. The *wedge* is a thinner pencilled raised portion on the inside heel. These modifications are not common now as studs can be used instead.

Grass tips – are modified shoes made to fit the toe area only to protect this part of the foot against splitting and cracking when the horse is at grass for any length of time.

They also reduce the risk of injury to other horses through kicking and fighting.

Remedial Shoes

A good Farrier will be able to improve faulty action, defects in conformation and assist in the Veterinary care of the foot and leg.

Feather-edged shoe – used on a horse that brushes. The inner portion of the shoe is thinned down and tapered to reduce the effect of *brushing* injuries. There are no nails on the inner side of the shoe but some may be placed around the toe area. The weight of the shoe on the outside of the hoof encourages the horse to carry his foot outwards and so correct the action that causes brushing.

Three quarter shoe – this shoe is reduced in length having no inside portion. The shoe usually ends just after the toe. As in the feather edged shoe, the lack of an inner portion reduces the effects of *brushing,* as there is no shoe to strike the opposite leg. Again the weight of the shoe is positioned to encourage the horse to carry his foot and correct the action that causes brushing.

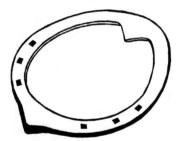

Bar shoe – this type of shoe is designed with an extra portion (a bar) across the heels.

The shoe is continued around the heel area with a small shaped addition to cover part of the frog. Used for cases of *corns or low heels.*

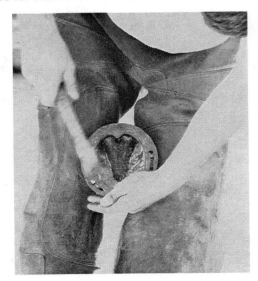

The farrier fitting a bar shoe

There are variations in the bar shoe design.

Egg bar shoe – the bar continues in a curve joining the two heels. This reduces the wear on that part of the foot encouraging the heels to grow. It also increases the bearing and ground surfaces, distributing the horse's weight more evenly over the foot. Used for horses who suffer from *long toes* and *contracted or collapsed heels, strained tendons* and *navicular syndrome.*

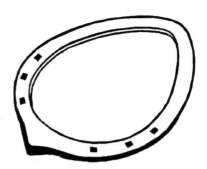

Heart bar shoe – is similar in design to the egg bar shoe but with an extra piece extending inwards to cover part of the frog. This increases the pressure on the frog and encourages correct blood circulation in the leg. Can be used for *long toes, contracted* or *collapsed heels, strained tendons, navicular syndrome, withered or small frog.* This shoe is also used for cases of *laminitis* as the bar supports the frog and the pedal bone without restricting the blood supply to the foot.

T bar shoe – has an longer extension over the frog putting more pressure on that area. Useful for a horse with *upright boxy feet* where the *frog is not in contact with ground.*

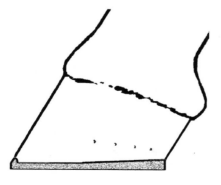

Gradiated heels – *the heels of the shoe are thicker in depth* to raise the back of the foot. This reduces the pressure on the deep flexor tendon and the navicular bone. Used for *long toes, contracted or collapsed heels, strained tendons, navicular syndrome.*

Wide webbed

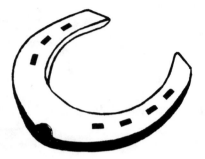 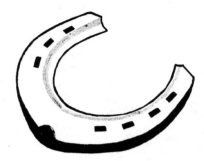

The web is the width of the shoe and in this type of shoe the width is greater. This protects part of the sole by keeping it away from the ground. For horses with *bruised or thin soles*.

In some cases the wide webbed shoe is bevelled, that is shaped around the inside, in the sole region to avoid the shoe touching the sole. This is called a *seated out shoe.*

Rocker bar shoe – the toe and heel of the shoe are made slightly thinner so that the ground surface resembles a rocker.

This helps the horse to roll his foot on the ground. Used for *stiff joints, side bone, ring bone and navicular.*

Squared toe – the toe of the hind shoe is squared off so that the hoof overhangs the shoe. This helps in cases of *overreaching, forging* (the hind shoe hits the front shoe).

Rolled toe – the toe is shaped at the front and may lie slightly behind the hoof. This again reduces the risk of *overreach injuries* if fitted on the hind feet.

Pads and Studs

On occasions the horse needs extra protection to the foot to help with a medical problem or as an aid against slipping.

Pads

The pad is a flat-shaped piece of leather made to cover the foot. It is placed under and secured by the shoe. Pads are occasionally made of plastic or synthetic materials; these are cheaper but may make the foot sweat. Leather allows the foot to breathe but is affected by weather conditions; too wet and the leather contracts, too dry and the leather becomes hard and may crack.

Pads are used as a protection in cases of bruised soles and corns, or puncture wounds. Most pads are temporary but sometimes pads have to be used on a permanent basis for a horse with a particularly thin or weak sole. Pads can also be used in snowy conditions to prevent the snow balling in the foot.

The pad needs to be removed periodically as dirt and mud can seep in underneath and cause infection. Stones may become lodged between the foot and the pad, and may cause bruising. The frog and sole may sweat becoming spongy and soft. Before the pad is fitted the sole and frog may be treated with Stockholm Tar. A soft gamgee may also be placed underneath the pad to prevent dirt entering.

Studs

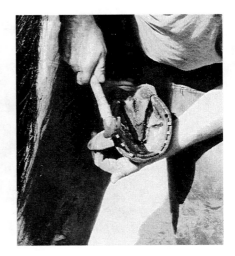

A road stud fitted permanently. The tungsten tip is visible

This shoe has a special hole for the competition stud

There are times when the shoe does not provide sufficient grip for the horse; in soft, wet or hard dry ground, on roads, when jumping cross-country or hunting. To improve the grip, studs are fitted. Studs are may be fitted to the outside heel of the hind feet only or on the inside heel as well. Occasionally, for a horse who tends to slip studs may be fitted on the front feet.

❖ **Road studs** have a tip made from tungsten, which is hard wearing. This type of stud is fitted permanently but, as it is almost flush with the shoe, it hardly affects the balance of the foot.

❖ **Competition studs** are used temporarily and can be removed from the shoe. The Farrier makes a special screw hole in the shoe and the stud is fitted and removed with a spanner. This stud should always be removed after use, as its size does affect the balance of the foot. The horse may damage the floor of the trailer or horsebox if he travels wearing the studs.

There are various shapes and sizes of competition stud. Square studs are used in soft ground and sharp studs are used on hard ground.

The screw hole in the shoe should be cleaned out and then packed with cotton wool when not in use. The studs should be cleaned after use and kept in an oily rag to prevent rusting.

Studs do affect the balance of the foot and increase the wear of the shoe at the toe. The Farrier should be asked for advice first before deciding to use studs. If necessary the shoe can be balanced by having a higher heel on the inside of the foot. The toe of the shoe can be reinforced with steel insets to protect it from abnormal wear.

The Farrier's job includes more than shoeing the horse every six weeks. Though this, in itself, is essential, a good Farrier will also be able to help the horse at times of his life when he needs medical attention, to improve action and prevent injuries.

That well known drinking spot
'The Farrier's Rest'

Exam Tips

Preparation for this section means observation. Look at different horses' feet and check the shoes. Assess approximately when the horse was shod. Look at the state of the feet. Check to see what type of shoes the horses are wearing, and if any have special shoes, pads or studs.

A great deal of information can be obtained from watching the Farrier. He or she will probably be only too pleased to answer questions. (As you have probably already done this for Stages I and II, see the relevant books, the bribe should now be something a little stronger than a cup of tea!) If you stand and hold the horse whilst the Farrier is shoeing, he will talk you through the procedure. It is amazing what information you can learn about horses' feet. Most Farriers are willing to talk about their profession especially to someone who shows a genuine interest.

C H A P T E R   21
The Yard

Most yards or riding establishments originate with a few looseboxes and develop with additional facilities as demand increases. Other yards have the advantage of being situated in old stable blocks, as part of a farm, country mansion or stately home. The stables may then be built of brick and placed around a central yard but may have little room for modern facilities such as an indoor school or jumping paddock. Few establishments are built to design specifications with future expansion planned.

Whatever the circumstances, owners of yards should always try to improve their facilities. They should be trying to create an environment where the horses, workers and clients are offered safety, efficiency, comfort and enjoyment.

Planning the Yard

The first consideration when planning to design or purchase a yard is to decide what type of yard is required and for what type of business. There are Riding Schools catering for novices, Educational Centres dealing with riders training for careers and examinations. Some schools cater for a specific discipline, dressage, show jumping, eventing, racing, whilst others are trekking centres dealing particularly with holidaymakers.

There are livery yards that only cater for livery owners either a 'DIY' or part 'DIY' basis and there are Stud farms dealing particularly with stallions, mares and breeding. Some centres will hold competitions whilst others offer a wide range of activities, children's rides, hacking, working or full liveries and training for various disciplines.

Depending on the type of yard, the facilities need to be thought out carefully to fulfil the needs of the clientele.

The Site

The location of the yard is important. From a business aspect the yard should be close enough to potential customers yet offer a variety of good hacking within easy reach. It needs access from a road but not so close as to be an invitation for thieves.

The type of yard will be important when choosing the situation. Sometimes the site comes first and the type of yard is chosen to suit the site. For instance a yard away from the main routes but with good hacking country within easy reach would be ideal for a trekking or hacking centre. A yard offering competitions will need to be near a main road or motorway to offer easy access. Ideally the yard will have both but this is not always possible.

Geography

The geography of the site is important. The yard area needs to be relatively flat yet well drained. Some yards do suffer from flooding in wet weather, if the ground is low lying or near a river.

Ideally it should be fairly well sheltered from the worst of the weather. A yard situated on top of a hill may be well drained but can be extremely uncomfortable in the wind, rain and the cold of winter.

The fields need to be suitable for horses. Gently undulating ground is best; this gives good drainage and the horses will be able to exercise themselves when grazing. Flat land can be boggy and encourage the growth of the wrong types of grasses. Extremely hilly country may be suitable for moorland ponies but for finely bred horses this could be too bleak, the grass too coarse and the steep hills may cause problems if the horses gallop around.

Catchment Area

The establishment ideally will need a resident population within easy access or the ability to offer holiday trekking. A further point of research would include other yards in the area. Whilst competition in any field of commerce is beneficial, trying to start the same type of yard near one or two other successful ones will make the going tough. The catchment area should be investigated, potential customers, likely competition, road networks, hacking and extra facilities such as cross-country courses for hire.

Planning Permission

When building a new yard, planning permission may be required. The planning officer at the local Council offices should be contacted. One loose box in the back garden may not need planning permission in some areas but to construct a number of buildings on a site will definitely require permission.

The local authorities have to consider the impact of such an establishment on the surrounding area; the increase in the volume of traffic, the change of character in the area; the effect on local wildlife, the extra demand on facilities such as sewerage, electricity and mains water.

In some areas if purchasing an existing plot, the owner has to apply for a 'change of use' or inform the local authorities that horses will be kept on the land. Some authorities are now reluctant to allow a 'change of use' from agricultural to equine.

Facilities

Designing a new yard needs careful consideration if all the facilities, and further expansion, are to be included. Drainage may need installing and the yard surface making solid and non-slip, either with concrete or hard core.

The looseboxes, tack room, feed room, isolation boxes, office, toilet facilities, water taps, hay and straw storage are planned and then, depending on the type of yard an indoor school and outdoor menage. The yard may also need a lecture room, staff quarters, car park, first aid room and rug room.

The isolation boxes will need to be down wind, a little distance apart from the yard to prevent the spread of infectious diseases. The hay and straw storage should be apart from the looseboxes to prevent the spread of fire. The muck heap will need to be down wind of the stable yard, preferably out of sight of clients but within convenient reach of the staff.

Once it has been decided what type of facilities are needed, the yard as a whole should be considered, its aspects, its appearance, its convenience and the impression that the owner wishes to impart to the clientele. One good idea is to visit yards and note the favourable points, the first impressions, what makes it look a good yard. This will give ideas on how to design and plan a yard and the pitfalls to avoid.

The Yard

The **yard** should have an **inviting appearance**, look tidy and clean at most times of the day and have an atmosphere of efficiency and friendliness.

∗   The looseboxes need positioning carefully. They need to be sheltered, with doors and windows away from prevailing winds. The boxes ideally should not face direct sunlight, which can make them quite hot. Looseboxes facing south-east or south-west are best. They can be arranged in rows facing each other for easy access and so that the horses can see each other.

∗   The floors of the looseboxes should slope gently to the back of the boxes to allow for drainage. The flooring of the boxes may include herringbone drainage channels or small holes to allow free drainage.

∗   The **office** should be well situated for clients and staff, look clean and well equipped.

∗   In training yards a **lecture room** is useful together with equipment such as television and video for teaching purposes.

* The **tack room** should be centrally situated with easy access. In establishments that have two or three separate yards, one tack room for each area is useful.

* The **feed room** should be large, airy, dry and clean. The feed room should be central to the yard with easy access.

* **Hay and straw** must be stored where they are kept dry, clean and convenient for staff. They should not be stored in the stable block because of fire risk.

* **Mounting blocks** are very useful to help the clients and save the horses' backs.

* There may be a **leisure area** for clients and staff, where drinks and possibly food are available.

* Toilet and washing facilities are essential.

* The **car park** must be situated with safety in mind. So many yards have cars driving straight through the yard or through areas where people and, in particular, children need to go. The car park should be outside the yard with a safe access from the road yet convenient for clients to reach the office and stable area.

* **Water** should be easily available within the yard. Ideally there should be one tap to each six boxes with a special area for hosing down or bathing horses. Good drainage is essential to prevent the yard and boxes.

* Important rooms such as the tack room, feed room, medical room and office need to be secured at night. These should be padlocked and have an alarm system.

* The yard should have a **gate** between it and the public highway. This should be kept closed at all times except for admittance to the stable. This is to prevent any horse straying or running onto the road and causing an accident.

Most importantly, all yards must have adequate **fire precautions**. Fire extinguishers should be easily accessible and everyone on the yard should be instructed on how to work them. A fire hose should reach every box in the yard. The Fire Prevention Officer will offer advice for any yard or establishment.

Stabling

Revision

Stage I and II – stable design, loose boxes, sizes, construction, materials, positioning, fixtures and fittings. Special purpose boxes.

There are different designs of looseboxes, the most popular is the wooden box bought ready for assembly. These can be constructed quickly and are relatively inexpensive to buy.

The American Barn system is gaining in popularity. A number of stables or stalls are situated within a large barn normally down both sides, leaving a central aisle. This does keep the horses, owners and handlers dry in wet weather and allows good ventilation. Space can be restricted though especially when several horses are tied up in the aisle whilst their stables are being mucked out.

Brick built stables whilst being the best, (strongest, fireproof, horseproof, weatherproof) are the most expensive to build.

Stalls, mostly for ponies and small horses, can save space. They are arranged in a small building with a passageway giving access. The stalls are normally only large enough for the pony or horse to turn around. A chain is fitted, instead of a door, to each stall. These can be efficient, easy to muck out and convenient. They do not allow much room for the horse to lie down or move, though and fights often break out because the ponies or horses are close to each other.

Fixtures and fittings within the box or stall should be kept to a minimum. The less there is in the box the less likely the horse is to hurt or injure himself. Two securing rings, either side of the box, good lighting and an automatic waterer, if required, is really all that is needed. If water is given in buckets, these should be large to offer the horse a good draught of water and sturdy enough not to be kicked around the box. Alternatively placing the bucket in a tyre keeps it secure.

There has to be lighting in the box. A light properly fixed high on the ceiling and covered with a protective guard in case the bulb explodes. Electric wiring has to be properly encased in a conduit and insulated. Switches are situated outside the box away from the reach of horses and protected from the weather by a covering. The yard may have a circuit breaker so that in the case of a problem the electric current is cut off immediately.

A hayrack has to be high enough to be safe for the horse. The height though, does allow hay and spores to fall onto the horse's head, into his eyes and nostrils. The height can also be problem for the person putting the hay into the rack. Hay is better fed from the floor or by a haynet properly hung from a securing ring.

A chain across the doorway is convenient so that the door can be left open in hot weather. The chain should always be left unfastened when the door is shut. If the horse has to be brought out of the box quickly (in the case of fire) trying to unfasten the chain can lose precious time.

Sometimes rugs are kept in the box, being hung over a piece of rope or a wooden bar suspended by ropes from the ceiling. Though this is convenient it is better to take the rug out of the stable in case the horse pulls the rug down, tramples on it and tears it. Rugs can also become dirtied if left in the box. Damp rugs may cause condensation. A rug room for drying rugs or a place in the tack room is more hygienic.

When planning a stable yard the points of importance are; safety for workers, staff, clients and horses; efficiency and convenience of the facilities and their position in relation to each other. For instance to have a car park situated where cars have to drive through the yard with people bringing horses out of the boxes and mounting would not be safe or convenient. To position the muck heap by the side of the yard entrance would not give a good impression to clients. The establishment needs to be inviting, the yard should look clean, efficient and safe.

Most equestrian establishments are run for commercial reasons; choosing the site and designing the yard is the first step towards a successful business. Ultimately the yard does need to be successful if the horses are to be kept in good condition, if the staff are to be paid their wages and the enterprise made worthwhile for the owner.

Exam Tips

In the Stage III you may be asked to assess the looseboxes and the yard. You will need to revise from the Stage I and II books on the materials and construction of the stables and looseboxes. You will also need to observe various establishments and be critical about their qualities, their different designs.

Make notes about the aspects of the yards you visit; first impressions; office or reception area, facilities for clients and staff. Look at the stabling for the horses, the schools or exercise areas. Notice the convenience of access to the feed room and tack room.

Decide on the points you like and those that subtract from the efficiency or safety of the yard. For instance there may be bad drainage in the yard, uneven, slippery ground surface; the schools may become waterlogged in wet weather. If you practise being observant and critical of a few yards you will soon learn to appreciate the points you like and dislike.

Looking through advertisements in magazines will give you an idea of the materials, buildings and designs available on the market and the prices. Materials for stabling, tack or feed rooms, flooring, roofing, types of fixtures and fittings.

You could then imagine that you have just won the lottery or have a million pounds to spend on building your own perfect Equestrian establishment; the type of buildings and facilities you would want. Add some really useful customer facilities. Design a yard for convenience, efficiency, appearance, good drainage and most importantly a yard in which the clients, staff and horses will be safe and comfortable.

C H A P T E R   22
Grassland Management

Maintaining pastureland is an important aspect of horse management. A neglected field or paddock constitutes a threat to the horse's health, is costly for the owner and reduces the value of the whole property. Whatever the size of the land, from a small starvation paddock to a large field for horses and ponies living out permanently, the routine of maintaining and improving the grassland area is an important factor in the horse's care.

Quality of Grazing

There are various factors that influence the type and quality of grazing in pasture.

* Soil type and composition
* Climatic conditions
* Geography
* Grassland management

Soil Type

Soil is formed from the disintegrated residue of rocks, minerals and decayed organic matter. There are different types of soil depending on the types of rocks present in that location.

Soil is important as it supports plant life, which in turn supports animal life. Different plants grow in different types of soil. Knowing the type of soil can determine what plants to grow and the kind of fertiliser required for improved growth or the growth of different plants.

Soil can be analysed for type and nutrient level. This may be done either by a Fertilising Company or by ADAS (the Agricultural and Development Advisory Service of the Ministry of Agriculture).

An analysis will indicate the level of acidity or alkalinity of the soil. This is graded by a pH (potential of Hydrogen) scale; pH 7 is neutral. Lower scale levels indicate that the soil is acid, higher levels are alkaline. For horses the measurement needs to be around pH 6 - 6.5; the ideal grade for grasses.

An analysis will be able to indicate what type of nutrient is present in the soil.

❖ Soils that are sandy are lighter and allow free drainage. The ground surface maintains its structure more easily, being less prone to poaching and damage from horses. Sandy soils do, however, lose nutrients through leaching; the water passing through takes the soluble nutrients with it.

❖ Soils that contain more clay are only slightly porous and so retain nutrients. Clay though can become waterlogged and is very prone to poaching and damage from horses.

❖ There are soils that are a mixture of these two in varying degrees.

❖ There are also soils containing other sediments such as chalk. Chalky soil is high in calcium carbonate and will be alkaline.

Soil Composition

Nutrients are present in the soil as minerals or elements. These include **lime**, which contains calcium, necessary for the formation of bones and teeth and **phosphates**, which includes the element phosphorus. The **calcium/phosphorus ratio at 2:1 in the soil** must be carefully controlled. **Potash** is a compound of potassium vital for plant growth. **Nitrogen**, a gaseous element is converted and absorbed by plants. Nitrogen is essential for plant growth. A lack of nitrogen results in the grass being weedy and slow growing. Excess nitrogen can make the pasture too rich for horses. Clover is rich in nitrogen and so pasture full of clover can, in some cases, be harmful for horses. A glut of nitrogen can also cause the grass to grow too quickly resulting in a shortage of other nutritional substances.

Climatic Conditions and Geography

Soil composition and nutrient level are influenced quite drastically by climatic conditions and geography, that is, the situation of the land and its surrounding areas.

Weathering, determines to what degree the rocks are broken down physically and chemically by snow, ice, rain, wind, cold and heat. This affects the type of nutrients present, their quantity and whether or not the ground is stony.

The **amount of rainfall** will not only affect the dryness or wetness of the land, but the amount of nutrients that are lost through leaching; the drainage and removal of nutrients from the soil. **Temperature** and **degree of evaporation** of water will also affect soil quality, as will **wind direction**, **speed** and **erosion**.

The **geography** of the land will determine to some extent **climatic conditions**, the **aridity** of the soil, the suitability of the **terrain** for horses, the amount of **erosion** and **conditions such as flooding**.

Grassland Management

One of the most important factors affecting quality of pasture is grassland management. This will either improve or degrade any type of land.

Drainage

Some types of land will drain naturally; undulating fields and sandy soils. Land that is drained maintains the soil texture, encourages root growth, aerates the ground and encourages growth. Drier ground is able to withstand poaching; damage to the soil from the horse's hooves.

Other areas need artificial drainage, clay soils and low-lying land, particularly fields adjacent to rivers. Waterlogged land encourages the growth of the wrong types of grasses and is prone to damage by poaching. It can also cause foot and skin problems for the horse; thrush or mud fever.

Putting in artificial drainage is expensive but, in some cases, necessary to improve the land. Attempting to improve badly drained land by reseeding or cultivating, without first improving the drainage, is mostly a waste of time and expense.

There are ways of improving drainage economically.

*   Ditches and drainage pipes around the field can be kept clear.

*   Streams or watercourses can be kept free flowing by removing obstructions clogging the water.

If the land is prone to flooding it may be necessary to employ a Drainage Company or contractor to lay pipes or drainage channels under the surface. This is expensive but worth the improvement to land and stock.

Fertilising

Soil that has never been cultivated usually contains adequate amounts of nutrients necessary for the *plant growth of that region*. This varies between areas, depending on what type of soil is available.

Soil needs fertilising for three reasons.

*   The soil present does not contain the right balance of nutrients to sustain the grasses needed for horses.

*   The nutrients have been taken out of the soil by the growth year after year of the same type of plant.

*   The quality of the plant growth needs to be improved.

Types of Fertilisers

Organic Fertiliser

Farmyard manure is the best organic fertiliser for horses, being milder and safer than chemicals. This type of fertiliser can take a long time to soak into the ground; treated pasture should not be used for grazing for 6 weeks afterwards. Avoid using horse droppings as these are acidic and contain the waste materials that horses do not need. This type of fertiliser can encourage the spread of worm larvae.

Inorganic Fertiliser

Chemical fertilisers have been used for decades but now it is considered that these may have caused some pollution. The chemicals wash out of the soil into streams and rivers.

Semi-organic Fertiliser

Semi-organic fertilisers include a mixture of organic and inorganic matter. This gives the advantage of having 'natural' matter returned to the ground with the added chemical nutrients necessary, but not in excessive proportions.

The most common type of fertiliser needed is one that contains nitrogen, potash and phosphates. There are times when land may need a specific type of nutrient; for instance a dressing of lime or chalk. This is useful periodically on all types of pasture grazed by horses to neutralise the acid from the droppings.

Nitrogen, normally available in the soil, can be leached out in wet weather or flooded areas. When a fertiliser is used which contains nitrogen, this is applied during the growing season so that the plants can take the nitrogen up into their roots.

Types of Grasses

The ideal pasture for horses should include a variety of grasses.

Perennial rye grass – constituting the majority of the pasture. Grows quickly and easily.

Timothy grows quickly, is hardy and can withstand cold weather.

Tall fescue.

Creeping red fescue good ground covering plant.

Cocksfoot can become tough when older.

Crested dogstail.

Clover in small quantities, excess can make the pasture too rich.

Common bent grass and Yorkshire fog are often found in pasture as they grow like weeds, but these are poor grasses for horses.

Note: good pasture grasses that make quality grazing do not necessarily make good hay.

Pasture should also include herbs such as **dandelion, plantain, garlic, yarrow, chicory, sheep's parsley and burnet**. These offer a variety of vitamins and minerals.

Poisonous plants

Revision

Stage II poisonous plants.

Good pasture management should definitely include ridding the land of poisonous plants. Whilst horses rarely eat these plants if the pasture is rich in grass, they may be tempted when the pasture is poorer, for instance during a hot, dry summer. An abundance of weeds and poisonous plants inhibit the growth of the grass to some extent. **Ragwort, buttercup, foxglove, horsetail** and **bracken** can be quite common in pasture. Bushes and trees such as **yew, laburnum, privet, laurel** and **rhododendron** are also toxic if eaten. The yew particularly is highly poisonous to horses. **Acorns from oak trees** can also be fatal to horses if eaten in quantity and some horses find them quite appetising.

The plants should be uprooted before they seed, taken away from the pasture and ideally burnt. Some plants become more palatable and toxic when withered, ragwort for instance. Pulling the plants out singly may be feasible for a small field or paddock with few plants but for large areas or heavily infested land a local Weed Control or Agricultural Company may need to treat the pasture.

Chemicals can be used to kill the plants. For small areas one person can spray individual plants. For larger areas spraying can be done from a tractor or by a Company dealing with this type of problem. The type of chemical used needs careful thought, as some kill the plants needed in the pasture. When using chemicals, read the manufacturer's instructions carefully. The horses will need to be kept away from the pasture for a few weeks.

Poisonous trees and bushes can be enclosed by fencing. The enclosure should allow plenty of space so that the horses cannot lean over and eat the leaves from the branches. If the trees or bushes are cut back, the cuttings should be removed from the area.

It is easy to become complacent about poisonous plants and trees. Horses often graze in fields covered in buttercups and ragwort with no apparent desire to eat them. Acorns are often eaten by horses with no apparent after effects. It may be time consuming and expensive to destroy the plants or enclose areas of danger but for those who have experienced a horse's death from poisoning, have gone through the agony of this, the importance of preventing this hazard is only too clear.

Weed control

Some plants, whilst not being particularly toxic, grow as weeds and inhibit the growth of grass. Weed control is also an important part of grassland management, helping to improve the land and make every portion economically viable. Plants such as nettles, docks and thistles can be cleared or cut back. The cuttings should be removed from the paddock.

Even in the starvation paddock, though the grazing is necessarily sparse, there will be a need for a variety of grasses. It is even more important for a small area to be cleared of weeds, poisonous plants and shrubs, where a lack of grazing may influence the horse or pony to eat plants.

Maintenance of pasture

Once the basic measures have been taken to improve the quality of the pasture, this standard is maintained by pasture management and constant attention.

Rotation

This is the method by which the paddocks and fields are divided into different areas. Each area is alternately rested, grazed by horses or stocked with other animals. This reduces the amount of land on which the horses graze, allowing the other portions to recuperate and produce new growth.

The field, depending on its size, can be divided into two, three or four portions.

One portion provides grazing for the horses. The horses should have a change of pasture every six to twelve months. Horses are destructive grazers cropping the grasses down to almost nothing and leaving rough patches where the unpalatable grasses grow. Areas around the water and the gate become deeply poached. One portion can be grazed by sheep or cattle. One portion is allowed to rest. It may be fertilised at this time. If there is a fourth area this can be used for hay.

Even if there is only sufficient land to divide into two areas, as long as the horses are periodically moved and a portion of the land is rested this will improve the pastureland and the quality of grazing.

Size of pasture

The area needed for horses and ponies depends on whether they are living out permanently or part time. For those animals living out full time, each horse needs around 1½ to 2 acres and each pony about 1 acre. Overstocking pasture not only causes the land to deteriorate it also greatly increases the risk of worm infestation.

For horses living out part time, for longer periods during the summer and shorter periods during the winter, approximately 1 acre will be sufficient with about ½ an acre per pony.

The starvation/isolation paddock is smaller but the horse or pony will not be expected to live permanently on this area. These paddocks are normally around a quarter of an acre in size.

Annual maintenance

Every season the grassland will receive attention to keep the pasture up to standard.

Spring

During the spring, providing the ground is sufficiently firm to take the weight of the machinery, the field will need **harrowing**. The spiked and linked chain harrow pulled by a tractor removes the matted, dead grass. This layer of dead material covers the ground, stifling new growth and preventing the sun from warming the soil. The spikes aerate the soil. Harrowing also helps to flatten out poached areas and spread any remaining droppings in the field. The first harrowing is done around late February or early March depending on the weather.

Parts of the field may need **re-seeding** to replace winter damage and prevent the spread of weeds and poisonous plants. Only in extreme circumstances is the whole field ploughed and re-seeded. This makes the pasture unsuitable for horses for at least a year, possibly two.

The ground will need **rolling** about a week after harrowing. This may be done before or after re-seeding. Rolling makes the ground firmer, flattens out poached areas and pushes nutrients into the ground encouraging new grass growth.

Fertilising can be done before or after rolling. The soil can be analysed first to decide what type of fertiliser is needed. The fields should be given a general inspection for winter damage. The fencing can be repaired, ditches cleared, water troughs cleaned out and checked, fallen trees or branches removed and other hazards dealt with, such as filling in pits and holes.

Swampy or boggy areas should be fenced off and poached areas made firmer with hard core, gravel, straw or shavings.

Summer

Harrowing can continue monthly during the summer to help grass growth and, during hot dry spells, to kill off worm larvae.

Topping is done to cut down the tall plants in the rough patches, encouraging the growth of the more palatable grass. The plants should be topped prior to seeding.

Topping can be done by hand with a scythe if the area is not large. In fields a mower or cutter on a tractor will be required. Apart from clearing the area, topping also improves the appearance of the fields, an important factor in a commercial business hoping to attract new clients. The cut plants will need removing immediately from the field.

The fields will need inspecting daily and necessary repairs done to fencing, gates, water troughs, poached areas. Any hazards should be removed or safely fenced off.

Autumn

Fertilising can be done in autumn if necessary.

Maintenance includes the field being prepared for winter; drainage needs checking and possibly clearing. The field shelter will need checking. Fencing, water troughs, poached areas, will all need attention. Hazards such as oak trees shedding their acorns need enclosing.

Winter

If possible, the fields should be left free of horses in the winter, or at least have a reduction in the grazing time. Horses damage the ground in wet conditions making next year's growth more difficult. Many horses and ponies do winter out though and with careful maintenance the damage will be kept to a minimum. Water will constantly have to be checked and possibly brought into the field. The water in the trough may be frozen; water may be supplied in buckets to replace this temporarily.

Safety

Creating, improving and maintaining pasture is an important aspect of managing horses and ponies at grass. The other essential factor is keeping the animals safe and secure. Anything that may harm or injure the horse, that poses a hazard, should be removed, enclosed, repaired or replaced. Fencing and gates need to be very secure. The fields and boundaries should be inspected daily. To prevent horse thieves, gates should be padlocked. These can be padlocked or secured at both sides; thieves have been known to take the gate off the hinges to gain access to the field.

Clean water should be constantly available. Horses will drink contaminated water if nothing else is available. All the animals in the field should be inspected closely at least once a day. Any wounds, injuries or illnesses can then be treated promptly. If the starvation paddock is used for schooling and jumping then the cones, blocks, poles and cups should be cleared out of the area when the horses are grazing.

Keeping horses safe at pasture is mostly common sense. Horses do tend to injure themselves in the fields and the aim is to minimise the risk as much as possible. Anything that may cause an injury or wound needs to be given immediate attention.

Horse Behaviour at Grass

Understanding how horses behave in the fields helps us to take measures to keep them safe. Horses are herd animals. If left alone a horse may become anxious and restless. He may canter or gallop around the field, injure himself on the fencing or strain a muscle. He will rarely settle to eat but will continue to become stressed.

Every herd has its 'pecking order' of seniority. New horses introduced to the herd can be bullied, they will certainly be 'tested' until they are accepted and have found their own level. In some cases horses can be severely injured. They may be stressed, restless and lose condition because they will not eat.

A new horse needs to be put into a field or paddock with a quiet companion first. This will prevent the problem of being on his own. He can then be introduced to the herd gradually over a period of weeks until he becomes 'known' and accepted. This minimises the risk of fighting and injuries.

A young horse should begin in a field with an older quieter companion. If young horses are put in together they will dash around, have 'mock' fights, tease or annoy each other. Though a young horse may try and 'play' with an older one, the older companion normally carries on eating. If the young horse annoys the older one, continuing to ask for play, the older one will generally show an aggressive posture, baring teeth, ears flat back or swinging the hindquarters around to face the younger horse. This normally puts the younger horse off, who becomes bored and decides to start eating.

When there are younger horses with the herd they will often chase each other around whilst the older animals continue with the more serious pastime of grazing. It is, therefore, an advantage to have older and younger horses together, providing there are a greater number of older horses than younger ones.

Geldings and mares should be separated and, if possible, have at least a field between them. Mares in season cause all sorts of trouble. An aggressive gelding will fight any other gelding in the field and can cause extensive injuries. He will constantly chase off, kick, bite and fight geldings near the mare or mares. He may trap another gelding in the corner of the field and proceed to kick him violently.

A horse with an aggressive nature should be watched or even kept in a separate field with one or two quieter companions. Aggressive horses can cause problems in the herd, fighting, kicking, bullying, biting, teasing, tormenting and generally causing injury to others. Putting an aggressive gelding in a field with two mares, or an aggressive mare with a gelding should cause the least problems. Often in a yard an aggressive animal of this type can cause difficulties between the owners as well.

Another problem occurs when a mild tempered gelding is constantly bullied. This type of gentleman (no, not a wimp!) is safer to be at grass with the mares. Two or three geldings of this nature are quite happy to be with the mares.

Caring for the Horse at Grass

Revision

Stage I – grassland management, shelters, fencing and boundaries. The horse-sick field, turning horses out and bringing them in from grass.

Stage II – caring for the horse at grass, daily care, inspections, grooming, trimming, winter care, rugging. Safety at pasture, flies, parasites, skin ailments. Riding the horse at grass.

Once the pasture has been made as safe as possible, care of the horse and pony at grass involves observation and daily routine. The horse is inspected at least twice daily, one of these being a close inspection. He may be brought in, groomed, checked and exercised. He may need a daily feed, particularly if he is being worked or during the winter months. If he is wearing a rug, this will need checking and probably adjusting. If the rug is wet this will need changing for a dry one.

He will need his feet attending to at least every six weeks and his normal worming dose given at the same time. He may need extra care if flies are a nuisance in the field. A fly fringe, fly repellent, garlic in the food all help to reduce this problem. He may be brought in during the morning and evening when certain flies are at their most active. Flies can be a problem especially in fields near water and trees. If there is a higher field with less trees it may be better to put the horses in this field during the spring and summer.

Some horses and ponies, particularly native ponies, thrive on being out at grass. They seem to be happier and more relaxed in their natural surroundings. Even finer bred horses such as Thoroughbreds can be kept permanently at grass with good care and attention. Many competition horses are kept at grass in a fit condition and compete successfully. Keeping horses and ponies at grass does *not* mean less work. They may need more care, time and attention. It can be time consuming for an owner who has to trek over fields to catch the horse, clean or dry him and wait an hour after he has grazed before riding him. This can be even worse if the horse is difficult to catch.

For some owners it is more convenient to keep the horse stabled. Every horse though should have some time at pasture and care should be taken to make sure that this time is both safe and relaxing.

Exam Tips

Candidates will need to know the basic methods of creating a good pasture and of maintaining that quality throughout the year. Knowing the difference between good and bad pasture is essential for those who will be caring for horses and ponies. Animals can be affected by many problems, illnesses and injuries, in the field. Some of this is just bad luck, but many difficulties arise through bad management, negligence or ignorance.

As part of the preparation for the Grassland Management section of the Stage III, observe different fields and how they are kept. Watch horses and ponies at grass, see how they behave; when being turned out, brought in, introduced to the herd, how they sort out the pecking order and how they react to their companions.

A revision of Stage I and II may be helpful as the Grassland Management section is such a vast subject covering many aspects of keeping, caring for and handling horses and ponies at pasture.

C H A P T E R   23
Lungeing

Lungeing is an important and useful skill. All horses and ponies benefit from lungeing whether as part of their training or as an alternative form of exercise. It adds variety to the work routine, allows the horse to move without a rider, exercises the horse if the rider cannot ride through illness, bad weather conditions or lack of time. It tones and develops the horse's muscles, increases suppleness and balance. It is also useful as a warming up or 'letting off steam' exercise before being ridden.

The Art of Lungeing

Learning to lunge takes good instruction, practice and experience, and is as much an art as riding. Often referred to as 'riding from the ground', horses can be trained on the lunge from a young age up to a high standard, which makes this aspect of horsemastership just as exciting and enjoyable.

Revision

Stage II Reasons for lungeing, where to lunge, lungeing equipment and fitting, basic methods of lungeing. Using the lunge equipment, lungeing aids, position of lunger. Fitting the side reins, functions of the side reins, working the horse on the lunge, use of body language. Basic assessment of the horse on the lunge.

Stage III Requirements

The basics of lungeing were covered at Stage II; the Examiners are now expecting candidates to lunge with more proficiency showing that they can work the horse as part of his daily exercise.

The Stage III candidate will need to:

✳ Check the tack and lungeing equipment, alter if necessary.

✳ Use the equipment competently and effectively.

✳ Show skill, control, good voice projection, good stance and use of body language.

✳ Work an experienced horse on the lunge.

The Tack and Equipment

The horse is normally tacked up as if for riding apart from removing the noseband from the bridle. The lunge cavesson needs to be fitted snugly so that it does not slip when in use and catch the horse's outside eye.

The cavesson headpiece fits over, on top of, the bridle headpiece.

The cavesson cheekpieces may either fit on top of or underneath the bridle cheekpieces. Either method is correct, but there is a trend of thought that having the lungeing cavesson cheekpieces on top of the bridle cheekpieces is more comfortable for the horse. If the cavesson cheekpieces fit underneath the bridle cheekpieces, this distorts the straps and may interfere with the bit.

The lunge cavesson noseband fits underneath the bridle cheekpieces. The bridle reins are twisted and normally secured through the throatlash.

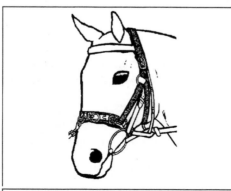

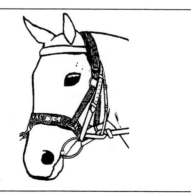

Method 1. The cavesson cheekpieces fit on top of the bridle cheekpieces	Method 2. The cavesson cheekpieces fitted underneath can distort the bridle cheekpieces and move the bit

If the horse wears his saddle, the stirrup irons need securing by means of the leather straps. This prevents them from slipping down and banging on the horse's sides. The side reins are threaded through the girth straps, under the first strap and around the second, so that they do not move when in use. A horse being lunged should always wear brushing boots on all four legs to protect against brushing and speedicutting whilst the horse is moving on the circle.

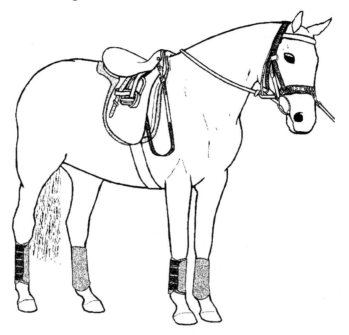

The lunge line should be at least 8 to 10 metres in length, in good condition and strong. There are different types on the market, the more usual are the light coloured webbing types or the thicker 'lead rope' type. Side reins are available in a variety of materials, leather, nylon, synthetic webbing. Nylon is strong and inexpensive, synthetic side reins with elasticated pieces allow 'give' but the elastic becomes worn with age and loses its elasticity. Many trainers prefer leather, as it is strong, quick to clean and the straps are more easily adjustable than some other reins. The lunge whip needs to be long enough to encourage the horse forwards, but not so long so that it is difficult for the lunger to use.

Lunger's Clothes

The lunger does need protection, lungeing can be extremely dangerous. A protective riding hat, correctly fitted and fastened, and a pair of thicker, protective gloves are vital. Strong footwear that will not slip, preferably riding boots, are also essential. A long sleeved jacket or shirt, and trousers protect the arms and legs in case of accidents.

Using the Equipment

The aim is to control and exercise the horse so that he moves forward with impulsion, balance and rhythm. To achieve this the lunger uses the equipment and his own skills effectively. The whip, lunge line, side reins, the lunger's voice, stance and body language are all used in a similar fashion to the 'natural' aids when riding.

The lunger works the horse so that he is moving from the whip (as with the leg aids) into the lunge line and side rein contact (as with the reins). The whip and lunge line are also used to work the horse into the correct bend on the circle. As the horse is bending around the circumference of the circle so he will be working into *the contact of the outside rein aid in a similar way as into the outside hand.*

The Lunge Line

The lunge line is held in the hand softly but firmly. It is used in a similar fashion to the inside riding rein with the lunger exerting a feel on the line to ask for bend. To do this and to achieve control through the line there has to be *a contact with the horse's head*. The lunger needs to feel the 'weight' of the horse through the line.

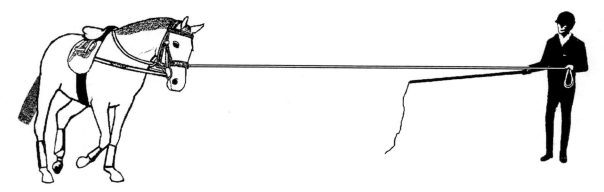

This contact is extremely important.

* The lunger needs to be able to convey messages down the line either by using a 'squeeze and release' feel or sometimes an actual 'resist and release' action.

* The lunger needs to make the horse work *into the contact* coming through from the hindquarters.

* The lunger may need to encourage the horse to bend into the circle.

If the line is loose the lunger will have no control over the horse and will not be able to make him work correctly.

The Whip

The lungeing whip is used to send the horse forward and to drive the horse into the lunge line contact. **The whip, in effect, is used in place of the rider's legs and should be used as effectively as the leg aids**. The whip is used in a variety of ways.

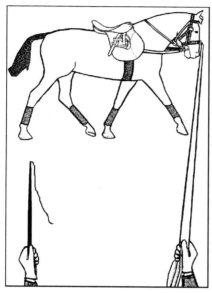

* ❖ Held pointing towards the hocks and kept still if the horse is responding well.

* ❖ Keep the elbow bent and the wrist supple so that the whip is not rigidly held out to the horse.

* ❖ Held pointing towards the hocks and used in a rolling, circular movement to encourage the horse forwards.

* ❖ Keeping the elbow bent, this circular motion is produced by the lower arm with supple wrist movement.

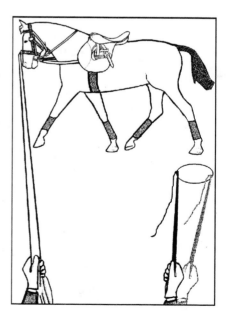

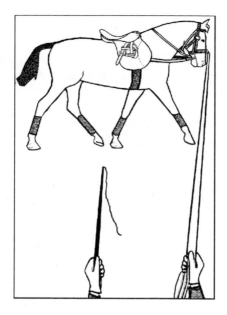

❖ Held towards the girth to ask for bend and to send the horse out onto the circle.

❖ Held towards the girth or the shoulder if the horse 'falls in', to insist that he keeps out on the circle.

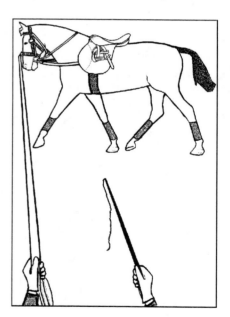

❖ Held towards the shoulder if the horse insists on swinging out when halting.

❖ Used to touch the horse just below his hocks to send him forwards if he is sluggish or lacks respect for the whip.

The whip can therefore be quite versatile. When it is used effectively the whip is an important part of the lungeing skill used to teach the horse obedience and submission to the lunger's commands.

As the horse is taught to respect its use, the lunger should keep it away from the horse when he is handling him at close quarters. It is then reversed and tucked underneath the arm furthest away from the horse.

The Side Reins

The aim of the side reins is to teach the horse to seek and accept the bit contact. They offer more control to the lunger and encourage the horse to develop a steadier head carriage. The reins also keep the horse 'straight' in his frame, improving his balance and building his muscles across his crest and back.

The **height and length of the side reins should be as equal as possible** to encourage the horse to work in balance and into an 'outside rein contact'.

In effect with the lunge line acting as 'inside rein', the horse is worked into the *outside side rein* contact just as outside riding rein. It is important therefore, to keep the side reins equal in length and not to make the inner rein shorter. It is quite correct when lungeing for the inner side rein to become *slightly* slack because the horse is working into the outside contact with the correct bend through his body.

The horse's head needs to be in a 'natural flexed position'. His neck should be curved, relaxed and bending at, or slightly behind, the poll. His face should be just in front of the vertical. The lunger can persuade the horse into this position before altering the side reins.

The height of the side reins should be level with the horse's mouth, parallel to the ground, when his head is flexed into this 'natural' position. They may be positioned slightly lower, but not so low as the force the horse's head down unnaturally.

In length the side reins should **just** reach the bit. This length is often influenced by personal preference; some prefer the rein slightly shorter and some slightly longer. With an unknown horse it is advisable to begin with this length and alter if necessary. A strong, fast horse may have the reins slightly shorter, a sluggish horse may work more effectively into a slightly longer rein.

The important points are:

* The reins should never be so tight that the horse is forced into a 'bent' head position with a cramped, tight jowl.

* The reins should never be so loose that they are ineffective.

To check that the side reins are equal, clip the reins to the bitrings and stand in front of the horse keeping his head in the flexed position and straight. If the reins do need adjusting, unfasten both reins from the bitrings first.

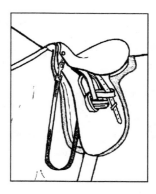

When starting to use the side reins, clip the outside rein onto the bit first. Both side reins are fastened onto the bit BELOW the bridle reins.

Side reins should always be unfastened when leading the horse into and out of the arena or when a rider is mounting. They are clipped onto the D rings of the saddle for safety until required.

The Lunger's Skill

To lunge effectively the lunger needs:

* a good stance.

* to use the whip, lunge line and side reins effectively.

* to use the voice aid clearly and consistently.

* to develop the technique of body language in lungeing.

* to develop an 'eye' and a 'feel' for the horse's movements.

The Stance

The aim is for the lunger to stand in the centre of the circle and, with a minimum amount of movement, control and work the horse through various paces and transitions.

To achieve this the lunger first needs a solid base from which to use the aids effectively. Think of the position as similar to the riding position.

- The feet are flat on the ground with the weight dropping into the heel.

- The knees are relaxed and slightly bent.

- The upper body is straight.

- The shoulders are level and straight, down and relaxed.

- The head is held up.

- The arms are kept softly by the lunger's side **with the elbows bent**.

In this position the lunger uses his own balance to control the horse. The horse is kept on a contact through the lunge line and the lunger uses his shoulders and back just as in riding, almost as if giving a 'half halt' aid. The lunger straightens his back muscles, maintains the contact on the lunge line and encourages the horse forwards from the whip.

The Voice

This is an important aid when lungeing. The voice should be clear and audible. The lunger needs to learn to project the voice as when instructing a lesson. Stance is important and will influence the sound of the voice. The lunger stands with the head up, neck straight but relaxed and the chest slightly expanded. Even for a person with a quiet voice, it is amazing how much good posture improves the voice.

The tone is important; through this the lunger conveys his commands, his praise or reprimand to the horse. The commands should be given with authority. A command given meekly in a whisper can easily be ignored.

The flexion in the voice illustrates the commands, raised for upward transitions, 'walk ON' and lowered for downward transitions 'AND whoa' or 'WA-alk'.

Body Language

Mental ability and belief is essential to all aspects of horsemastership. *'The mind knows; the body shows'*. If the lunger believes in his own ability and competence this will be apparent to the horse through the lunger's body language. This does not mean aggressiveness or loudness, but a quiet confidence, firmness and determination.

Body language can be extremely effective; the lunger uses subtle movements of his body to encourage the horse to work correctly.

Moving the whip position to different areas of the body, or just slightly extending the whip arm so that the end of the whip comes nearer to the horse's body, can have quite an effect.

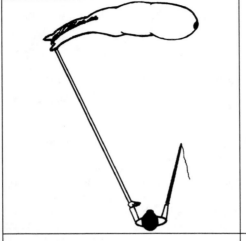

The 'normal' lungeing stance.

The lunger can move the whip shoulder towards the horse's hindquarters, using the body to drive the horse forwards. The arm should still be relaxed with the elbow bent.

Positioning the body can have a restraining affect on more active horses, as much as a driving affect on sluggish horses.

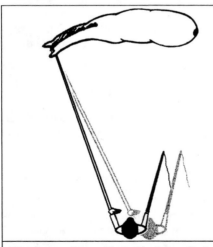

The lunger is positioned in line with the shoulder. This can persuade an active horse to steady his pace. (The lunger should not become 'in front' of the horse.)

The lunger is positioned more in line with the horse's hip. This can have a driving affect on a slow or sluggish horse.

These alterations of position are slight, a step or two. The contact should still be maintained with the lunge line.

'Eye and Feel'

To cultivate an 'eye and feel' for the horse's movement takes observation, experience and practice. The lunger needs to gain knowledge of how the horse moves when he is working properly. Good instruction from a knowledgeable teacher and observing horses being lunged will expand the experience. Practise will increase the lunger's technique and ability.

Working the Horse

The first consideration is the lunge area. The ground should be flat and fairly soft. A good surface will prevent the horse from stumbling or losing his balance. Hard or stony ground may bruise his feet. Slippery or steep ground may cause the horse to slip and injure himself.

Ideally the area should be enclosed and safe at least 20 metres by 20 metres but no larger than 20 x 40. Often at competitions or shows lungeing has to be done in a field or open area, but as long as the horse has been fully trained to be obedient on the lunge this does not normally cause a problem.

To Start

The lunger starts on the left rein as normal, holding the loops of the lunge line in the left hand. The whip is tucked under the left arm. The lunger walks a few steps with the horse onto the circle.

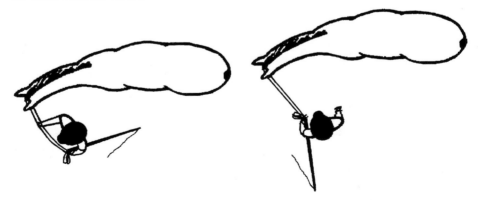

Once the horse is walking on the circle, the lunger turns to face the horse's side. The whip is brought *behind the lunger's back* into the right hand and encourages the horse forwards.

- The lunger *should never step backwards* either to manipulate the horse onto a larger circle or to deal with a problem.

- The lunger should *never be positioned in front of the horse.* This will encourage the horse to nap or swing around.

- The lunger should *never come within kicking distance of the horse's hindquarters.*

The lunger stands facing the horse's side with the horse, line, lunger and whip maintaining the triangular 'slice of pizza' shape.

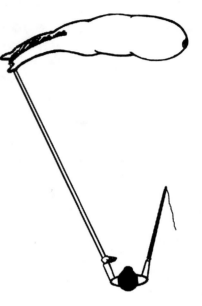

Paces and Transitions

To work the horse effectively on the lunge, he needs to go forwards into trot fairly soon. Allow him half to one circuit in walk at the beginning, then make the transition to trot.

The horse should be allowed to warm up in trot. He needs to loosen and stretch his muscles, and relax into a balanced trot rhythm before beginning transitions. The horse needs to be going forward first before he can perform good transitions.

Once the trot is established and the horse is relaxing, stretching forwards and down, the lunger can ask for transitions to and from walk. Keep the walk periods down to a maximum of half a circuit. Make changes of rein quite frequently to exercise both sides of the horse.

Assessing the Horse

The horse needs to be assessed in his paces, his transitions and his general 'way of going'. In this way the lunger can assess when the horse is going well and in which areas he can be improved.

*   He will stretch his frame through his loins, his back and his neck reaching forwards and slightly downwards with his head.

* He will also need to bend through his body around the circumference of the circle.

* The paces should be rhythmical with the footfalls even, then the horse will achieve balance.

* Ideally he will be tracking up or over tracking without losing balance or rhythm.

* He needs to 'round' his hindquarters to bring his hindlegs underneath the body and to bend his hocks.

* He will respond to the lunger's voice quickly, he may even be watching the lunger, showing an awareness and attention.

* He will be taking the contact on the lunge line and side reins.

The horse will probably work more efficiently on one rein, his softer side. The lunger will recognise which is the horse's stiff side. The contact on the lunge line will be stronger. The horse may be more reluctant to bend and may swing his hindquarters out. The lunger should continue to ask for bend by feel and release on the lunge line and use of the whip.

Time

The horse is normally exercised sufficiently in 30 to 35 minutes if this is his exercise for the day. If he is to be ridden after lungeing then 10 to 15 minutes will settle or make him more supple.

Lungeing on a circle is quite a strenuous exercise; excess may put strain on his joints, muscles, tendons and ligaments. The rein should be changed frequently so the horse is exercised equally on both sides.

All these points show how intricate and effective lungeing can be in training and exercising the horse.

Stage III Lungeing

Each candidate will be required to lunge an experienced horse in a 20 x 20 metre arena. In an arena of 20 x 40 metres there could be two candidates; if 20 x 60 there could be three lungeing simultaneously. The separate lungeing areas are normally divided by poles on the ground or poles and blocks. The horses, prepared for lungeing, will be brought to the candidates in the lungeing areas.

There are two important points in this Examination, the time allowed for lungeing and the efficiency of the candidates. Each candidate is given between 12 to 15 minutes to lunge. This means that checking the tack and equipment has to be completed quickly. The candidates need to be proficient at checking and altering tack; organising the lunge line and the side reins.

Start

The tack and equipment should be assessed for fit, security, condition and suitability. The cavesson can be tightened if necessary, the girth will probably need tightening; check the stirrup irons are correctly secured. The side reins can be assessed, check the height when tightening the girth, check the length by quickly measuring each side rein to the appropriate bitring.

Though condition and suitability of the equipment are out of the candidate's control, the Examiners may ask questions about this and request suggestions for improvement.

At the start of the lungeing session, once the lunge line is clipped onto the central ring of the lunge cavesson, the line needs to be organised into loops. The candidate should, if possible, straighten the line by passing it from hand to hand. If the line is so tangled it cannot be organised efficiently by hand the candidate may, whilst holding onto the line near the horse's head, throw the excess on the ground. The line should be thrown behind the candidate and organised into loops efficiently. (Using loops is more advisable than folds, as the line can be handled more easily.)

The loops should be even and of a suitable size, not too small so that the line may become wrapped around the hand, not too long as to hang down by the candidate's feet. The lunger should hold onto the loop at the end of the line. If there is no loop to hold, there should be a knot. This is to prevent the line being pulled easily out of the lunger's hand.

The Warm up

The horse should be warmed up first without side reins. This gives time for the candidate to assess the horse. The warm up should be quite brief, walk one circuit, two circuits at trot then walk, halt and change the rein. In the new direction walk half a circuit, trot for one then walk and halt. Bring the horse into the centre and fit the side reins.

If, during the warm up, the horse is eager and lively the side reins can be put on immediately. The horse is obviously ready to work and the side reins will give the lunger more control.

Side Reins

The side reins are measured either at the start of the session or when the candidate wishes to start using them. The length of the side reins is a subject surrounded by controversy and discussion. They should not be too loose to be ineffective or too tight to restrict the horse. The aim is for the horse to feel the contact and to work into this contact.

Persuade the horse to hold his head in the 'flexed' position. The tip of the clip of the side reins may just reach the bitrings. The reins can be slightly shorter, if the candidate judges this to be suitable for the horse.

If the horse is forward going and responsive, as assessed in the warm up period, the side reins can be shorter. If the horse is sluggish or finds it difficult to flex, perhaps he has a thicker neck, the side reins can be slightly longer to just reach the bitring.

If the candidate does work the horse and find the side reins too loose, then he or she can alter them during the next change of rein. The inside rein may show a little slackness if the horse is working into the lunge line and outside rein contact.

Working the Horse

The horse is worked in trot for most of the period. The candidate can start by asking the horse to walk for up to half a circuit after the warm up period.

The horse should be given some time in trot to allow him to warm up. He should be encouraged to trot actively, by the effective use of the whip and the lunger's body language. Watch for him stretching forwards and down into the side rein contact. Watch his pace, allow him a few circuits to establish a good forward rhythm. Once the horse has settled into trot, he can be asked for some transitions to walk and into trot again.

The horse should not be cantered at Stage III. If the horse is sluggish and the candidate pushes him to work properly, at which point he canters, this is quite acceptable and may even help his forwardness. After half a circuit the candidate can ask the horse to trot.

He should work on a good circle without falling in or pulling out. If the horse does 'fall in' around the circle, smoothly move the whip so that it points at the horse's girth at the point where he comes in. It is usual for the horse then to pull out at the opposite side of the circle. If this occurs the candidate should anticipate this and hold onto the lunge line firmly. The candidate should use their body weight to hold the line and horse on the circle. Just as quickly the horse will be round to the spot where he falls in so the candidate needs to be alert.

If the horse is sluggish and refuses to go forward the whip should be used with effect. Try the movements of the body to drive the horse on. Try the wrist movement to circle the whip. If the horse is still not forward going, the candidate should use the whip and flick the horse below the hocks. Keep the contact with the lunge line and send him forwards.

Change of Rein

The direction should be changed fairly frequently to keep the horse from being 'one-sided' and to keep his attention. The candidate brings the horse to walk and halt with a firm command. If the horse swings his hindquarters out at this point the candidate should step a little sideways and towards the horse's hindquarters and tell him to walk on. Remember to keep a safe distance from the horse's hindquarters.

To avoid twists in the lunge line when changing the rein, the candidate can place the lunge line into the other hand before walking to the horse. For instance, if lungeing on the left rein; bring the horse to halt, reverse the whip and tuck it under the right armpit. Change the lunge line from the left hand into the right hand. Whilst walking towards the horse take up the slack with the left hand and make sure that the line is placed flat into the right hand.

On reaching the horse, pass in front of him onto his off or right side. Then, holding the line near the cavesson in the left hand, proceed to walk the horse into the centre of the circle for a change of rein.

When changing the rein, the side reins do not have to be unfastened. The candidate should walk the horse from the circle to the centre in a wide arc so that the horse does not turn too quickly and exert a pull on the bit through the side reins.

If the candidate prefers, the outside side rein can be unfastened and clipped onto the saddle D ring until the horse is in the middle of the circle when it can be refastened.

The Examiners may inform the candidates when the time is nearly finished. The candidate may wish to make some more transitions at this point, or continue to keep the horse working in trot if he is going well. If there are a couple of minutes remaining there may be time for a quick change of rein before the candidate asks the horse to walk and halt. The horse should then be brought into the centre of the circle and the side reins unclipped and fastened to the D rings on the saddle.

Exam Tips

During the lungeing session, you need to show that you are accustomed to using the lunge equipment and to lungeing horses effectively. This mean practice and more practice until you have gained competence and ability.

You will *not* have a lot of time, 12 to 15 minutes passes quickly, so you will need to crack on and work the horse.

The voice should be loud, clear and authoritative. You need to sound confident. Nervousness, lack of confidence and experience will show in the voice. Imagine you are talking to the other person lungeing, someone over in the gallery, or by the fence so that you project your voice. It will not matter if your voice is a little loud. It will be noticed if it is too quiet!

Keep the contact with the lunge line and if the horse does try and come into the circle, insist he stays out by positioning the whip and using the voice.

Avoid holding the whip out like a 'fishing rod' with a straight, rigid arm. Effectiveness of the whip is an integral part of the skill of lungeing, use it to its best advantage. The horse will be watching the whip out of the corner of his eye; slight body movement may be enough to persuade him to work. Often those who use their voice too much are not driving the horse with effective use of the whip.

One point over which candidates agonise is whether or not to use the whip on a sluggish horse. The answer is – yes, do. If the horse is clearly not responding, refusing to go forward, he does need to be reprimanded. Keeping the elbow bent, stretch the arm out slightly and using a flick of the wrist touch him on the hindlegs below the hocks.

Avoid, though, cracking the whip or swinging it about continuously with little effect. Subtle use of the whip with discretion, that is, when it is needed, demonstrates the lunger's ability.

In the Stage III examination, a good deal of emphasis is placed on the lungeing. So it is worth the time practising, learning and increasing your knowledge of this skill.

Besides, when you have mastered the use of the equipment and have developed the ability to work the horse on the lunge, you will be amazed at how you can influence the horse's paces by voice and body language. You will also learn that you can create a close rapport with the horse through lungeing and that both of you can really enjoy this form of equitation.

C H A P T E R   24
General Knowledge and Safety

The horse is a living creature with a mind and temperament of his own. He reacts to situations instinctively which, through his size and strength, occasionally results in injury to the rider, owner or handler. Fortunately most of the time horses and ponies are relatively good-natured (apart from some small ponies who can be a real pain!). There will always be the time though if the horse is frightened or defending himself when he reacts in an injurious way.   The point about safety is to keep these circumstances to a minimum; preventing a situation is far better than dealing with an accident.

The British Horse Society places great emphasis on safety. Knowing the basic rules of safety can save so much stress and pain not only to the human handler but also to the horse or pony himself.   For this reason the safety section is covered comprehensively within the British Horse Society's examination training scheme.

Safety

Revision

Stage I and II. Safety rules and regulations; safety precautions in the yard, in the stable, when hacking, for children, fire precautions and regulations. Safety on the Public Highway, riding on the road. The Country Code.

Every student for the Stage III is strongly recommended to revise the safety sections from the Stage I and Stage II books.

By Stage III the candidates will know the rules and regulations for safety around the yard, in the loose box, when teaching, when hacking, on the Public Highway and in the countryside.   Students can now go one step further to prevent injuries and accidents before they occur.

Anticipation and Prevention

Students at this level should be able to anticipate and avoid situations where an accident is likely to occur. The theoretical information learnt from the previous Exams should now be applied practically in everyday situations. For instance, a pitchfork left on the ground would be a potential danger.

Seeing a small child trying to tack up a large, unrestrained horse in a stable would immediately be cause for concern. The horse could spin round, knock the child down and kick or trample him.

Anticipating these potential dangers is the first step to prevention of accidents. Students working towards their Preliminary Teacher's qualification are learning to take charge of staff and yards. They will have the competence to control situations. For instance, they will ask someone to remove the pitchfork and put it away safely. They will prevent the child from entering the horse's stable alone and either tack the horse up or ask someone else to do it. As well as awareness the student can be active in preventing accidents. This is putting the theoretical knowledge to practical use.

Safety at Shows and Competitions

Most accident prevention is common sense. Everyone who enters a competition, show or sponsored ride should read the rules of that particular event prior to the day. Take time and care over parking, unloading, tacking up, working the horse in, cooling him off afterwards, loading and leaving.

Visiting shows, competitions, horse sales and even some yards is a real eye-opener and, in some cases, distressing. Seen at a competition recently two adults were sat on straw bales watching the show, each with a lighted cigarette. When challenged they sheepishly stated that they knew it was wrong and dangerous. There are so many horror stories and as many, if not more, narrow escapes.

Fire Regulations

The potentiality of fire within a yard is very high. The stables are normally made of wood, have straw bedding; there are hay and straw bales stored in bulk. The electricity may not be as safe as it should be and a spark can set off a fire, which within a few minutes will spread around the yard.

The Fire Prevention Officer should inspect the yard regularly. Fire extinguishers should be checked periodically and renewed when necessary.

The fire drill notice should be posted around the yard at several visible areas to inform everyone of the fire drill. It will give the designated collection area for that part of the yard, the nearest telephone and the next nearest telephone to contact the Fire Brigade. It will inform the staff to let the horses out of their boxes starting from the box nearest to the fire and working away from this area. Fire extinguishers, fire buckets filled with sand should be easily accessible and everyone should be taught how to use this equipment.

There should be regular fire drills at different times of the day so that staff, helpers, clients and riders know exactly what to do. Panic can be as great a risk to life as the fire itself.

This may sound common sense but many yards completely ignore fire precautions. Some yards allow their staff and clients to walk around smoking, even mucking out a box with a lighted cigarette in the person's mouth.

It is worth being over cautious and insisting on fire precautions. Being a witness to a yard fire is one of the most devastating and distressing experiences, especially when the fire costs the lives of horses.

Road Safety

According to statistics there are approximately 3000 accidents on the roads every year involving horses. Many of these incidents could be avoided. Unfortunately most motorists seem to have little regard or understanding of horses and will drive past them far too fast. Amazingly this is particularly so on winding, narrow country lanes when drivers come screeching around corners into the back of horses.

Wearing bright clothing, fluorescent during bright days and reflective during dull days or in the evening, will help riders to be seen more easily. In groups, riding with a grey horse positioned at the front and back also helps.

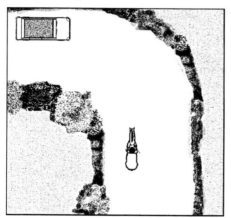 

Positioning on the road can make horse and rider more visible, encouraging drivers to take more care. When riding around corners, particularly on narrow lanes, position the horse further to the right towards the middle of the road, on left-hand bends. On right hand bends position to the left, further in towards the kerb. Riders will also be able to see motorists sooner. Keep alert, keep listening and keep looking, anticipate and be prepared.

Follow the rules of the Highway Code, looking, signalling and positioning the horses at junctions and roundabouts. Keep the pace active but not fast; avoid trotting around corners or roundabouts and where the road surface can be slippery.

Avoid hazards if possible, anything that may make the horse spook into the road. If absolutely necessary, dismount and lead the horse past the hazard.

Unfortunately riding on roads is a necessity for most yards, livery stables and hacking establishments. Being aware of the dangers and following the safety rules is essential to prevent an accident.

The British Horse Society has launched a new education programme the *'Safety 2000 Campaign'* aimed at motorists. In conjunction with the Department of Transport, the BHS has produced a leaflet, *'Horse Sense for Motorists'* to make them more aware of the vulnerability of horses and riders on the road. They are also encouraging more riders to take the Riding & Road Safety Test. The BHS are hoping through this campaign to reduce the number of road accidents involving horses.

Safety Training

Many accidents are caused by ignorance, negligence or plain stupidity. Everyone who begins work in a yard; working pupils, helpers, part-time, temporary staff and especially children should be given lessons on safety rules and regulations.

For those who have been in the equestrian industry for years, most safety rules are second nature, almost instinctive. It is then easy to forget that a child or an adult who has never worked with horses previously, has no idea of the dangers. For instance, children will run around the back of ponies, adults will slap a horse on its rump when turning him out in the field. Riders often try and mount with a loose girth or hold the whip in the wrong hand when being given a leg up and hit the assistant in the face. People genuinely need to be taught these points, simple as they may be.

Accident Report Book

Whenever there is an accident in the yard, on the road, out hacking, the instructor in charge must complete an Accident report form. This will include the date, time of the incident, names of the persons involved, their addresses and the horses, where and how the accident occurred.

It will also include the name of the instructor and exactly what attention or action was taken. This form should be witnessed. Any after care, such as hospital treatment, should be noted in the Report book.

Accident procedures

There are recommended procedures to follow in the event of an accident.

1. **Assess** the situation
2. **Prevent** further accidents
3. Assess the **casualty**
4. Send for **help**

Remember the mnemonic

Assessment – Prevention – Assess Casualty – Help = APACHe

Assess the situation

Always take a few seconds to assess the situation first. This is absolutely vital if further accidents are to be prevented. Stop; use this time to gather information by observation and by asking people for information if it is not clear what occurred.

In all situations KEEP CALM. It is those first few seconds when the adrenaline pumps in, the stomach goes cold and common sense seems to fly out of the head. The person in charge can use these seconds to take a deep breath, clear the head and tell the others to keep calm. Seeing the instructor or leader take control and remain calm will prevent panic.

Prevent further accidents

Having collected information the next step in the procedure is to prevent anyone else becoming injured. **Never put yourself or others into danger**. Make the area safe and keep the others under control. Take charge.

Assess the casualty

Once the area is safe, now is the time to assess the casualty. **Ask** the casualty how they feel. **Observe** their appearance and reaction to your questions. The decision is then made whether or not to send for help.

Send for help

The decision to send for medical help will be based on the first three procedures. **If in any doubt always send for help**. If there is a life threatening injury or wound then this may be given first aid, until help arrives. Never try to deal with a situation on your own.

In cases where there are several casualties, always attend to those that are quiet first. Someone who is groaning, moaning or screaming is obviously able to breathe. The one lying quietly may have an obstructed airway, which could be fatal within minutes.

First Aid

Revision

Stages I & II – Basic first aid, minor wounds, to stem bleeding. Unconsciousness, opening the airway, recovery position. The ABC procedure, checking the airway, breathing and circulation. Body check, treating unconscious and conscious casualties. Treating shock, broken bones, strains and sprains.

Simple first aid procedures were covered in the Stage I and II books and again the Stage III candidate should be able to use this theoretical knowledge in real life situations. The Examiners are now looking for practical ability as well as knowledge.

Assessing the Casualty

Once the situation has been brought under control, the injured party can be assessed. This is achieved by observation and assessment of reaction.

The casualty may be or appear uninjured. Even in these cases the casualty should be monitored for a while afterwards. Delayed shock, unnoticed injuries such as internal damage or concussion, may not be apparent immediately. If the casualty remains obviously injured then an assessment is made.

If the casualty is conscious:

+ tell the casualty to remain still.
+ ask if they have any pain and if so where.
+ if complaining of pain in the neck or back keep them still, **do not move them**.
+ send for help and watch out for shock.
+ do a body check for injuries.
+ talk to the casualty calmly and quietly. This could be asking them about the accident or giving an explanation of the body check. For example 'I am checking you for injury. I shall start at your head, tell me if you feel any pain. Does it hurt in this area?'
+ stem any obvious bleeding particularly if arterial or venal.
+ keep the casualty warm and keep talking to them until help arrives.

The priorities are: breathing, bleeding, bones and shock – BBBS (the three B'S).

Breathing   Check for difficulty in breathing this could be serious, possibly fatal. Check if the casualty suffers from asthma or another respiratory problem. Keep the casualty quiet and still to reduce the demand on the heart and lungs. If the casualty has an inhaler and is able to, he can administer this himself. He should not be given anyone else's inhaler (possibility of incorrect drug or cross infection) nor have the inhaler administered by someone else. Send for help.

Bleeding   Check wounds for the type of bleeding, arterial, venal or from capillaries. Stem any bleeding by direct pressure. Severe bleeding may lead to shock. If the casualty has no broken bones and the bleeding is not associated with a broken bone, the injured limb may be elevated to reduce the blood flow. If necessary it may help to lay the casualty down reducing the blood flow and the effects of shock. Send for medical help. If there is an object embedded in a wound, do not try to remove the object, this may cause more serious bleeding.

For minor wounds, stem bleeding, clean, dress and protect. If the casualty is likely to need stitches do not apply a dressing.

Bones

Check for difficulty in moving a limb, pain, swelling, bruising, bleeding, abnormal limb position. A grinding sound (crepitus) may be heard. In a **simple fracture** the bone is **broken in two**. A **comminuted** fracture is where the bone is broken into **fragments** and in a **greenstick** fracture the bone **splits and bends** rather than breaks. This is more common in children. When the **broken bone breaks through the skin**, this is an **open or compound** fracture. When the surrounding **skin is unbroken** this is a **closed** fracture. A **dislocation** occurs when one bone is **displaced at a joint**.

Do not move the casualty, steady and support the limb if possible. Use a sling for an arm, broken ribs and shoulder injuries. For leg injuries, place padding (a coat) between the legs and tie the legs together above and below the injury. Send for medical help.

If the bone broken is in the neck or back do not treat, send for help immediately.

Shock

This is serious and could be fatal. Symptoms are a pale, sweaty, cold, clammy skin; shallow rapid breathing, yawning, gasping for air. The casualty may feel dizzy and weak, nauseous; may become aggressive or anxious. Causes of shock include a heart attack, severe bleeding, loss of body fluids as in vomiting or diarrhoea, severe fright or pain. Basically the circulatory system fails to deliver oxygen and nutrients to all parts of the body, in extreme cases this affects the vital organs such as the heart.

Treat any injury. Lay casualty down and raise his legs so that they are above the level of his head, do so carefully if any bones are broken. Loosen tight clothing, shirt, tie, belt. Keep casualty warm, cover with a coat or blanket. Send for medical help immediately.

In all cases where the casualty suffers breathing problems, a serious wound, a broken bone or from suspected shock, **do not allow the casualty to eat, drink or smoke**. The casualty's lips may be moistened with water if absolutely necessary. Do not move the casualty unless absolutely necessary, give emergency treatment in the position found.

In all cases, even if the fallen rider immediately rises and insists that they are well, it is still wise to take a few minutes and to make absolutely sure. Always advise the casualty that should they feel unwell later in the day they should contact a doctor immediately. Delayed shock may occur some time after the accident.

Body Check

An injured casualty should not be moved except in an emergency, where his situation would place him in danger. A body check for the above priorities can be made without moving the casualty.

+ Starting at the head, feel gently around the skull for wounds, bleeding, swellings or indentations. Do not move the head. In cases where a riding hat is being worn, do not remove the hat unless absolutely necessary, for instance when the hat is obstructing breathing. Feel the base of the skull and the neck.

+ Feel around the face, the cheekbones, forehead and the chin.

+ Observe the eyes looking for dilation of the pupils and whether the casualty is focussing normally.

+ The colour of the skin; pale or flushed.

+ Nostrils and ears for any discharge of blood or fluid.

+ Check the mouth for any obstructions, for rasping or noisy breath and for bleeding.

+ Check the neck. Gently feel under the neck from the base of the skull to the shoulders where the body has a natural hollow.

+ Pass the hands across the tops of the shoulders, feel both collar bones.

+ Check each arm, first one then the other with both hands. Check the fingers, can the casualty move the fingers normally?

+ Check the trunk, feeling the ribcage, does each rib feel normal.

+ Check the hips, pass both hands down each leg, looking for swellings, wounds or deformity of the limbs.

Compare one side of the body with the other for abnormalities.

This 'top to toe' check can be done smoothly and fairly quickly. *Talk to the casualty all the time giving reassurance and keeping him calm.* He will probably be able to pinpoint any pain in his body, but it is wise to check the whole body for further injuries. It also gives an order to follow, which will keep everyone calm. Inform the doctor or paramedics when they arrive of any injuries found on the body.

Unconsciousness

There are various degrees of unconsciousness, from a brief fainting spell to a person who is fully unconscious over a period of time. The unconscious casualty will not be aware of his or her surroundings and will be unable to respond to stimuli.

If the casualty is unconscious the procedures are Dr. ABC – danger, response, airway, breathing and circulation.

Danger: assess the situation and prevent further accidents, never put yourself or anyone else into danger.

Response: check the casualty for consciousness and their level of response. Call out the casualty's name, gently shake their shoulders. Check if the eyes remain closed or the casualty opens them on command. Speech: does the casualty respond at all and if so is the speech slurred or confused? Action: will the casualty make any response at all and if so are the movements slow, painful or will he obey commands?

ABC routine: airway, breathing and circulation.

Open and clear airway, even if the casualty is breathing, when a person is unconscious the tongue can slip backwards and block the trachea.

With one hand on the forehead or hat and the other hand under the chin, very gently tilt the head backwards so that the airway is open. Check the mouth for obstacles.

Check breathing by listening and by watching the ribcage for movement.

Circulation, press two fingers gently on the neck by the side of the windpipe to feel the carotid artery.

Send for help.

+ No breathing; no pulse send or go for help immediately: 999.

+ No breathing; yes pulse: opening the airway may encourage breathing. Send or go for help immediately 999.

+ Yes breathing, yes pulse, treat any life threatening injuries such as arterial bleeding. Send or go for help immediately. In this situation, if the casualty has to be left alone, put into recovery position.

If it is possible, stay with the casualty until help arrives. The paramedics may need information about the accident, the persons involved and any treatment that has been given.

Emergency Action

The important point about any situation is that *under no circumstances should anyone who is not professionally trained give medical treatment of any kind.* First Aiders are trained to deal with emergency situations. They are there to assess the situation, treat any life threatening injuries, send for medical help and to give early appropriate treatment when necessary until help arrives.

In most cases the most essential part of First Aid is controlling the situation, preventing further accidents and keeping everyone calm. It is having the confidence and competence to keep cool especially in the first vital seconds after the accident has happened. It is taking charge, informing people of what to do, sending for help and reassuring the casualty.

Always send for help if the injury is anymore than minor. A cut or graze can be dealt with quite quickly and easily in the First Aid department or the office. If you suspect anything more, a wound that may need stitching, a broken bone, internal bleeding, concussion, **always, always** send for medical help. It is better that you err on the side of caution than send someone home with a serious, undiagnosed condition.

Remember to complete the Accident report form.

Practical Ability

Learning about First Aid and how to deal with situations from a book is never the same as having to deal with actual accidents. Whenever an incident occurs, take your time. Remember the procedure APACHe and put this into operation. By that time you will be calm and in control.

Example

Rider falls off horse at canter in the indoor school, crashes against school wall. Casualty is now lying on her back groaning.

Assess situation. Six in group trotting round. The loose horse is cantering round wildly upsetting the others.

Prevent further accidents. Command everyone to walk. Command whole ride to turn into centre of school and dismount. Catch loose horse. Ask someone to hold it.

Assess casualty. Talk to casualty. Ask if she is in pain and where. Ask what happened and check responses. Speech is fine, casualty obviously conscious. She says her back hurts and her leg looks at a strange angle.

Send for help. Casualty is obviously injured, could be spinal and possible broken leg. Turn to ride ask someone to go to the office and ring for an ambulance. Ask person to return when this done. Ask the rest of the ride to take their horses out. Make body check very gently without moving casualty. Check for bleeding; keep checking responses.

Keep talking to casualty; put coat over her and keep her warm. Keep her still and do not move. Wait until help arrives.

Once the casualty has been taken to hospital, fill in Accident Report Form.

In this case, as in most circumstances, the most important action is to take control of the situation, organise the rest of the ride and send for professional help. Following the accident procedures gives people a routine, it provides action and keeping people busy prevents panic.

Exam Tips

It is an excellent and useful exercise to take a First Aid course. This gives confidence when dealing with situations. Even if there are no casualties, having the confidence means that all types of incidents, even minor ones, can be dealt with calmly.

The St John's Ambulance Association and Brigade, St. Andrews Ambulance Association and the British Red Cross Society all offer courses. The telephone numbers of the local offices can be found in the local telephone book or Yellow Pages; alternatively enquire at your doctor's surgery.

C H A P T E R   25
Exam Information

Candidates at Stage III level are expected to have more competence and confidence when handling horses than in the Stage II. They will need to show practical experience when dealing with horses in a variety of situations, have the ability of making their own decisions when necessary and of handling staff tactfully.

Training Preparation

Having successfully taken the Stage I and II examinations and possibly the Preliminary Teaching Test, the candidate at Stage III will have experience in training for examinations. The theory needs home study and lectures, the practical and practical oral need experience with horses.

If the candidate can widen their scope of experience in any way, for instance accompanying a friend who is competing in a show or assisting a Vet or Farrier for a period, this will increase the candidate's skill and ability.

The equitation training consists of developing physical and mental fitness. There is no short cut, this needs hours in the saddle. The rider needs to develop a confidence in their own ability in flatwork and jumping.

A qualified, experienced and knowledgeable instructor is vital. So too is experience; of riding with others in a school, of riding Stage III standard horses and of jumping various show jumping and cross-country courses.

Students should plan their own timetable, working towards the date of the Exam and including weeks for revision. At this standard, candidates will need to show more maturity in their manner, have confidence in their ability and qualities.

Applying for the Exam

For those candidates who wish to check on available dates and venues, or who need further information about the Examination, the staff at the British Horse Society are always helpful and informative.

The application form for the Stage III is available from most Examination Centres or from the British Horse Society.

For information and application forms contact:

> The British Horse Society,
> Training and Education Department,
> British Equestrian Centre,
> Stoneleigh Deer Park,
> Kenilworth,
> Warwickshire, CV8 2LR

> Telephone Number: 01203 696697

Examination Day

Plan to arrive 30 minutes to 1 hour before the Examination begins at 8.30 – 9.00 a.m. Some riders may decide to take a private lunge lesson before the Exam, to loosen and supple the muscles.

Candidates do need to walk the show jumping and cross-country courses before the Examination starts. Though at most Exam Centres candidates are allowed to walk the courses immediately prior to their jumping session, this is not always preferable. It is more of a benefit to the candidate to arrive early at the centre and have time to walk the courses.

Clothing

As with the other Stage Exams, neat, suitable and practical clothing is required. The new standard riding hat is now compulsory at all BHS Examinations, a PAS 015. There are now a variety of designs incorporating this standard of hat, some of which are elegant in appearance. Anyone not wearing such a hat will not be allowed to take the Examination. The hat should also fit the rider.

Other clothes needed for the equitation are a hacking jacket, jodhpurs, a long sleeved shirt, with tie or stock. Gloves are essential and a long riding whip for the flat work and a short whip for the jumping. Long boots are also necessary. New leather boots will need at least six weeks wearing in before they are comfortable.

For the cross-country phase all candidates will need a current standard body protector. This is normally worn on top of the jacket, occasionally underneath. On hot days, Examiners permitting, the hacking jacket can be removed and the body protector worn on top of a shirt.

For practical sessions, a waterproof or windproof jacket may be worn, provided it is safe, comfortable and properly fastened. On hot days candidates may be permitted to remove their jackets, but they have to be wearing a long sleeved shirt.

No jewellery, apart from a wedding ring, may be worn; not even studs, in pierced ears. Long hair should be tied back for safety.

Format

The format will be similar to Stage II. The equitation, flatwork and jumping, is normally organised in the morning together with some sections of the Horse Knowledge and Care part of the Exam. There will be a break for lunch after which the remaining sections will be completed. The Examination finishes at approximately 4.30 p.m. and the results will be given as soon as possible.

Example of Stage III Timetable. Riders to walk the courses before 8.40 a.m.

British Horse Society Stage III Examination						
Timetable 14 Candidates						
Times	**Flatwork**	**Theory**	**Ailments paper**	**Ride & Lead**	**Lungeing**	**Jumping/X country**
09.00	Group A	Group B	Group C			
09.50	Group B	Group C	Group A			
10.40	Group C	Group A	Group B			
11.30				Group A	Group B	Group C
12.10				Group C	Group A	Group B
12.50				Group B	Group C	Group A
1.30	*L*	*U*	*N*	*C*	*H*	
	Practical	**Practical/oral**				
2.30	1-7	8-14				
3.30	8-14	1-7				
4.30	Exam	Finishes				

The timetable may vary depending on the facilities of the Centre and the number of candidates.

The British Horse Society

In 1947 the National Horse Association and the Institute of the Horse and Pony Club combined to become the British Horse Society. Since then the BHS, a registered charity, has worked unceasingly to promote the welfare of horses and ponies. Many of the workforce are volunteers including all committee members. The Society's policy of 'open communication' means that any individual member may express their views to the BHS via their local representatives or Development Officer.

The Aims of the BHS

The Society provides an organisation that works on behalf of all those who breed, own, ride and drive horses and ponies. It **promotes the views of the equestrian industry** to local and central government and to the European Community. In this capacity it deals with issues such as the live export of horses for slaughter.

The Society promotes the policy of access and rights of way for horses and riders. They **campaign for new rights of way**, the **improvement of existing bridle paths** and the **return of unrecorded ancient routes as bridleways or byways**. They also publish a number of books dealing with bridleways and paths across the country.

The Society works towards the **protection of horses and ponies** promoting their welfare by encouraging the expansion of knowledge throughout the equestrian industry.   It does this by producing publications covering the management and handling of horses, and by organising progressive training and education schemes.

The British Horse Society's **training programme** is considered one of the best in the world. Many countries in Europe, Asia and the USA are now training staff towards BHS qualifications. The Society **seeks to educate** by setting standards of training and by offering qualifications through examination and vocational courses.

It also **sets standards** of horsemastership **by approving, through regular inspections, educational and riding establishments throughout the UK and other countries**. Those of the public who then wish to train or ride for pleasure, know what type and grade is offered by any approved school.

Safety is one of the most important aims and objectives of the BHS. The Society is concerned with ensuring that the **health of all BHS members**, staff and members of the public who work and visit premises or attend BHS events should be safeguarded as far as is reasonably possible.   The Society is committed to its responsibility to fulfil the legal obligations of the Health and Safety at Work Act 1974.

The Society has made **safety for personnel and horses an integral part of its training schemes**, as part of the Examinations and by offering a specific Riding & Road Safety Test for riders and horses using the Public Highway.

All accidents, particularly those that are serious or fatal, have to be **reported to the BHS**. This information is collected and used by the BHS as **statistical data** to show how and where improvements can be made for further safety measures. One result of this is the launching of the 'Safety 2000 campaign' to reduce the number of road accidents involving horses by the year 2000.

Another area covered by the Society is the breeding of horses and ponies. Many Breed Societies have nominated members on the Horse and Pony Breeds Committee. This committee looks after the **interests of breed societies and matters affecting breeding**.

The **British Horse Database** was created to collect information about the performance of British bred horses and ponies. A permanent record is made of the horse or pony with distinguishing features and breeding information. When the horse or pony is successful at affiliated competitions this is also recorded. Breeders can therefore monitor the progress of their stock; buyers can check the record and ancestry of any horse they wish to purchase. Registration is compulsory for horses competing in Dressage or Horse Trials.

One of the British Horse Society's main aims is to **prevent cruelty to horses and ponies**. Most cruelty and neglect is caused by ignorance. Training and education are therefore a high priority to combat this type of suffering. Unfortunately not all suffering is caused by ignorance and BHS members are asked to be vigilant and to report any cases of cruelty to the BHS offices at Stoneleigh, to the local Welfare or Development officers.

Organisation and Structure

The British Horse Society headquarters is based at Stoneleigh in Warwickshire where the Society membership and organisation is run by permanent staff, together with regional Development Officers.

The Council, together with the General Purposes and Finance Committee, govern the Society's activities. There are committees at National, Regional and County level, some of the volunteers on these committees are elected and appointed from the membership.

The Committees pass on the plans and policies of the Council to the membership and in return pass on the wishes of the members to the Council. Members of the Committees are there to provide advice, promote welfare and training, and to communicate with local authorities on equestrian related matters.

There are also Policy Committees

> **Access and Rights of Way**
>
> **Safety**
>
> **Welfare**
>
> **Horse and Pony Breeds**
>
> **Training and Education**

Changes within the BHS

As with any large organisation that keeps in step with present and future times, the British Horse Society is changing.

The Examination structure has recently been altered so that those passing their Exams up to Stage III, including the Preliminary Teaching Test will become a Preliminary Instructor. The PI then continues to gain practice and experience at teaching, so that after a number of hours they can qualify for the Assistant Instructor Certificate.

The British Horse Society included various disciplines such as show jumping and driving under its banner. In recent years these disciplines have decided to branch our and organise their own finances and maintenance. The disciplines of Horse Trials, Endurance Riding, Vaulting, Dressage and Horse Driving opted out of the Society to set up as individual companies.

Benefits to Members

Membership of the British Horse Society allows those involved with horses to belong to a body that seeks to influence, and frequently does, National Governments, regional councils and authorities in the best interest of the horse. The Society represents its membership on many issues such as instigating more awareness amongst motorists for riders and improving the standard of care for horses and ponies.

The Society offers an advice service to all members. There is free 24 hour legal helpline for members who need advice on legal matters and a free tax helpline (office hours) for advice on tax, VAT and related subjects. Indeed any member with a problem can contact the BHS for guidance and advice on subjects ranging from training to pasture management, breeding to euthanasia for horses.

Full membership includes free insurance; Personal Liability Insurance and Personal Accident Insurance for equestrian related incidents.

Members receive an annual Yearbook and a colour magazine 'British Horse' three times a year. They are also entitled to a 10% reduction on all books, gifts and videos purchased from the British Horse Society Bookshop. They are allowed to use the BHS facilities at certain events and entitled to reductions at many BHS functions.

Full members are able to take the BHS Examinations and gain qualifications. Once qualified they are eligible to be included in the Register of Instructors. This Register confirms that the instructor holds the qualifications indicated and that they attend training sessions. The BHS recommend that members of the public receive tuition from a registered instructor.

The British Horse Society has a wide range of activities and functions, representing its membership on many issues with various bodies of government. Most importantly the Society is there to protect and promote the welfare of horses and ponies.

Exam Tips

Prepare as thoroughly as possible, put in the hours for riding practice, take lectures for the theory and practical sections and plan a timetable for studying at home. As with any Examination, putting in the work is essential.

At Stage III you will need to show practical experience around horses, an ability to organise horses and people, to deal with situations when they arise or to request help from someone more experienced.

With thorough practice and study, you will develop confidence in your own ability, and through that you know you will be successful.

Good luck

APPENDIX A

Recommended Lectures and Practical Sessions

Psychology and Anatomy

❖ Learn the muscles. Revise the skeleton.

❖ Discuss the formation and function of muscles.

❖ Discuss how the muscles work in combination with each other.

➥ Practical - watch horses working and observe how they use their muscles for different actions.

Anatomy

❖ Learn and discuss the circulatory and respiratory system.

❖ Discuss how the three systems, the muscular, circulatory and respiratory systems work together.

❖ Learn the structure of the horse's lower leg and foot.

➥ Practical – look at a horse's leg and foot, discuss the structure.

Minor Ailments

❖ Discuss minor ailments, their symptoms, treatment and prevention.

❖ Talk about minor wounds and their treament.

Health

❖ Discuss temperature, pulse, respiration and equine vaccinations.

❖ Discuss worming, importance of a worming programme and types of wormer.

➥ Practical – take a horse's respiration, pulse and temperature.

➥ Worm a horse or watch a horse being wormed. Discuss types of Wormers.

Minor Ailments

❖ Discuss the causes of lameness in horses; the methods of assessing lameness.

❖ Discuss calling the Vet, when and how.

↝ Practical – watch different horses being led in hand. Assess some horses for lameness. Trot a horse up in hand.

↝ Practise answering questions on written minor ailments papers.

Static Conformation

❖ Learn about static conformation, what points to look for and relating terms.

↝ Practical – check different horses for static conformation.

Dynamic Conformation

❖ Discuss action, points to assess and the equine terms for types of action.

❖ Discuss different breeds and their conformational characteristics.

❖ Relate dynamic conformation with muscular development.

↝ Practical – check different horses for dynamic conformation. Assess the paces, their action. Watch horses being ridden and assess paces and movement.

Behavioural Problems

❖ Discuss behavioural problems, their causes, effects on the horse's health, treatment and prevention.

❖ Discuss the horse's natural lifestyle, his perception, instincts and characteristics and the reasons why horses develop vices.

Ride and Lead

❖ Discuss the reasons for ride and lead, the method of leading a horse, mounting, dismounting with two horses and safety precautions particularly on the road.

❖ Talk about the protective clothing for the horses.

↝ Practical – practise ride and lead, at least two or three times and with different horses.

Travelling

❖ Discuss the theory of travelling. Talk about trailers, boxes and the new regulations affecting the transport of horses.

↪ Practical – prepare a horse for travelling.

↪ Load different horses and unload, checking the trailer, towing vehicle or box prior to loading.

Nutrition

❖ Discuss feed rooms, their requirements, safety and security.

❖ Discuss the nutritional value of different feeds, the importance of carbohydrates, proteins, vitamins, minerals, fats and oils in the diet.

↪ Look at some feed samples giving their respective values and uses.

Feeding

❖ Discuss the importance of water in the diet.

❖ Talk about the different forms of roughage and methods of feeding.

❖ Discuss the importance of grass in the diet.

↪ Make up feed charts for ponies and horses doing various types of work and for those off work, using both traditional and compound feeds.

Fittening

❖ Discuss the importance of a fittening programme and the variety in programmes designed for horses in different types of work.

❖ Learn and discuss the hazards of fittening work and the problems that may occur.

❖ Briefly discuss interval training, keeping the horse fit and preparation for shows and competitions.

Tack

❖ Discuss the requirements of a tack room, design and security.

❖ Discuss different types of bits, their functions, action and uses.

↪ Practical – look at different types of bit and discuss their functions and action.

Saddlery

❖ Discuss the fitting and uses of a double bridle.

↪ Put on and fit a double bridle.

❖ Discuss saddles, designs, fittings and attachments.

↪ Tack horses up for different disciplines using various bridles, bits, saddles and attachments such as a martingale and a surcingle girth.

Rugs and Bandages

❖ Discuss the fitting and uses of various rugs, particularly anti-sweat and cooler rugs.

❖ Discuss the uses of exercise bandages. Compare their advantages and disadvantages with protective boots.

↪ Practise fitting exercise bandages. Use different horses and a variety of exercise bandages and paddings.

Shoeing

❖ Talk briefly about shoeing procedures.

❖ Discuss the signs of a well shod foot and the problems caused by bad shoeing.

❖ Look at and discuss various types of shoes including remedial shoes used for corrective or medical purposes. Discuss the use of pads and studs.

↪ Watch the Farrier shoeing. Ask about remedial shoeing.

Stable and Yard Design

❖ Observe facilities on the yard; discuss their functions, advantages and disadvantages.

❖ Discuss stable design, siting and materials, fixtures and fittings.

↪ Design your own yard including facilities and space for future expansion.

Grassland Management

❖ Discuss size and type of pasture suitable for horses; soil analysis and types of grasses.

❖ Name and describe various poisonous plants and their control.

❖ Discuss maintenance of pasture on a yearly, monthly and weekly basis. Talk about daily inspections and safety in fields and paddocks.

↪ Observe paddocks and pasture pointing out good and bad points.

Horses at Grass

❖ Discuss the routines for keeping horses and ponies at grass.

❖ Learn about feeding during the seasons of the year and working horses from grass.

❖ Consider problems such as keeping a clipped horse or pony rugged during the winter; hazards such as flies and poisonous plants. Discuss security and safety for horses and ponies at grass.

Lungeing

❖ Revise the methods and reasons for lungeing, fitting lungeing equipment and safety.

↝ Practise lungeing different horses with the aim of working the horse for exercise. Fit the lungeing equipment.

Safety

❖ Discuss accident procedures, basic first aid and dealing with injured riders or clients.

❖ Discuss safety and fire precautions around the yard, in the stable, on hacks and on the Public Highway.

↝ If possible take a First Aid course.

General

❖ Discuss Exam procedure, routine and requirements, that is clothes and equipment.

❖ Discuss the British Horse Society, its history, its functions, structure and influence on the equestrian industry.

❖ Discuss the benefits to members, riders, owners and the general public. Talk about the current changes within the society and how this may affect the industry in the future. Discuss insurance cover for riders.

The Exam

❖ Attend a mock Exam day.

APPENDIX B

Worms and Worming Information

Name	Symptoms and Effects	Description	Life cycle
Large Redworm	Anaemia, loss of weight and condition, rough coat, loss of performance, blood clots, diarrhoea, damage and death of parts of the gut. Fatal colic. Effects; damage to inner lining of blood vessels.	About three types of large redworm, the most common is the *Strongyle vulgaris*. Grows to 1.5 - 4 cm.	Affects all horses, ponies and donkeys. Life cycle of 6-7 months. Eggs passed into pasture through droppings. Develop into larvae that are ingested by the horse. The larvae migrate through the wall of the gut to blood vessels and main arteries and back to the large intestine to mature. The adult worms live in the large intestine and caecum. Here they bite into the wall of the gut and feed by plugging into blood vessels. Eggs are laid 6 months after infestation, pass into pasture and remain viable for years.
Small Redworm	Anaemia, loss of appetite and weight, diarrhoea, colic. Inflammation and thickening of gut wall. Can be fatal.	About 40 different types of small redworm. Most common is the *Trichonema*. Grows to 0.5 to 1 cm.	Affects all horses and ponies. Life cycle of 2 - 3 months. Taken in by digestion. Larvae migrate to glands in the wall of the large intestine. Adults live in the large intestine and caecum. Plug feeders like the large redworms. The small redworm can remain dormant within the wall of the gut throughout the winter.
Large white Roundworm	Loss of condition, coughing, nasal discharge, unthriftiness, loss of appetite. In excessive infestations causes blockage and rupture of intestines and death.	Grows to 40 cm. White and thick. *Parascaris equorum*.	Affects all horses in particular up to 3 years old. It has a life cycle of 3 months. It is taken in by digestion and by coughing and swallowing. Migrates through lungs and liver. Adults live in small intestine. Millions of eggs are produced and these remain viable for years in the stable or pasture. They remain dormant until the conditions are right to hatch, so it is difficult to deal with these completely.

Tapeworm	Damage to caecum affecting the valves within the gut. Also causes intussusception; part of gut telescopes in on itself restricting blood vessels. Part of gut dies as a result.	Grows to 8 cm long and 4 cm wide. Grey-white, flat, segmented. *Anoplocephala perfoliata.*	Affects all horses. Life cycle of 3-6 months. Forage mites first ingest the eggs of the tapeworm in the pasture. These mites are in turn digested with grass by the horses. Adults live in the small intestine and the caecum holding onto the lining of the gut wall with four suckers. Tapeworms grow in segments. The segments contain eggs. These segments drop off, pass out of the horse with dung and the eggs are laid. NOTE. Some Wormers do not deal with tapeworms.
Lungworm	Persistent coughing, respiratory problems. Increased respiration during exercise.	Grow to 3.5 cm. White, long and thin. *Dictyocaulus arnfieldi.*	Affect donkeys in particular and sometimes horses. Taken in by digestion in pasture grazed by donkeys. Can sometimes be transmitted from one horse to another. Migrates through walls of intestine via circulation to lungs. Lives in the bronchi and bronchioles of the lungs.
Threadworm	A heavy yellow discharge from nostrils. Occasionally respiratory problems.	Size up to 1cm. Very small and thin. *Strongyloides westeri.*	Affects foals up to 6 months old and occasionally horses. Taken in by foal suckling from infected mare and by digestion through grazing. The larvae will also burrow into the legs of the foal. Migrates through to the lungs, is coughed up and swallowed. Adult worms live in the stomach and intestine.
Pinworm or Seatworm or Whipworm	Irritation around the tail, scratching and bare patches around dock.	Size from 1cm to 10 cm (females). Thin tapering tail. White grey in colour. *Oxyuris equi.*	All adult horses. Life cycle of 4 -5 months. Lives in large intestine. These worms float around in the intestine and feed as scavengers on food and tissue. Female worm migrates to anus, sticks tail out and lays eggs. These are visible as yellow wax around the dock. The eggs can live within wood in stable or fencing and re-infect horses when they scratch.
Bots	Horses can react quite wildly when the female bot fly is around, dashing around the field. Causes colic and loss of condition.	This parasite is a fly not a worm. The fly, yellow and black rather like a small bee lives for some weeks during the summer. The cold weather kills them off. *Gastrophilus intestinalis.*	The bot fly lays its eggs on the horse's body, usually around the shoulders, legs and stomach. The eggs are tiny bright yellow specks, which stick to the hair. The horse licks these off and the larvae hatch growing under the horse's tongue for 2-3 weeks. These are then ingested and live in the stomach for the winter, 10 - 12 weeks. They then emerge with the dung and turn into flies. Prevention, pick off or use a bot fly pad to remove eggs. Worm with a special bot wormer around October/November time.

Index